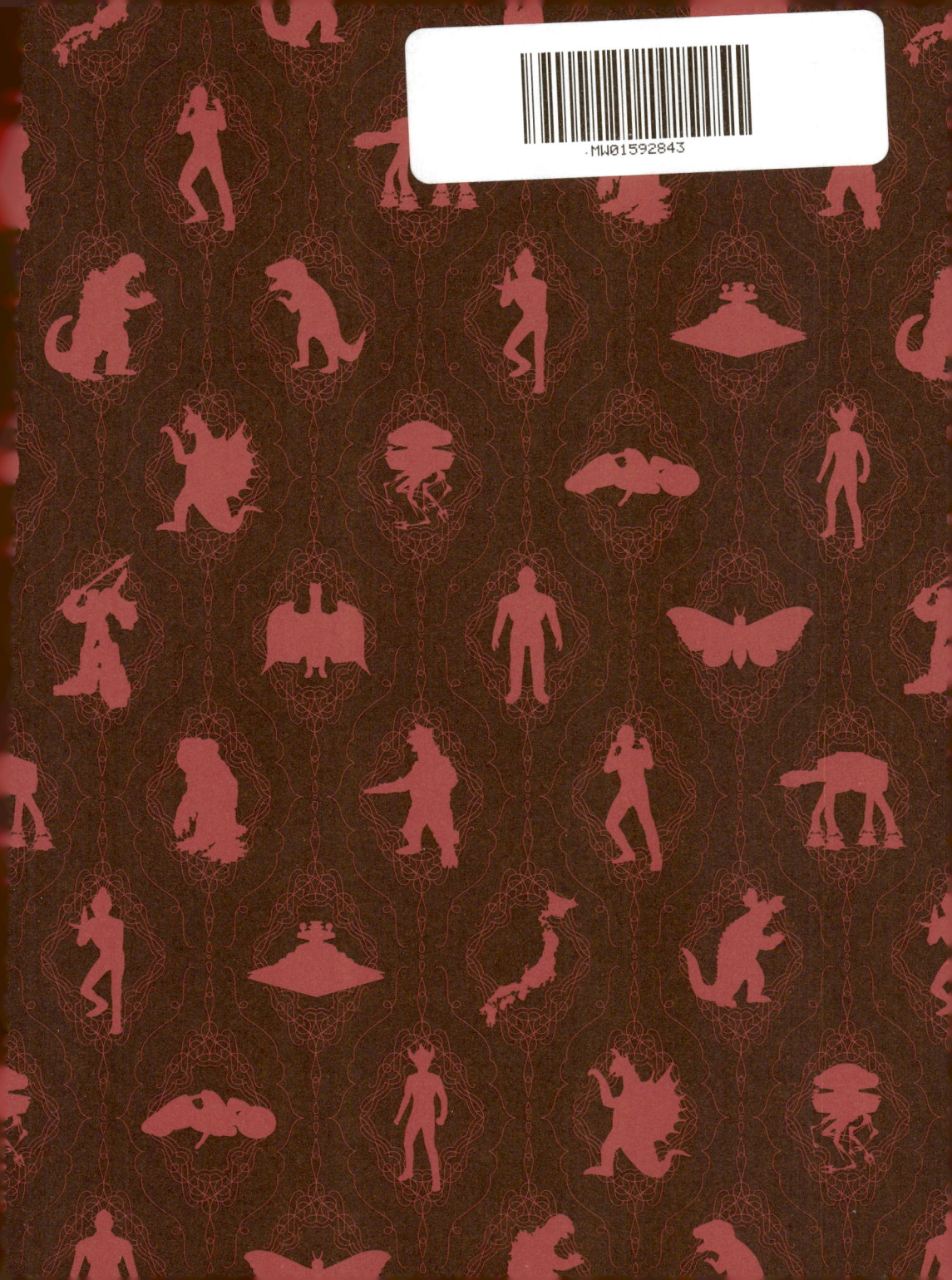

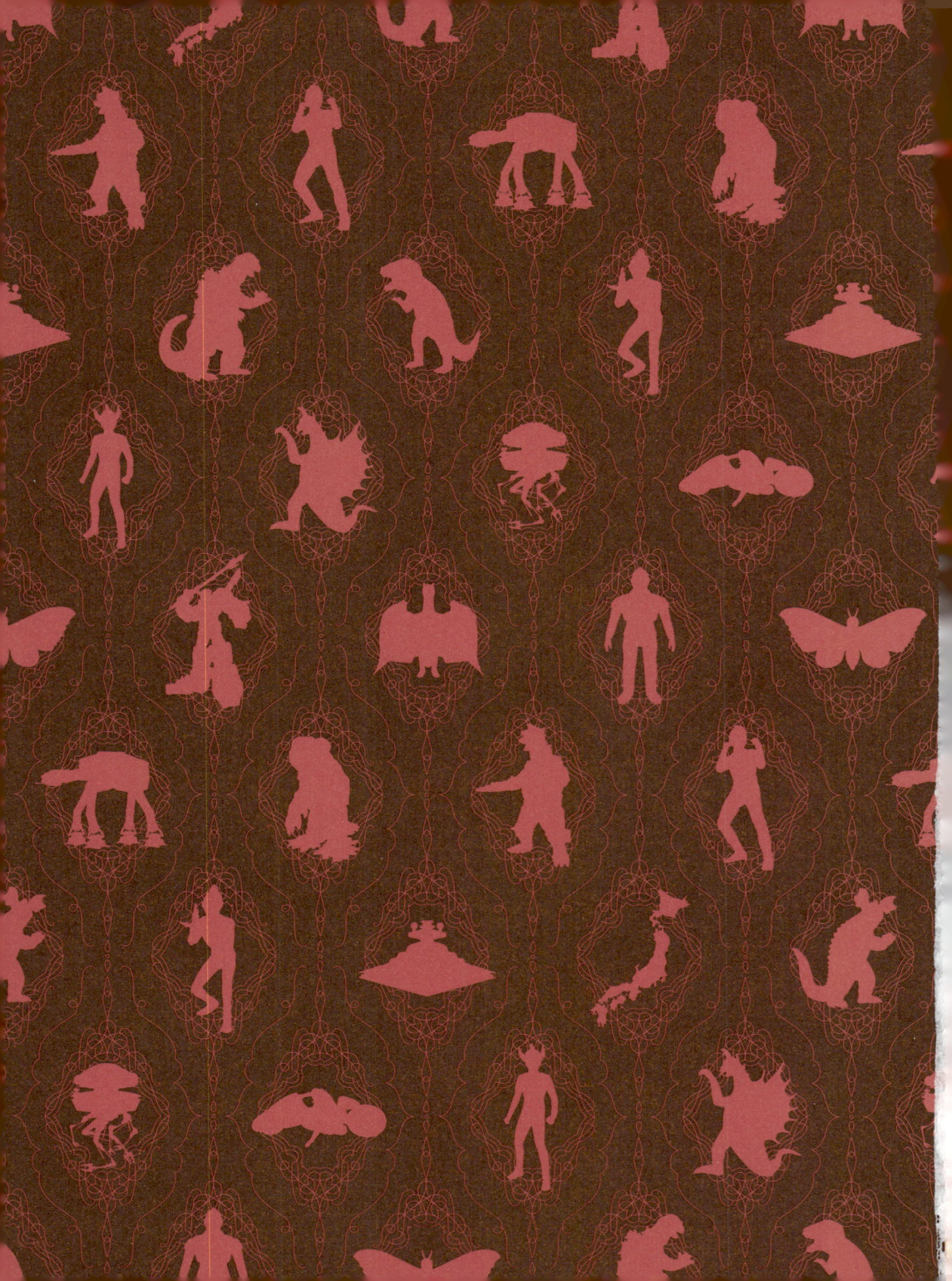

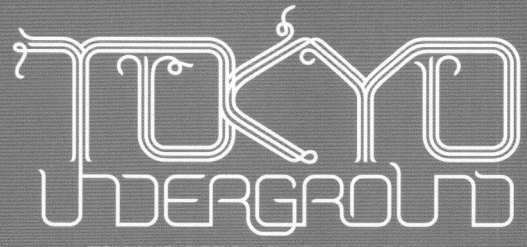

TOY AND DESIGN CULTURE IN TOKYO

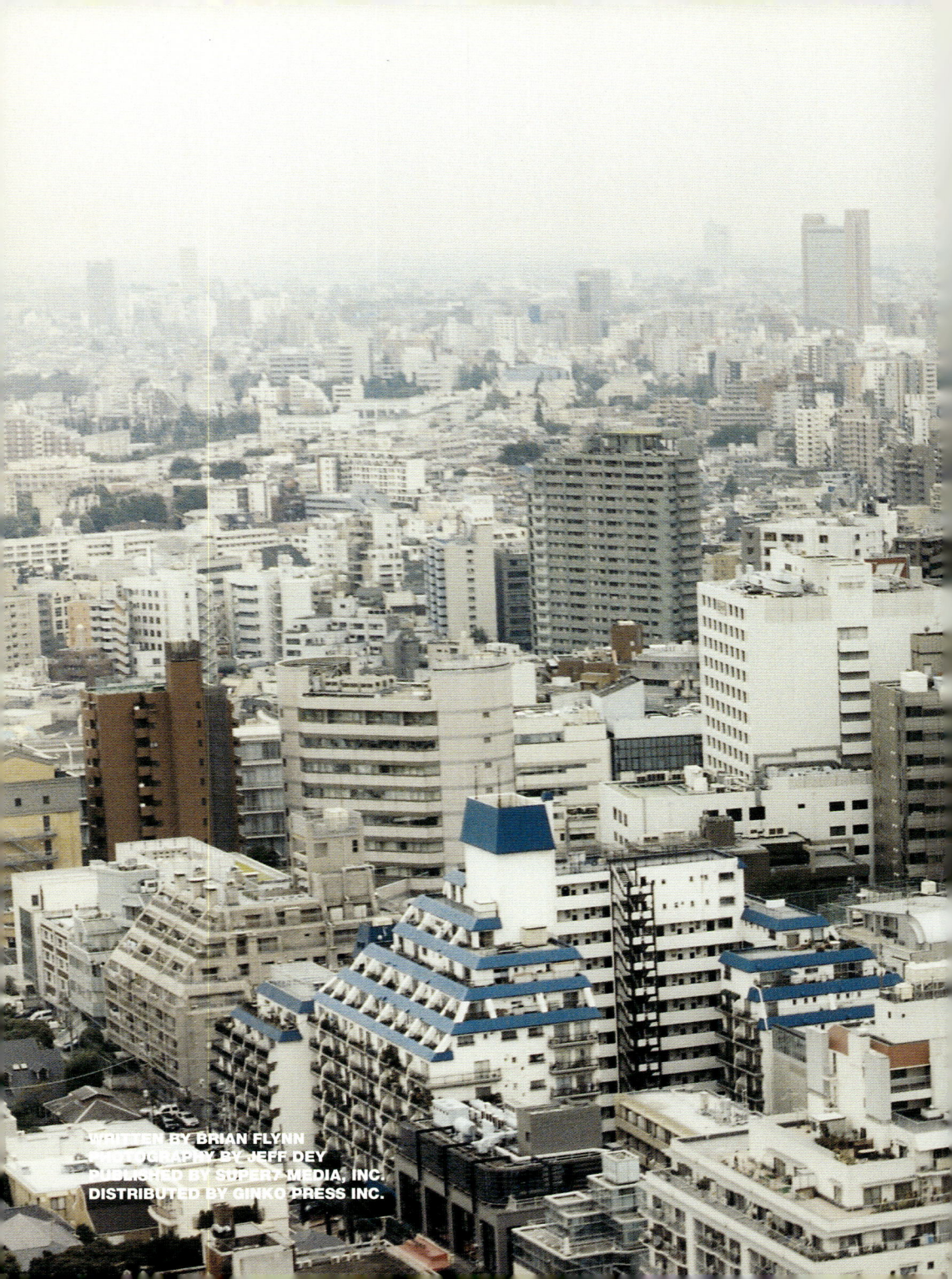

WRITTEN BY BRIAN FLYNN
PHOTOGRAPHY BY JEFF DEY
PUBLISHED BY SUPER7 MEDIA, INC.
DISTRIBUTED BY GINKO PRESS INC.

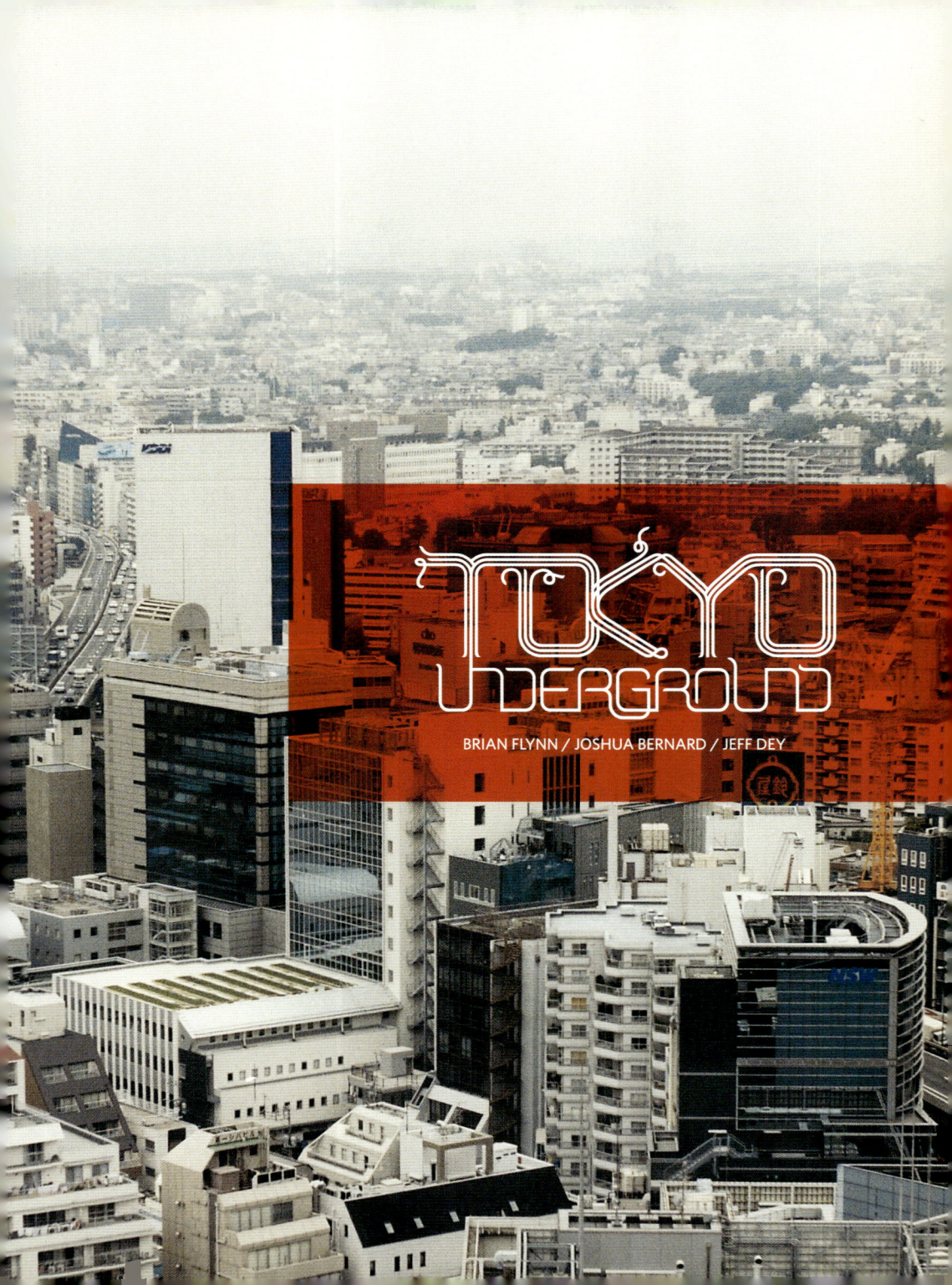

TOKYO UNDERGROUND

BRIAN FLYNN / JOSHUA BERNARD / JEFF DEY

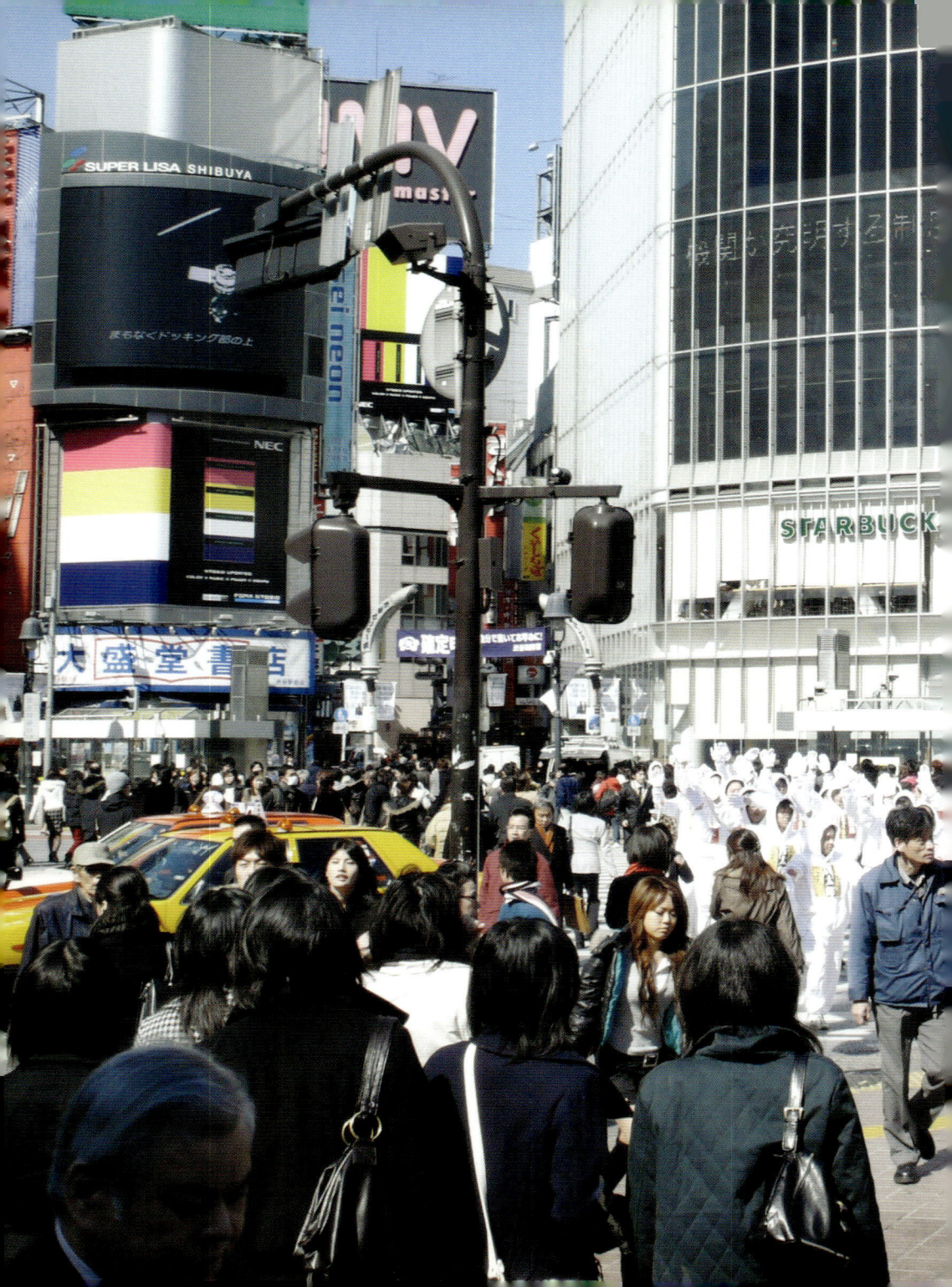

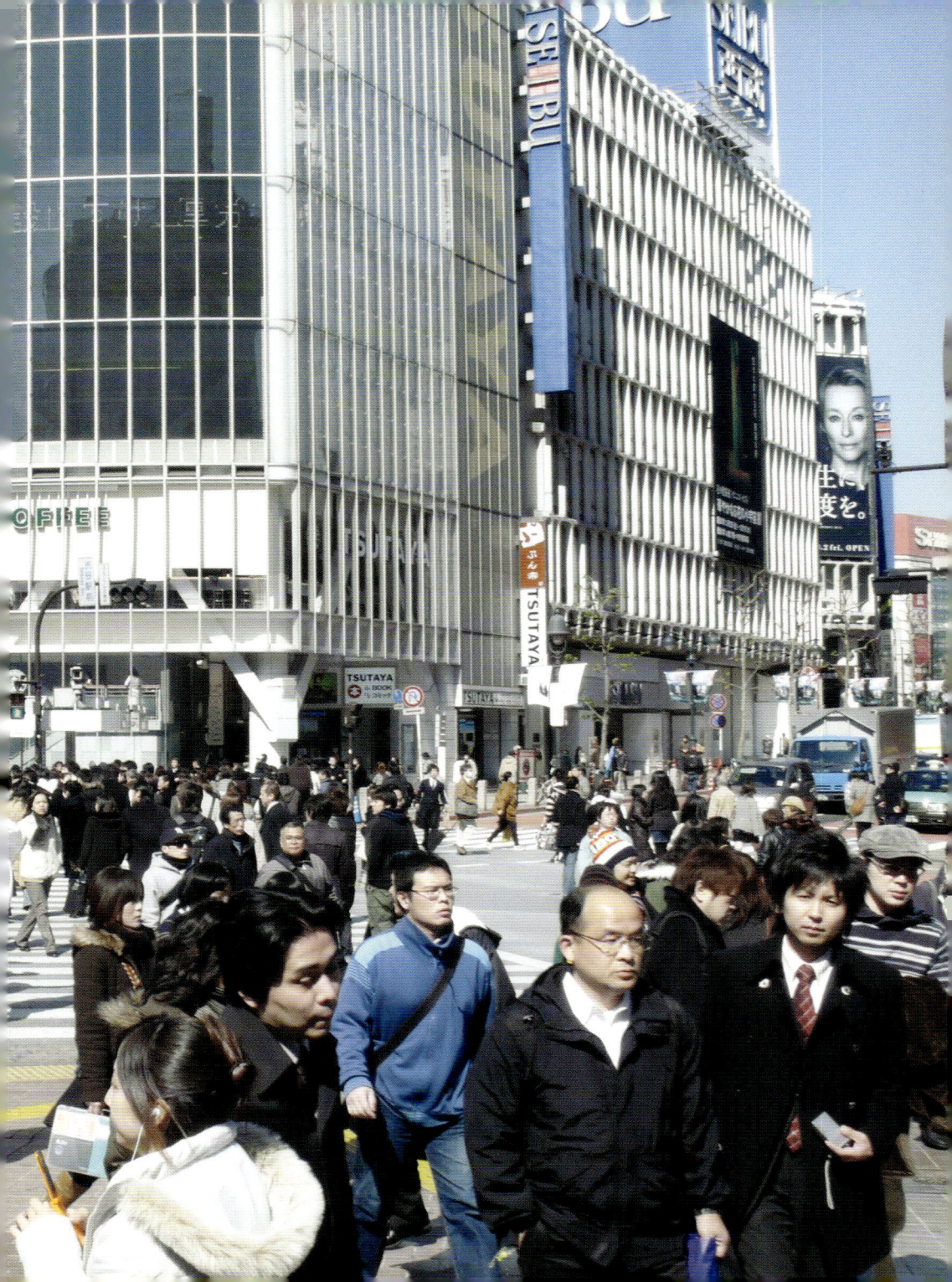

TOKYO UNDERGROUND:
TOY AND DESIGN CULTURE IN TOKYO

Published in 2007 by Super7 Media, Inc.
All text and artwork copyright ©2007 Super7 Media, Inc.
Distributed by Gingko Press Inc.

Gingko Press Inc.
5768 Paradise Drive, Suite J
Corte Madera, CA 94925
Telephone: 415.924.9615
Facsimile: 415.924.9608

books@gingkopress.com
www.gingkopress.com

ISBN: 978-0-9796678-0-0
ISBN-10: 0-9796678-0-1

Written by Brian Flynn
Edited by Annie Tucker
Compiled by Brian Flynn of Super7 and Joshua Bernard of CollectionDX.com
Design by Hybrid Design, San Francisco, CA – www.hybrid-design.ccm
Primary photography by Jeff Dey – www.jeffdey.com
Additional photography supplied by Brian Flynn, Joshua Bernard,
    Isaac Ramos, Dave Keymont, and Mark Helm

Super7 Media, Inc.
1628 Post Street
San Francisco, CA 94115
USA

Telephone: 415.409.4700
Facsimile: 415.409.4703

info@super7magazine.com
www.super7store.com
www.super7magazine.com

info@CollectionDX.com
www.CollectionDX.com

Printed in Hong Kong

CONTENTS

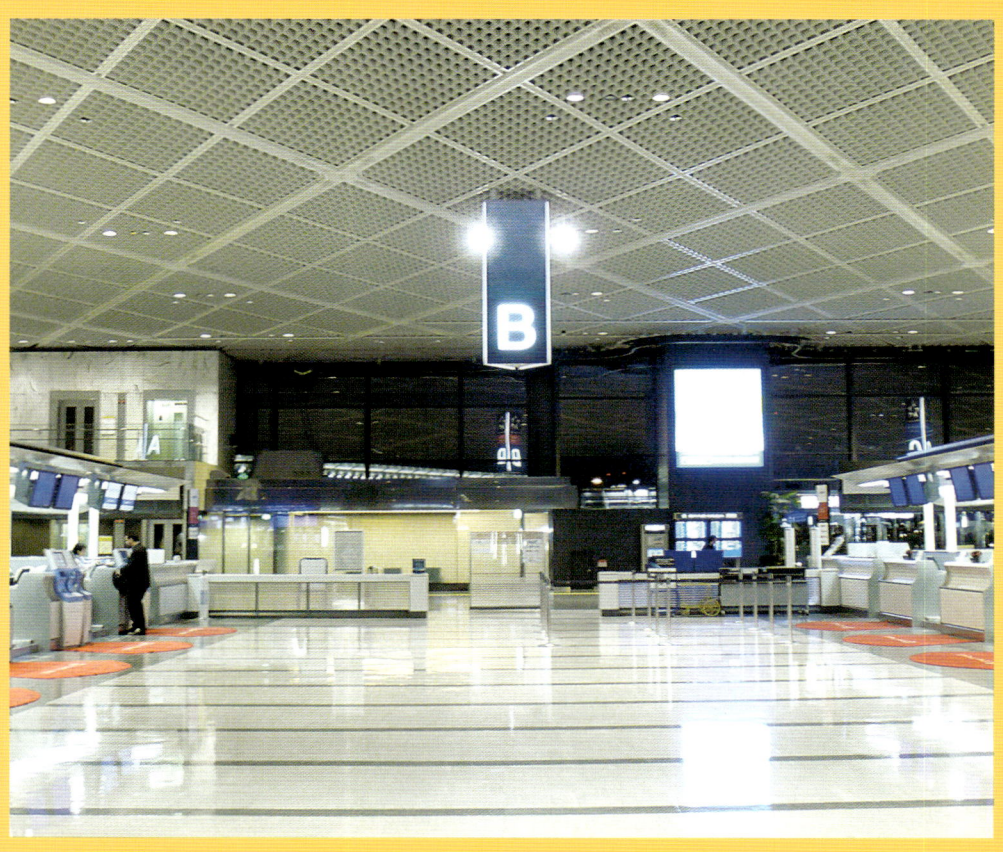

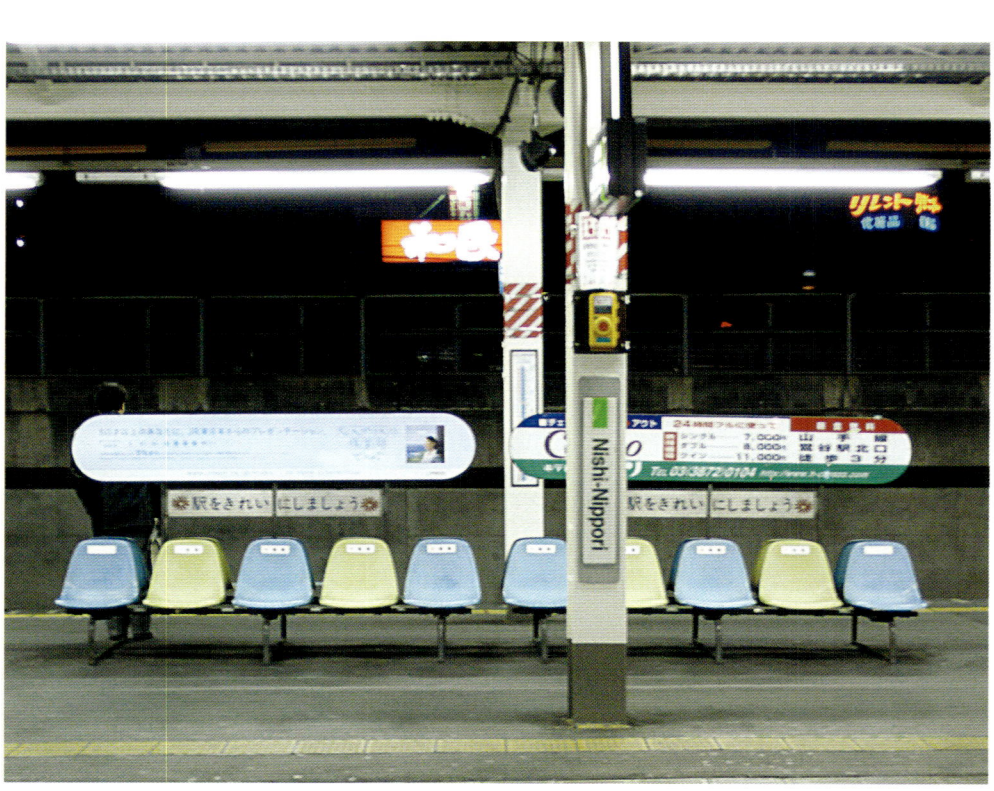

If there were ever a niche travel book, this is it. I am sure anyone with any "common sense" would never consider a project like this. Then again, Super7 has never really done much that makes any sense, and everything seems to work out for the better because of it. We are a bunch of stylish, misfit nerds who obsess about vintage toys, movies, punk records, hip-hop, sneakers, and half a dozen other forms of minutia that no one else in your family can relate to. If you can claim even the slightest predilection in your daily life for *Star Wars, Transformers, Godzilla, Ultraman, Macross, or Shogun Warriors*, or understand the terms *standard size, missile-firing, removable mask, mint on card, mint in box, DX*, or *completely trashed*, you're free to join the club.

To make this book, what were initially two separate sets of maps—one designed by *Super7* magazine, the other created by CollectionDX.com—were combined, elaborated on, and hopefully contextualized in a readable, enjoyable way. Shops old and new, as well as local landmarks, restaurants, and interesting places, were labeled and catalogued as simply as possible. In past years these maps would have been guarded like gold, hidden away from all but the toy-geek elite. So consider this your lucky day, and go forth on an unprecedented international shopping spree.

Finally, this book represents a collaborative effort, an accumulation of ideas and resources that would not have been possible without the help of Dora Drimalas, Geoff Allen, Caleb Kozlowski, Darlene Gibson and Suzi Nuti of Hybrid Design; Super7's Hiro Hayashi, Isaac Ramos, Karen Stanley, Josh Herbolsheimer and Joe Huerta; CollectionDX's Joshua Bernard and Dave Keymont; expatriates Matt Alt, Dennis Hamann, Yuriko Shirahata, and Koji Harmon; frequent flyers Mike Johnson, Pushead, Roger Harkavy, Omar Valles, and Denise Wong; and local legend Take-Shit of Cocobat—who all walked the streets of Tokyo in confused disarray, locating all of these shops and hot spots across the city. We hope you enjoy reading this book as much as we have enjoyed putting it together.

So what are you waiting for? Get going!

—BRIAN FLYNN, MARCH 2007

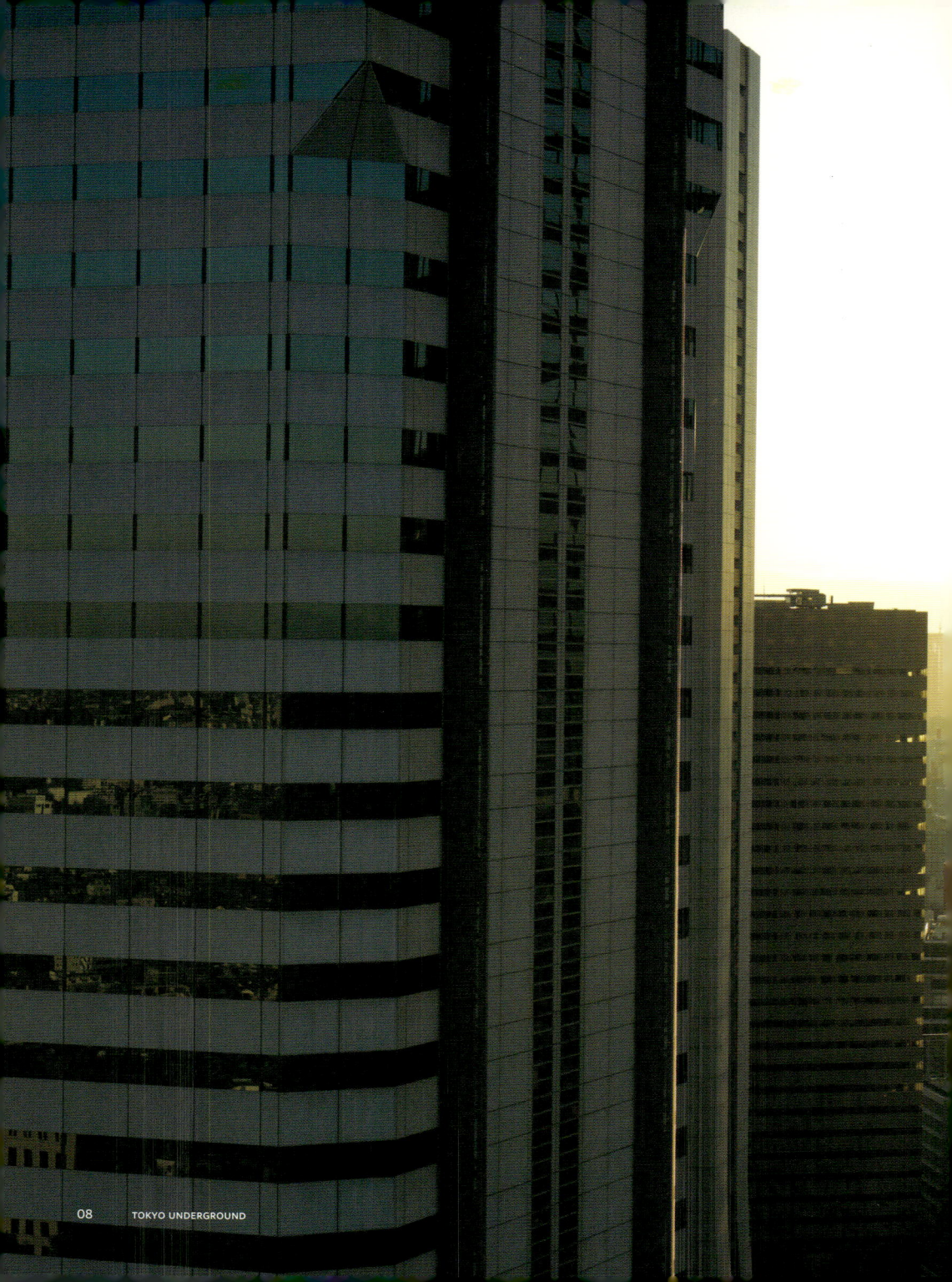

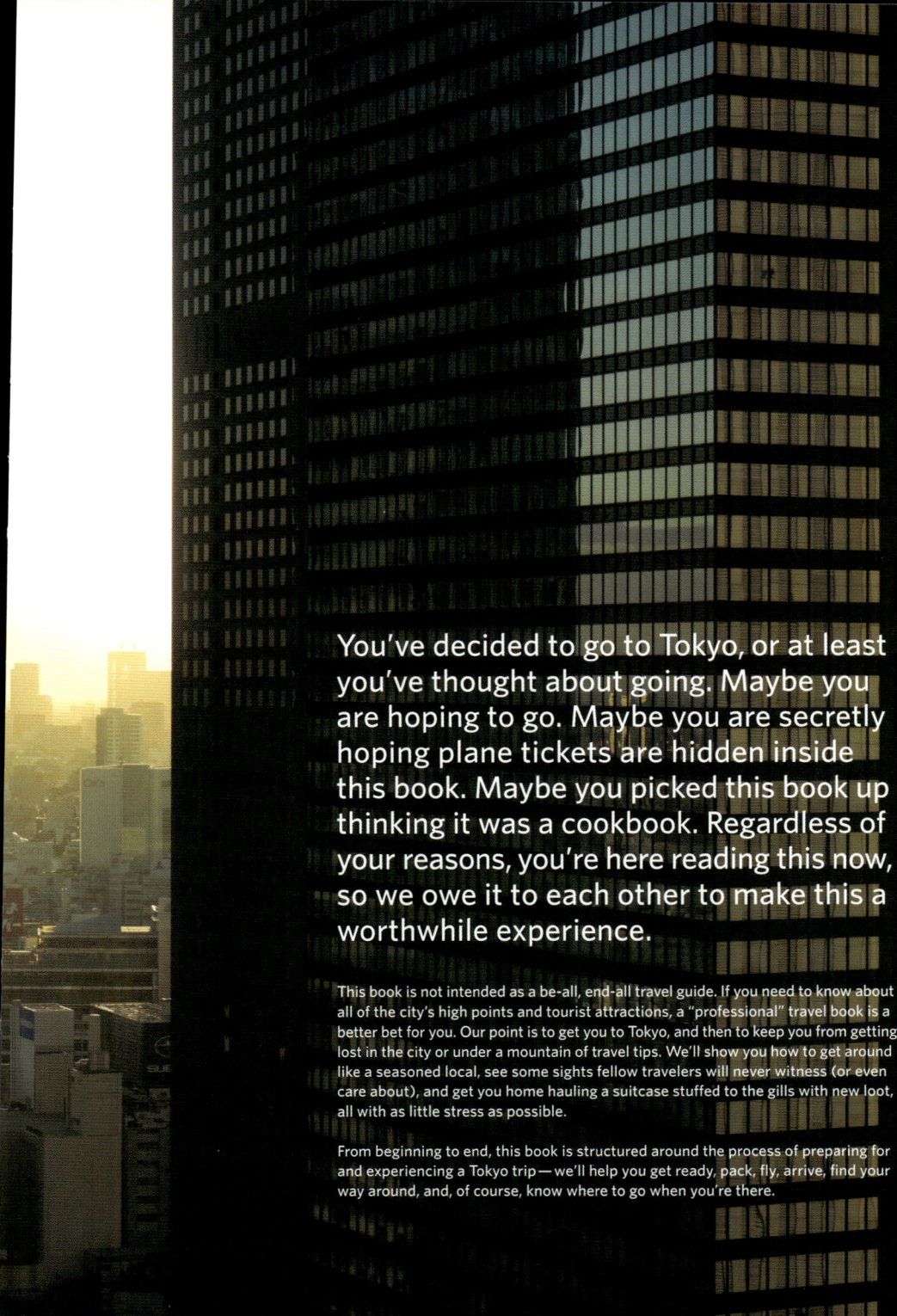

You've decided to go to Tokyo, or at least you've thought about going. Maybe you are hoping to go. Maybe you are secretly hoping plane tickets are hidden inside this book. Maybe you picked this book up thinking it was a cookbook. Regardless of your reasons, you're here reading this now, so we owe it to each other to make this a worthwhile experience.

This book is not intended as a be-all, end-all travel guide. If you need to know about all of the city's high points and tourist attractions, a "professional" travel book is a better bet for you. Our point is to get you to Tokyo, and then to keep you from getting lost in the city or under a mountain of travel tips. We'll show you how to get around like a seasoned local, see some sights fellow travelers will never witness (or even care about), and get you home hauling a suitcase stuffed to the gills with new loot, all with as little stress as possible.

From beginning to end, this book is structured around the process of preparing for and experiencing a Tokyo trip—we'll help you get ready, pack, fly, arrive, find your way around, and, of course, know where to go when you're there.

THE FIRST QUESTION

Why are you going to Tokyo? We're not being sarcastic; this is really important. If you don't know the reasons behind your trip, you probably won't know what to do when you get there. Sure, heading over for the adventure of it all is a blast, but at the very least, have a backup plan. Otherwise, you will spend your entire trip wandering from KFC to KFC, looking for Colonel Sanders pictures with Japanese captions. Trust us, we've done it. Do you want to go to the temples? Do you want to see the cherry blossom festival? Are you looking for the latest sneakers? Do you want premium denim? Are you looking for good sushi? Or are you looking to buy toys? Great! Now we can offer some help. But figure out how deep you want to go, because we can get real nerdy, real fast, and you'll probably only want to hang out with us for a little while, not for your whole trip.

Make a list. Check it twice. Give yourself plenty of time to hit the must-sees, and leave the rest to chance and spontaneity. On the one hand, you don't want to be so regimented that you act like a drill sergeant, but on the other hand, if you don't have enough to do, we guarantee that you will find a way to be bored, even in a city of ten gazillion people.

MYTHS

Everyone seems to have heard a myth about Japan. Yes, there are vending machines everywhere. Yes, you can buy beer from them. No, you cannot buy used women's underwear from them (at least not from the versions we've seen). Yes, the people are very nice. No, the Yakuza will not kill you if you look at them, nor will you know them when you see them. But yes, they are very real. Yes, almost everything has fish in it. Yes, they have everything you've ever wanted. No, there are not cyborgs everywhere (not yet at least). Yes, they put fried eggs on hamburgers and eat pancakes as a dessert. And no, you don't have to eat them the same way.

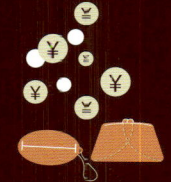

COIN PURSE:
YOU CAN PICK THE MALE OR FEMALE VERSION, BUT IF YOU HAVE ONE OF THESE, PACK IT. THERE ARE A LOT OF COINS IN JAPANESE CURRENCY, AND YOU'LL BE HANDLING THIRTY-POUND POCKETFULS IN NO TIME.

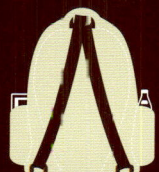

HANDS FREE:
TAKE A BACKPACK FOR YOUR DAILY SHOPPING ADVENTURES. TRUST US, YOU ARE GOING TO NEED IT.

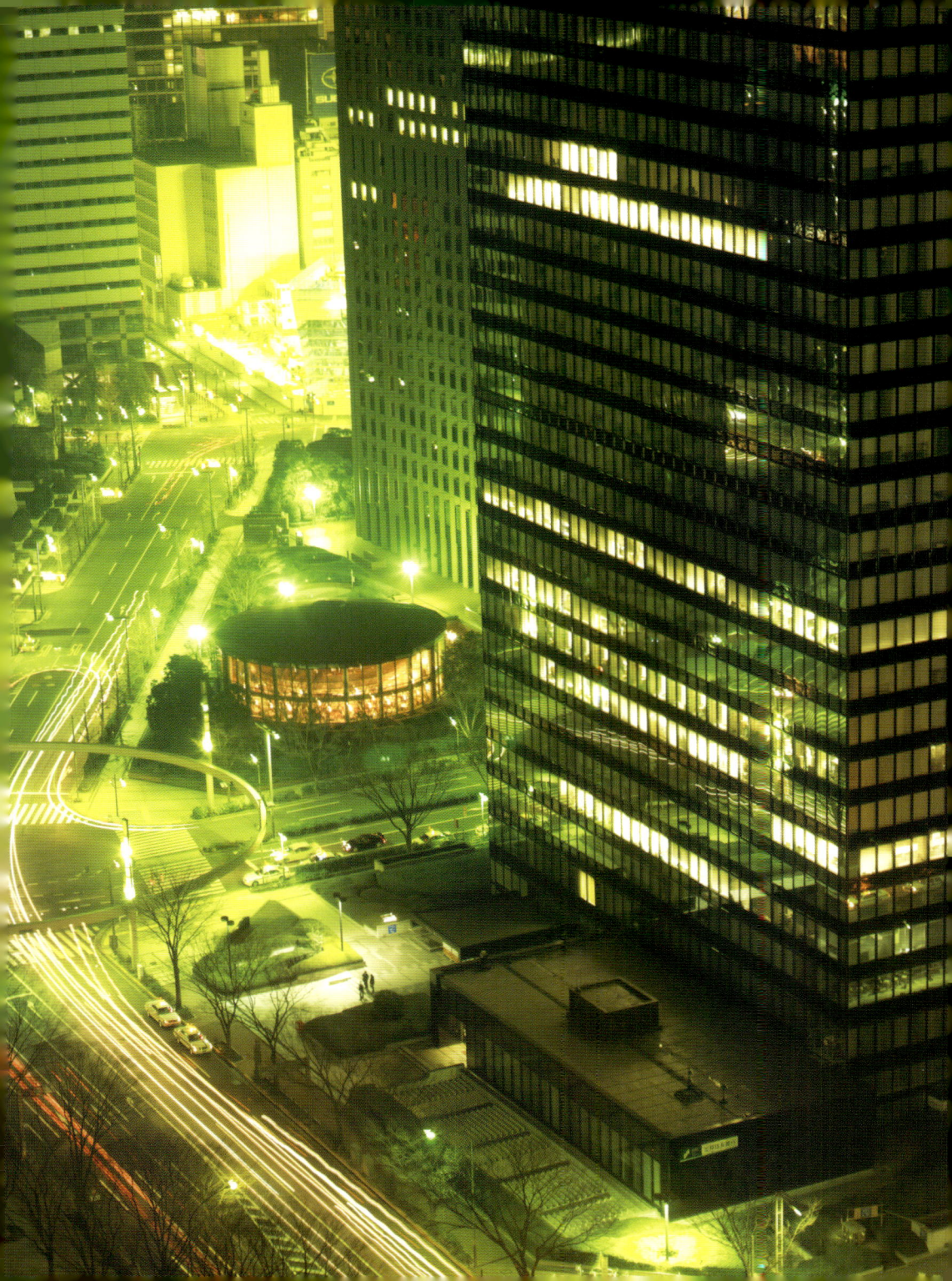

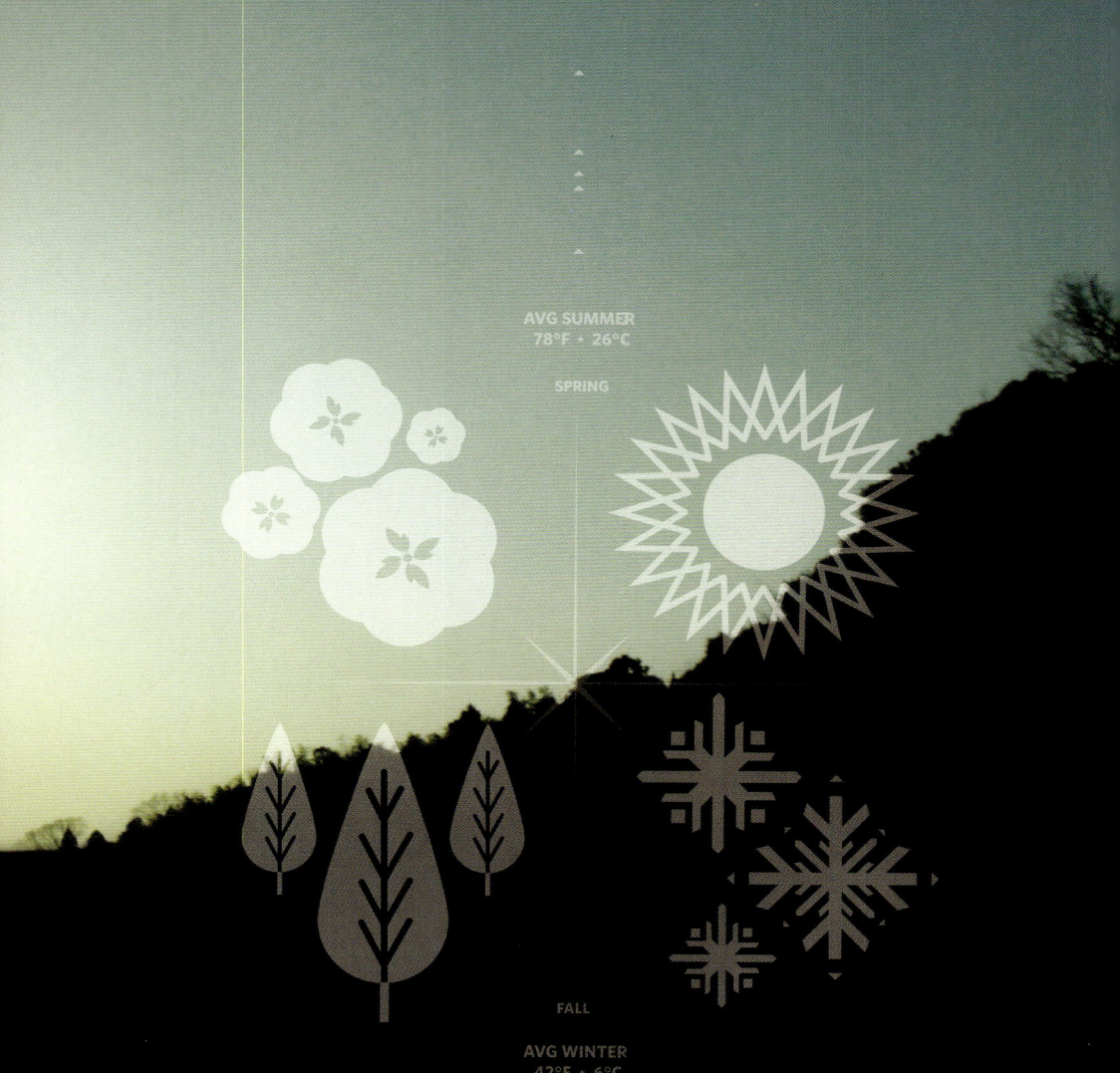

AVG SUMMER
78°F · 26°C

SPRING

FALL

AVG WINTER
42°F · 6°C

WHEN ARE YOU HEADING OVER?

We recommend fall over all other seasons. Spring is fine, but you do have to worry about rain and the coming monsoon season. Also, avoid Golden Week in early May, as most of Tokyo will close for the entire week. Winter is cold, but nothing like the North Pole, so it can make for a nice time as well, provided you take the appropriate layers. Avoid summer if you can. It's hot. Real hot. Then it's humid. Real humid. Imagine wearing thermal underwear while running a marathon in Richard Hamilton's tanning booth without the pearly white teeth and the free drinks. Those darn monsoons make it rough, and you will spend a lot of time walking from place to place or on outside train lines. Hot + humid + crowded train = a Degree moment waiting to happen. That said, we wouldn't pass up a free summer trip if you want to give us one.

MONEY AND CURRENCY

To quote the Wu-Tang Clan, "Cash rules everything around me," but less than it used to. In all major areas and shops, your credit cards and debit cards should work just fine. We do recommend calling your bank ahead of time to tell them to keep your cards activated when all your purchases in Japan begin to show up on their radar. But at some point, you will invariably get a call from your bank; when it happens, don't let it dampen your spirits. Just get in touch with them and clear things up.

If you'll be dealing with vintage shops, many still prefer to deal in cash, and a few even deal exclusively in cash, so make sure to carry some if you go to any vintage shops. Later in the book we will discuss the finer points of exchange rates, coins, and bills, as well as how to use an ATM.

DOUBLE UP:
BY PACKING YOUR FULL SUITCASE INSIDE A LARGER EMPTY SUITCASE, YOU ARE GUARANTEED TO HAVE ROOM TO BRING BACK ALL YOUR NEW PURCHASES.

A PLACE TO STAY:
YOU NEED TO WORK THIS OUT IN ADVANCE. DON'T THINK YOU CAN LOOK FOR A PLACE ONCE YOU GET THERE. IF YOU DON'T HAVE YOUR ACCOMMODATION INFORMATION, CUSTOMS WILL NOT LET YOU IN. NAME, ADDRESS AND PHONE NUMBER — DON'T LEAVE HOME WITHOUT THEM.

PACKING

Let's get you packed. There are some things you should take and some things you should not. Unless you are traveling with a porter service, we recommend a backpack for your daily trips, and a rolling suitcase for traveling from the airport to the hotel. If you plan on buying lots of toys while in Tokyo, we recommend that you pack your belongings in a slightly smaller suitcase that can fit into a larger suitcase, so that you have one to stuff full of, well . . . *stuff*.

During your trip you will probably walk more than you are expecting to, and it's a good idea to take at least two pairs of shoes. That way you can switch off shoes every day, or even during the day. You will be amazed by how much better your feet feel after changing into another pair of shoes that put pressure on different parts of your feet. By the same token, you don't need to take four or more pairs — unless, of course, your fitted hat matches only one specific pair at a time, in which case we expect you to go looking fresh to death.

EXCESS BAGAGE

Your cell phone won't work in Japan. It doesn't matter what international, hot-rod, multitasking piece of electronic genius you have. Japan has its own exclusive cellular network and your phone isn't part of the club, so leave it at home.

CHARGERS/ADAPTERS

We have mixed emotions about these. Yes, you need them, but they never seem to work well. Go ahead and pack them; it's worth a shot. Some of the hotels that cater to Western travelers even have U.S.- style plugs that make it a non-issue, but those are very specific.

If you plan on getting any work done, take your laptop. Internet cafés have alternate keyboards that have an option to type in English, but most of the time they get stuck in all-caps mode. It is frustrating beyond belief.

FOOD

If you have special dietary needs, you need to take some of your own food just in case. Supermarkets are not readily available, and while there are plenty of convenience stores, they don't offer a lot of specialized options. For the vegetarians in our group, we make a habit of packing plenty of extra granola bars. You won't be able to take fruit into Japan, much less meat and poultry, so pack accordingly. Most everyone will be able to eat just fine, but if you are "that person," take some edible entrées for the road.

MEDICINE

If you like a specific medicine, take it with you unless it is a controlled substance. How, where, and what you can buy changes dramatically from country to country, so your brand of cold or sinus medicine and headache or pain reliever may not be available. You don't need to take a pharmacy, but a few key items may keep you going versus cooped up in the hotel, feeling miserable. One thing you *can* stock up on in Tokyo is pink grapefruit HALLS. You can't get them in the States, and they seemingly cure colds instantly.

BIG IN JAPAN

We hear it all the time: "If you have [insert item name here], the Japanese are crazy for it and will pay you tons of money for it. [Distant relative or unknown friend's name] did it, and it paid for their entire trip." Trust us, if the Japanese want it, they already have it. In fact, they were stateside two years ago, buying the best versions of it before you even knew it was happening. This rule applies to all forms of sneakers, denim, Hawaiian shirts, toys, vintage t-shirts, records, and just about anything else you can think of. Don't believe the hype, and leave all this stuff at home.

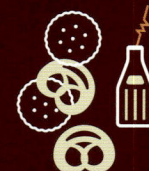

SNACKS:
ALWAYS PACK A SNACK. YOU NEVER KNOW WHEN THE HUNGRIES WILL HIT, AND YOU MAY BE ON A TRAIN OR OFF THE BEATEN PATH, WHERE A RESTAURANT IS NOT IMMEDIATELY ACCESSIBLE.

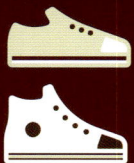

STEPPING OUT:
YOU WILL BE SURPRISED AT HOW MUCH WALKING YOU WILL DO IN TOKYO, SO BE SURE TO PACK A CHANGE OF SHOES. YOUR FEET WILL THANK YOU.

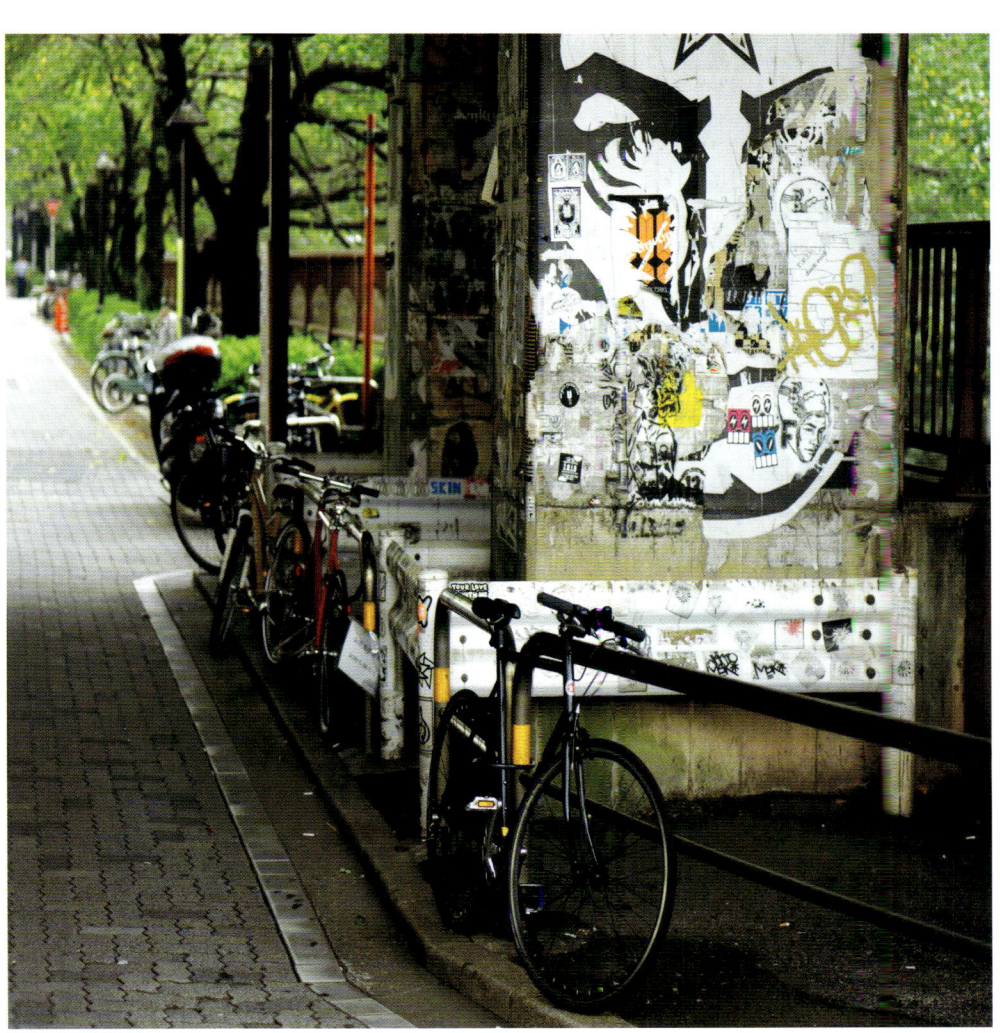

THE PLANE RIDE

Don't let anyone lie to you: This is a long ride, but you can survive it. Most travelers start in or connect through a West Coast airport on their way over. A few other cities offer direct flights. All approximate flight times are listed to the right. The return flight is shorter than the outbound flight, which will be nice when you are ready to come home.

In most cases, your flight will be 8.10–14.25 hours long, so take a few things to keep yourself from going crazy. Books, iPods, and portable game systems are all good. Magazines tend to last a short time and take up lots of space and weight. Laptops generally have low battery life and allow you minimal room in coach. Those of you flying business class or first class may have fancy gadgets that work like magic and make time disappear, but we don't know about them.

We also recommend snacks. Plane food has never been known to be epic, so unless you normally eat very little in ten-plus hours at home, pack what you like. One or two pieces of fruit make a huge difference and help balance out the soda and chips you'll end up eating out of desperation. PowerBars and nuts are also good traveling items that take up little space.

Beyond that, plan for your flight ahead of time, and you won't get stuck watching *Lassie* on the overhead projector three times in a row. Sleeping can be tricky, too, so don't count on it unless you are related to Rumpelstiltskin or Ambien. If you are taller or larger than your typical traveler, check your airline options, as some have more leg room than others. An additional two inches can make a huge difference on a long flight.

PASSPORT:
YES, YOU NEED THIS. IT TAKES
TIME TO GET ONE IF YOU
DON'T ALREADY HAVE ONE.
GET ON IT ALREADY, OR YOU'LL
MISS YOUR FLIGHT.

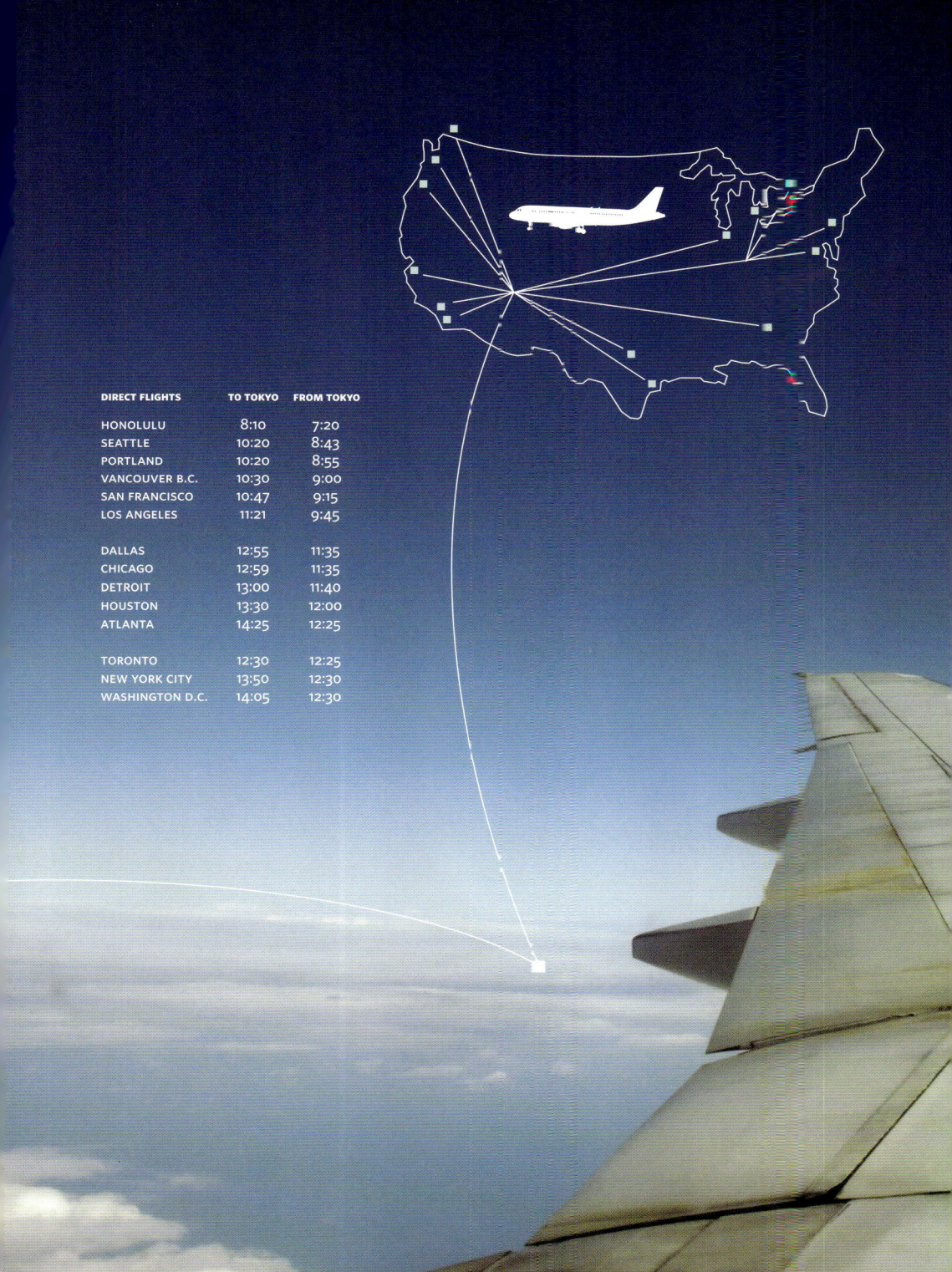

DIRECT FLIGHTS	TO TOKYO	FROM TOKYO
HONOLULU	8:10	7:20
SEATTLE	10:20	8:43
PORTLAND	10:20	8:55
VANCOUVER B.C.	10:30	9:00
SAN FRANCISCO	10:47	9:15
LOS ANGELES	11:21	9:45
DALLAS	12:55	11:35
CHICAGO	12:59	11:35
DETROIT	13:00	11:40
HOUSTON	13:30	12:00
ATLANTA	14:25	12:25
TORONTO	12:30	12:25
NEW YORK CITY	13:50	12:30
WASHINGTON D.C.	14:05	12:30

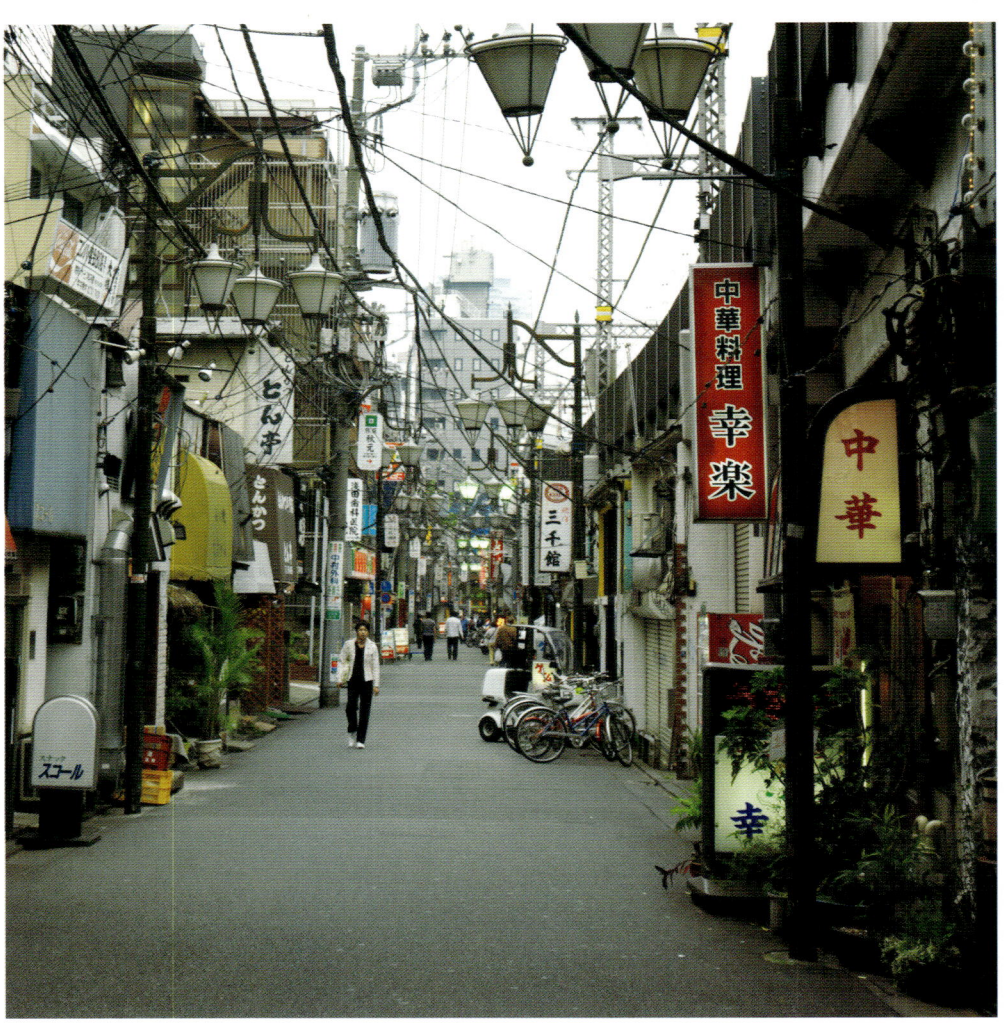

DRY LAND

Once you land at Narita International Airport (Tokyo Airport is domestic only), your next stop (after a long walk) will be customs. Use the restroom beforehand if you have even an inkling, because the lines can be long. Make sure you have filled out the entrance form they gave you on the plane, or pick one up here. Make sure you have your passport and know where you are staying in Japan. If you have these two things you will most likely get in, unless you are wanted for a crime (that they know of). There is no visa fee, so smile, say hello, get stamped, and head off to get your luggage. Once you collect your belongings, you will go through another set of customs. Make sure you throw out your fruit here (they have a place to toss it and anything else you need to). Everyone is nice, so just act cool, and everything will be fine. Wheel on out to the exit and begin your adventure.

MONEY

Once you exit customs, you are in the Narita International Airport, and officially in Japan. Conveniently located on either side of you should be currency exchange desks, which we usually use, as the rates are good. You will need to fill out a form for types of currency and then get in line, the first of many. When it is your turn, place your money and form in the small plastic tray, the first of many you will see. In fact, the small plastic tray might as well be the cultural ambassador of Japan. You will rarely hand your money or credit card directly to anyone; you'll place it in the tray, then they'll put your change and receipt in it and hand it back to you. Very presentational. Very formal. Very Japanese.

CASH FRIENDLY:
TO USE YOUR ATM CARD YOU NEED TO FIND AN "INTERNATIONAL" ATM. THEY ARE DENOTED BY THIS "POSTAL" SYMBOL.

ATMS

These are a little tricky, because local ATMs and even banks won't work with your ATM card. A bank can give you a cash advance, but you have to set that up ahead of time. Additionally, traveler's checks need to be cashed by a bank or hotel. To use your ATM card, you need to find an "international" ATM, denoted by the "postal" symbol shown at right. They are not very common, so all foreign expatriates know where they are. They usually allow a maximum daily cash withdrawal of 50,000 yen.

CREDIT CARDS

Assuming you have heeded our advice and called your credit card provider before traveling overseas, credit cards seem to work fine everywhere. One interesting note is that people in Japan rarely carry debt, so you might be asked if you would like a larger transaction to be divided into phases. What this means is that for a fee, the Tokyo merchant will spread your purchase price out over multiple billing cycles. This service is not typically preapproved for international credit cards, so we recommend avoiding it, no matter how desperate you are for an expensive item. Finally, just to make things sporty, there is a good chance that your card will be deactivated while you are in Tokyo. We know you called before you left, just like we told you to, but sometimes it happens anyway. If it does, don't panic. Take it in stride, call the credit card company at your next convenience, and use a different card if you have one.

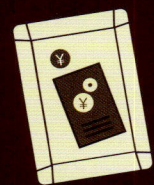

THE TRAY:
LIKE A SMALL PLASTIC SHADOW,
THIS TRAY WILL FOLLOW YOU
EVERYWHERE YOU GO. DON'T FIGHT
THE TRAY. THE TRAY HAS FRIENDS.
LOTS OF THEM.

JAPANESE CURRENCY IS CALLED YEN. THE EASIEST WAY TO THINK OF IT IS THAT ONE YEN IS THE SAME AS ONE PENNY. THAT MEANS 100 YEN ARE LIKE 100 PENNIES. IF YOU WANT TO THINK OF YEN AS DOLLARS, SIMPLY INSERT A DECIMAL POINT BEFORE THE LAST TWO DIGITS IN THE NUMBER, SO 100 YEN ARE THE EQUIVALENT OF $1.00.

DOLLARS TO YEN EXCHANGE RATE

	100 Y	105 Y	110 Y	115 Y	120 Y	125 Y
1,000 Y	$10	$9.50	$9	$8.50	$8	$7.50
5,000 Y	$50	$47.50	$45	$42.50	$40	$37.50
10,000 Y	$100	$95	$90	$85	$80	$75
50,000 Y	$500	$475	$450	$425	$400	$375
100,000 Y	$1,000	$950	$900	$850	$800	$750
Amount in Yen						*Amount in USD*

EXCHANGE RATE

To figure out your currency exchange rate, the easiest way to think of it is to assume that every number above 100 yen equals that percentage off the price. Therefore, a 110 yen exchange rate means you get 10 percent off of the price; a 120 yen exchange rate is like taking 20 percent off the price; and a 130 yen exchange rate signifies that you're getting an amazing rate, so you shouldn't even worry about it anymore — just buy everything you like.

ONE YEN >

THE JAPANESE VERSION OF A PENNY. THESE ARE COMPLETELY WORTHLESS, AND THEY FEEL LIKE IT. THEY MAY ACTUALLY BE MINTED OUT OF AIR. SILVER, LIGHT, AND SMALL, THEY WILL PILE UP LIKE USELESS TOKENS.

FIVE YEN

THE NICKEL OF JAPAN. ANOTHER WORTHLESS COIN. SO WORTHLESS, IN FACT, THAT THEY DID NOT EVEN BOTHER TO PUT A NUMBER ON IT. (OR MAYBE THEY DID THAT JUST TO CONFUSE THE TOURISTS.) REGARDLESS, YOU CAN'T USE IT FOR TRAIN FARE, SO IT IS ALMOST USELESS. LUCKILY, EVERYONE LIKES TO ROUND RETAIL PRICES TO THE FIVE YEN, SO YOU CAN GET RID OF IT THEN.

500 YEN

THE BIG JERK OF THE COIN WORLD, THIS OVERSIZE GOLD BRICK WEIGHS A TON. WITHIN THE FIRST DAY, YOU WILL BE DITCHING THESE EVERYWHERE OR PAYING FOR YOUR WHOLE GROUP'S TRAIN FARE WITH THEM. TOO EXPENSIVE TO IGNORE, AND TOO BIG TO LOVE.

TEN YEN

SIMILAR TO A DIME, BUT DECENT SIZE, BROWN, AND EVERYWHERE. EVERY TIME YOU REACH INTO YOUR POCKET, YOU WILL FIND A MILLION OF THESE. GOOD FOR TRAINS AND NOT MUCH ELSE.

50 YEN

A TRICKY LITTLE COIN, AND SMALLER THAN EVERY OTHER COIN EXCEPT THE 1 YEN, THE 50 YEN COIN IS SILVER AND HAS A HOLE IN THE CENTER. THIS IS THE COIN PEOPLE KEEP AS A SOUVENIR SO THEY CAN TELL THEIR FRIENDS, "LOOK, IT HAS A HOLE IN THE CENTER." (THEY ALSO WON'T TAKE IT AT THE MONEY EXCHANGE, SO YOU END UP WITH A SOUVENIR WHETHER YOU LIKE IT OR NOT.)

100 YEN

A MUCH HEAVIER, SILVER COIN, THIS IS JUST SLIGHTLY SMALLER THAN A QUARTER, MUCH THICKER, AND WORTH FOUR TIMES AS MUCH. THINK OF IT AS A SILVER DOLLAR. THESE WILL ADD UP QUICK, AND BEFORE YOU KNOW IT, YOU WILL HAVE 2,000 YEN IN CHANGE. GOOD THING YOU CAN EXCHANGE THESE.

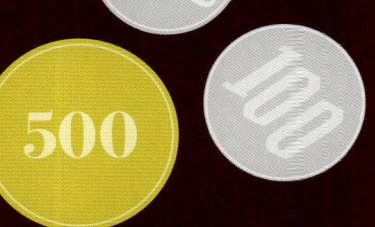

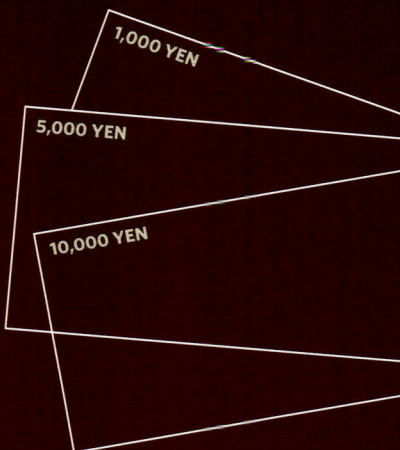

1,000 YEN >

YOUR FIRST BILL, ONE OF THESE EQUALS A WHOLE POCKET OF HEAVY CHANGE, SO ONLY BREAK ONE IF IT'S ABSOLUTELY NECESSARY.

10,000 YEN >

THE BIG BILL, THIS ONE CAN TRICK YOU, SO ALWAYS COUNT THE ZEROS. DON'T MISTAKE THIS FOR 1,000 YEN, OR VICE VERSA. FATTEN UP YOUR WALLET WITH A PILE OF THEM AND GET READY FOR A DAY OF SHOPPING.

5,000 YEN >

THE MIDDLE CHILD OF THE BILL FAMILY. QUIET, UNASSUMING, AND PLEASANT. THERE IS NOT MUCH MORE TO SAY ABOUT THIS BILL.

WHERE DO I GO FROM HERE?

We don't know where you're headed, so we can't tell you how to get there. Before you panic, though, here are a few common options that will probably work.

LIMOUSINE BUS: Probably the cheapest option from the airport, the bus counter is located right across from your exit from customs. The limousine bus travels from Narita Airport to all major city areas and hotels. They usually run every hour to ninety minutes, so you can always wait for the next one if you miss your bus. It generally costs about 3,000 yen per person and is a very comfortable ride. For more details, you can look them up on the web at: www.limousinebus.co.jp/e/index_route.html.

CAB: Cabs are available, but are very expensive.

CAR SERVICE: This is even more expensive than a cab. Then again, if you are considering this option, you probably flew first class anyway.

TRAIN: We usually end up taking the Narita Express. It runs all the time and costs 3,000–4,000 yen for a ticket, depending on your final destination. To get there, take the escalators downstairs. The hallways open up into an area with shops and a Starbucks. This is the right place. The Narita express ticket counter is located in the back right of this area. It heads to eight major neighborhoods in Tokyo, including Shinjuku and Shibuya. By riding the Narita Express instead of the limousine bus, you get to see the scenery instead of the highway, and who knew the airport was so far away from the city? If you take the Narita Express, you can transfer to most other train lines at its major stops.

NARITA AIRPORT

YOTSUKAIDO

CHIBA

TOKYO

SHINAGAWA

SHIBUYA

SHINJUKU

IKEBUKURO

OMIYA

YOUR FIRST TRAIN RIDE:
THE NARITA EXPRESS MAKES EIGHT STOPS THROUGHOUT TOKYO. THE TRAIN RIDE TO SHIBUYA/SHINJUKU IS ALMOST ONE HOUR FROM NARITA AIRPORT.

WHERE TO STAY

Oh, man, we wouldn't touch this one with a ten-foot pole. Use the Internet. Find out what is where, and how much you want to spend. We would suggest staying "central," so getting around is easy. We recommend Shibuya, as there is always something to do there, as well as Shinjuku, but there are lots of other places to stay. Staying in Roppongi is also popular, and anything on the JR Yamanote line is helpful. Because you have so many options, we'll leave it up to you to figure out your hotel on your own.

TRANSPORTATION

Now that you are in Tokyo, you have dropped off your luggage and are itching to get around. The easiest way to do so is by train. There are three kinds of trains: the JR system, the Tokyo Metro Subway, and private train lines. Before you panic, you don't really need to know most of it. Everything in this book is based on the main JR system, and of all the lines on the JR map, you really only need two; the JR Yamanote and JR Sobu.

Really, it's that simple. There are two trains, one that goes in a circle, one that follows a straight line. The Yamanote is always highlighted by a green line, and is one of the most popular train lines in Tokyo. It is easy to get to, and the trains show up every four minutes like clockwork. The Sobu line is a bit more local and runs in two forms: local (all stops) in yellow, and express (big stops only) in orange. For starters, ignore the orange express, and look only for the local yellow, which will get you everywhere you need to go. After you get comfortable with your new train, you can graduate to other train lines, but for now, keep it simple, and you will be just fine.

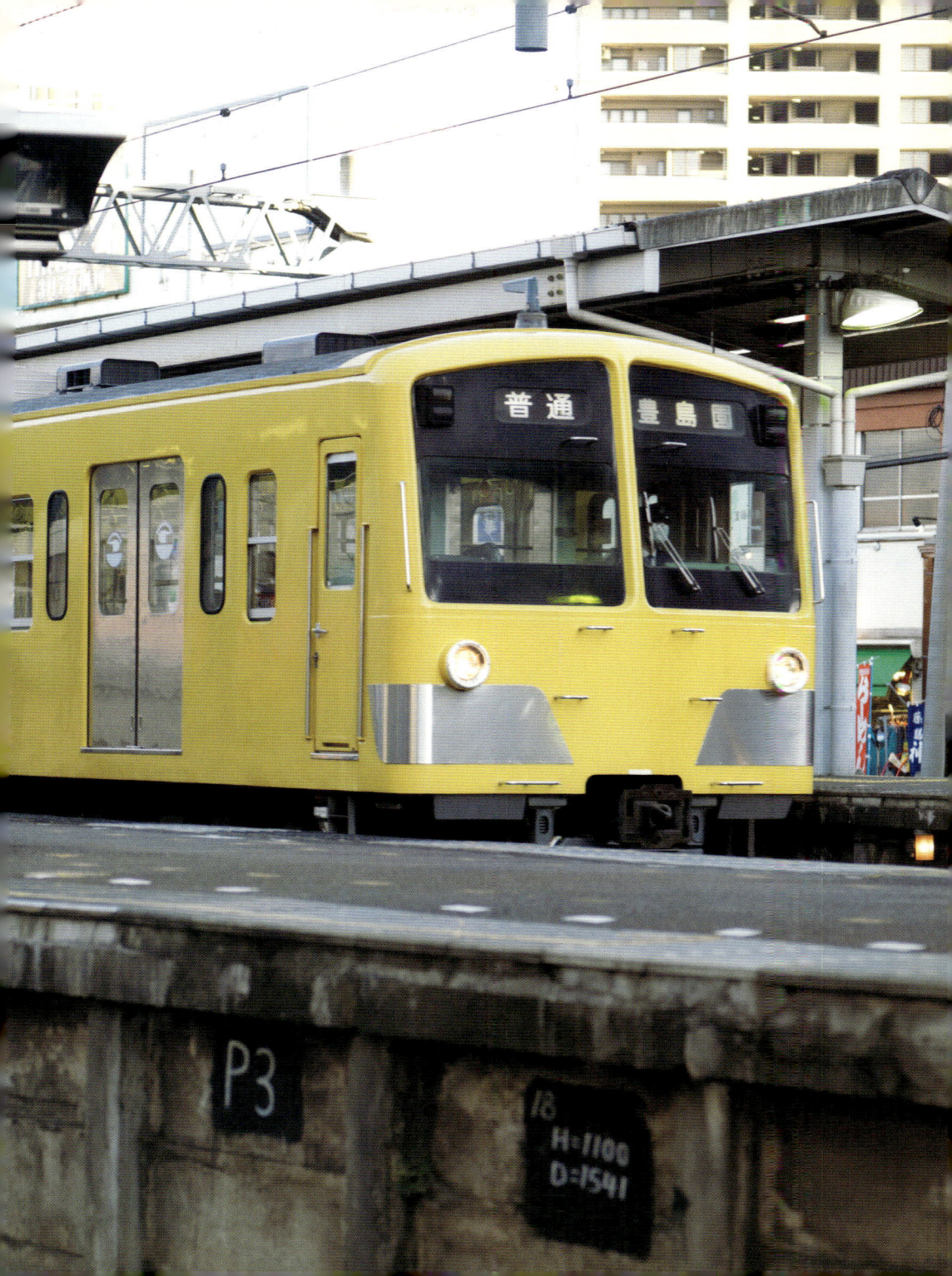

81

011 + 81 + 3 + TEL#

- US TO TOKYO -

01

01 + 1 + AREA CODE + TEL#
001 + 1 + AREA CODE + TEL#

- TOKYO TO US -

GETTING AROUND

Train stations are labeled in both English and Japanese on alternating signs, so anywhere along the way, you can check the station names. The super-fancy Yamanote line even has LEDs with the stop names, digital maps, and voice-overs telling you everything you need to know, as well as occasional English lessons. Trust us, it's almost too easy on the Yamanote.

HOW TO PAY FOR A FARE

Fares are based on the distance you are traveling. The minimum fare on all the JR train lines is 140 yen. To figure out how much you need to pay, consult the diagram in the train station. The bigger stations usually have an English version; some smaller local stations are only in Japanese, but you can count your stops from the diagram and figure out the price. If you are wrong, it's easy to correct the price at your destination. Just look for the circle (Yamanote) and the line through it (Sobu) on the diagram, and you will know where you are like a seasoned local.

TIME CHANGES

Tokyo is across the International Date Line from the United States, so it is one day ahead. If it is Friday in the States, it is Saturday in Tokyo. Toyko is eight hours behind the West Coast, or eleven hours behind the East Coast. This is always a little confusing, so we made you a handy chart.

TOKYO	HONOLULU	WEST COAST	MOUNTAIN	CENTRAL	EAST COAST
NOON SATURDAY	5 PM FRIDAY	8 PM FRIDAY	9 PM FRIDAY	10 PM FRIDAY	11 PM FRIDAY

MAKING A PHONE CALL

If you are calling into Tokyo, the country code is 81, and the city code is 3. Therefore to dial Tokyo, you need to dial 011+81+3+(telephone number). If you are calling from Tokyo to the United States, the country code is 01. So to dial back across the ocean, you need to dial 01+1+(area code)+(telephone number). In some places, you will need to dial 001+1+(area code)+(telephone number), based on varying phone providers.

CELL PHONES

Your cell phone will not work in Japan. Just reread the paragraph in the "Packing" section earlier in this book. Many places will have cell phones that you can rent for the trip, or you can buy international calling cards. You might also check to see what your hotel's phone rates are; many hotels have very good international rates, while some are very expensive.

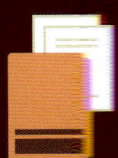

BACKUP PLAN:
BE EQUIPPED WITH YOUR HOTEL AND EMERGENCY NUMBERS AND PASSPORT INFORMATION, SO YOU'LL HAVE AN OUT IF ANYTHING HAPPENS. HOPEFULLY YOU WILL NEVER NEED THIS INFORMATION. SO PUT IT IN YOUR WALLET AND FORGET IT'S EVEN THERE.

BATHROOMS

Public restrooms are few and far between, so restaurants and department stores are your best bet. Most toilets have a dizzying array of buttons and functions that we have never figured out. What we do know is this: The toilets make noise or swirl water to help cover your "natural sounds," and one of those side buttons shoots precisely aimed water lasers, so watch out. If you end up at a public restroom out of desperation, you will be faced with a prehistoric squat toilet. Be sure to grab some of the giveaway tissues before heading in, as there are no paper or towels for wiping or drying.

SHIPPING

If you have bought so much that you need to ship it home, there are a few options for you. UPS and FedEx work if you have your own account already, and the Japanese postal system offers two forms of international shipping: Surface/Air/Land (SAL) and Express Mail Service (EMS). SAL is generally cheaper, but it has a maximum size you cannot exceed, and the packages take anywhere from five days to four weeks to arrive. EMS (Express Mail Service) is more expensive, but you can send much larger items than you can through SAL, and packages are automatically insured and arrive in just three days. Ultimately, finding a post office to mail these items from can be a pain, but your hotel can usually prearrange an EMS pickup from most locations.

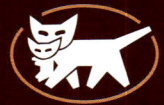

A HELPING HAND:
YAMATO DELIVERS EVERYWHERE THAT YOU DON'T WANT TO, QUICKLY AND INEXPENSIVELY. YOU WILL SEE THE YAMATO CAT LOGO ALL OVER TOWN. ISN'T THAT CUTE.

YAMATO SERVICE

You probably won't need this, but this is the greatest thing ever. Someone needs to bring this service to the United States. Yamato is a glorified courier service that allows you to deliver shipments within the city of Tokyo. For a very small fee, you can send unwieldy boxes or other items to your hotel or friend's house. Yamato delivers twenty-four hours a day, so you can pick your drop-off time in six-hour windows to guarantee that someone is available to receive your box when it is delivered. You will see the cat logo all over Tokyo. These guys deserve a medal.

LOCKERS

If you are running around and need to stash your loot for later, most train stations have lockers that rent for 100–600 yen, depending on the size of the locker. Drop off your stuff here and keep shopping; just make sure to come back and get it.

VENDING MACHINES

These are everywhere, and sell almost everything you could want. Some of the teas and coffees are even designed to heat up once opened. If you ever need anything to drink or snack on, these are lifesavers, and the only things open at 6:00 AM.

TIPPING

Gratuity is always included, whether in a restaurant, a cab, or a hotel. Most people will not accept a tip even if you insist, and some will even be annoyed at the concept. Keep the change, because they won't.

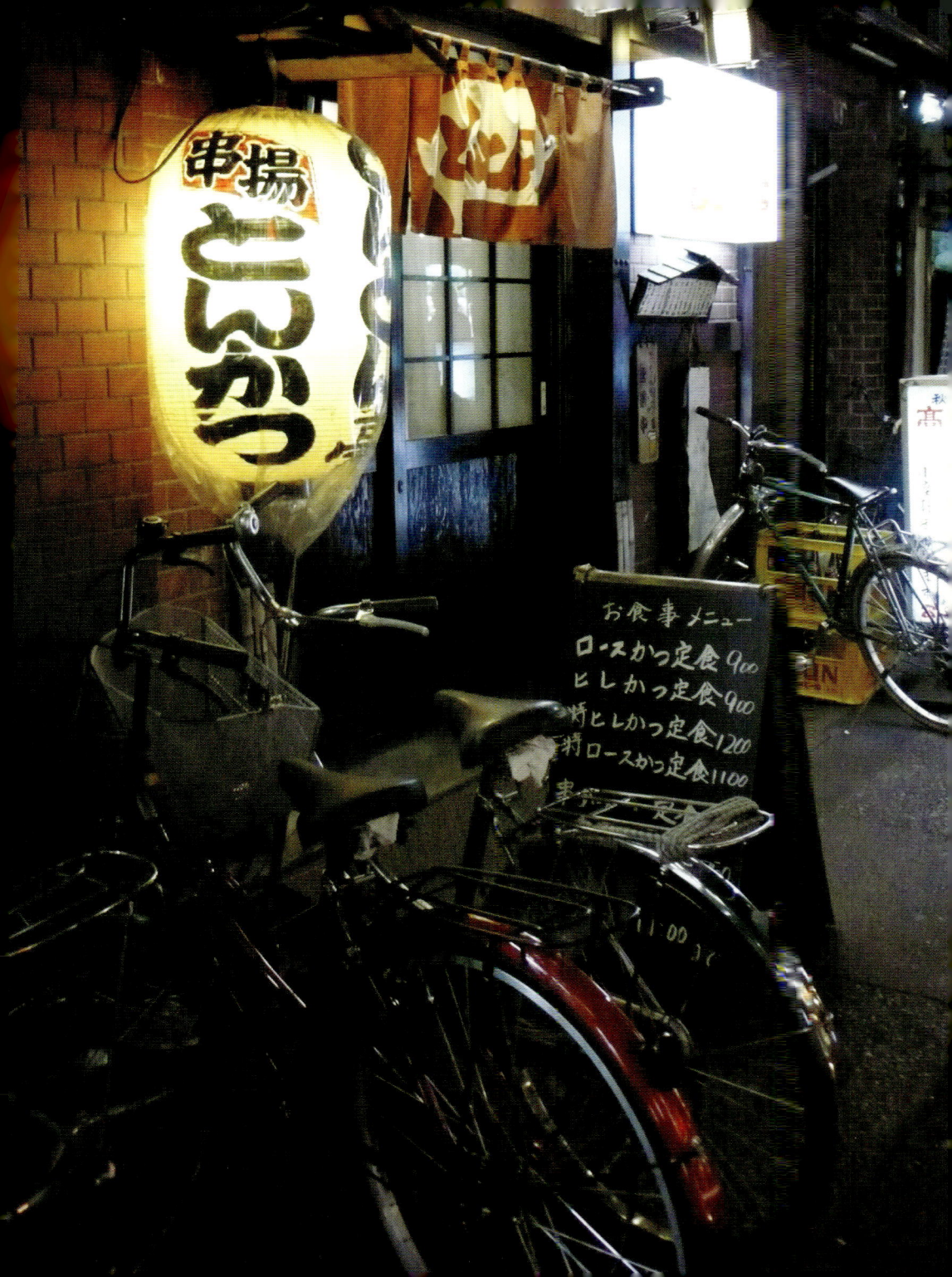

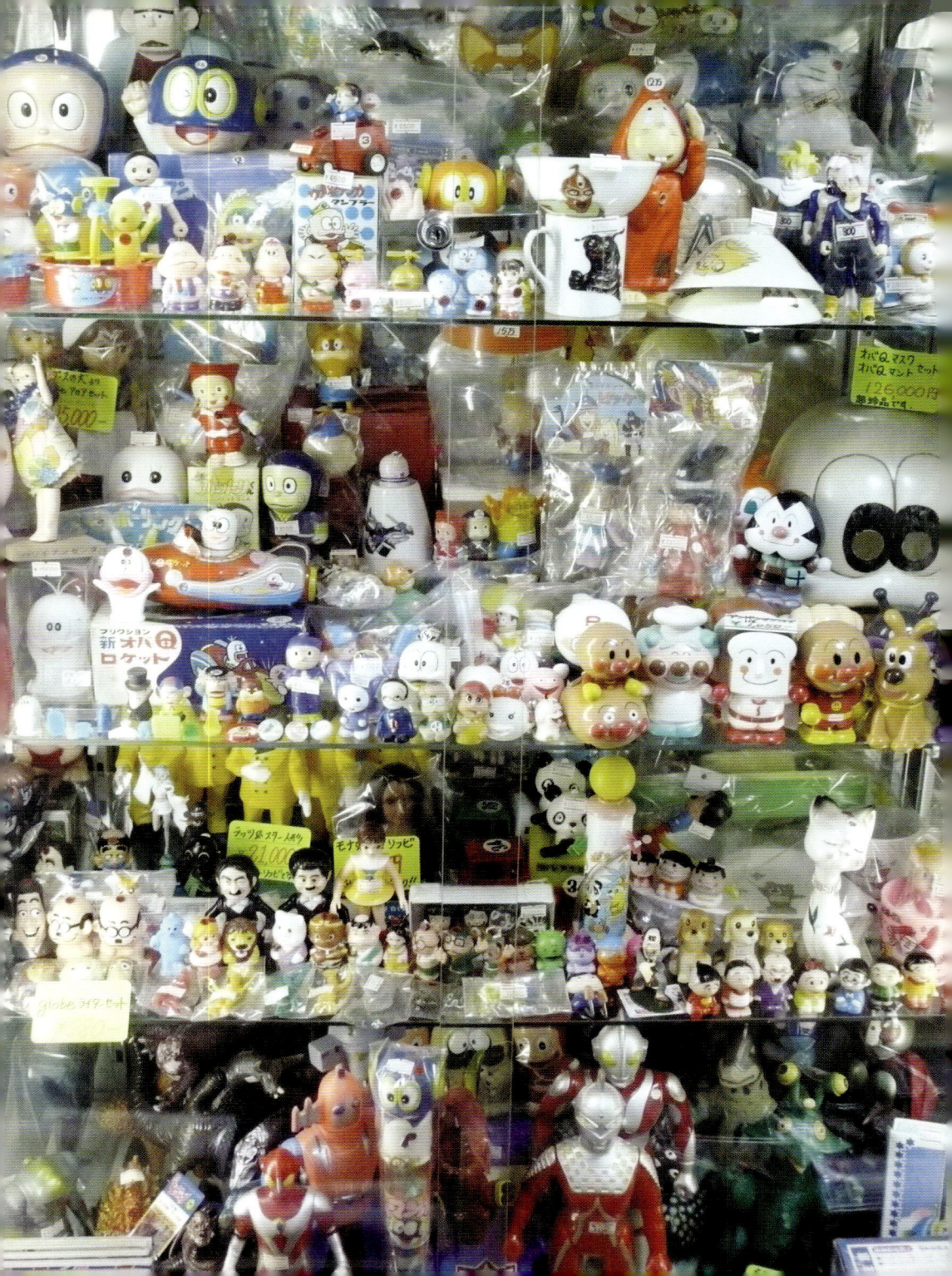

TRASH

There are very few trash cans, so expect to carry your trash with you until you find one. There is usually a trash can at most vending machine groups, as well as at the entrances to convenience stores. You won't see any litter, so don't start a trend—take your trash with you.

JAYWALKING

Most everyone waits for the light to cross the street in major areas, and uses the crosswalks. In residential areas, rules are much more lax, but expect to wait with the masses when you are around town.

SLEEPING

When you arrive in Tokyo, stay up as late as you possibly can. The later you stay up, the later you will be able to sleep in the morning. Once you go to bed, sleep for as long as you can. Toss, turn, roll over, and do whatever you can to keep your eyes shut. When you finally give up on sleeping, take a look at the clock. It will be 6:00 AM. We guarantee it.

WHAT TO DO AT 6:00 AM

In all honesty, there isn't a lot to do this early in the morning. Almost nothing is open—no shops, very few restaurants, and a handful of convenience stores (and that bookstore in Shibuya, but more on that later). So grab a snack, take a train ride, visit a temple, go for a jog, do Sudoku, call home . . . basically, keep yourself occupied until 10:00 or 11:00 AM, when shops will start to open.

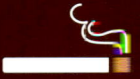

SMOKING:
EVERYONE SMOKES. IT'S A NATIONAL PASTIME. THAT SAID, PEOPLE USUALLY SMOKE IN VERY SPECIFIC AREAS OR INSIDE SMALL ROOMS WITH NO VENTILATION. YOUR CLOTHES WILL SMELL LIKE SMOKE AND THERE IS NOTHING YOU CAN DO ABOUT IT, SO YOU MIGHT AS WELL GET USED TO IT NOW.

Now that all that is behind us, let's move on to the good stuff. On the following pages are maps to different neighborhoods in Tokyo. Each map features the best stores, with dark green flags designating "highlighted shops," and light green flags indicating "secondary shops." Points of interest and other shops are shown with a light brown flag, with visual landmarks marked in gray. Last, the Koban, or neighborhood police boxes, are shown with blue hats. If you get lost or need anything, stop by the Koban. It's like a neighborhood information box that just happens to be staffed by policemen.

So get out there and have a good time. Wander down side streets, poke your head into tiny shops, and relax. Although Tokyo is a city that never ends, you are never far from a train that can get you back to wherever you came from. Now get going—you didn't fly all the way over here just to read this book, did you?

GREETINGS

Ohayou ....Good morning
Konnichiwa ....Good afternoon
Konbanwa ....Good evening
Oyasumi ....Good night
Sayonara ....Goodbye
Moshi Moshi ....Hello (on the phone)

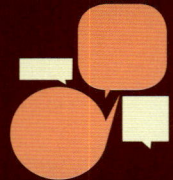

TALK THE TALK

In a surprising coincidence, everyone in Tokyo speaks Japanese. Some people speak a little English and are more than happy to try to work it out while you butcher their language. If someone knows English, they are more likely able to read and write it than speak it, so have a notebook handy. In the interest of fair play, here are a few key phrases you can use to impress your new Japanese friends.

TOY SHOPPING LINGO

Kaiju .... Monsters
Chogokin ....Die-cast robots
Sofubi .... Soft vinyl
Sentai .... Team series TV shows
Otaku ....Fans of anime, manga, and video games
Kore katte kureru? ....Will you buy this for me?
(Kore wa) ikura desa ka? ....How much?

HELPFUL PHRASES

Ha ....Yes
Iie ....No
Tabun .... Maybe
Tasukete! .... Help!
Domo ....Thanks (informal)
Arigatou ....Thanks (informal)
Domo Arigatou ....Thank you very much (formal)
Sumimasen ....Excuse me/Pardon me
O namae wa nan desu ka? ....What is your name?
Onegai .... Please
Mayotte shimai mashita ....I'm lost
Gomen nasai ....I'm sorry
Su goi! ....Cool!
Eigo wo hanashi masu ka? ....Do you speak English?
_____ ni wa dou ikebaii desu ka? ....How do I get to _____?
Kono densha wa _____ ni tomari masu ka? .... Does this train stop at _____?
Toire wa doko desu ka? .... Where is the bathroom?

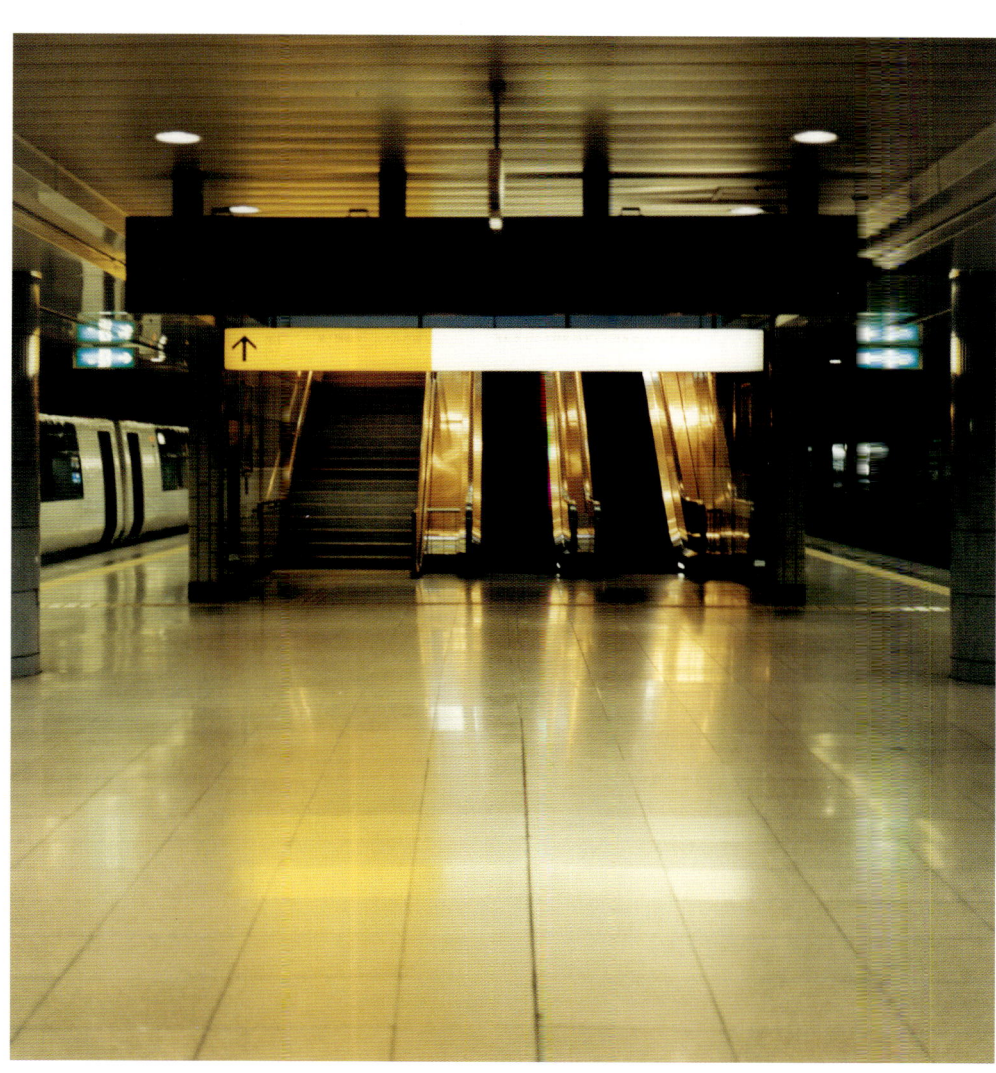

TOKYO
NEIGHBORHOODS

JR EAST RAILWAY LINES IN GREATER TOKYO

For your introduction to Tokyo, here is the map to the JR train system. Don't worry, though; you don't need to know all this. Just turn the page, and we will make it easer for you. Visit www.jreast.co.jp for more information.

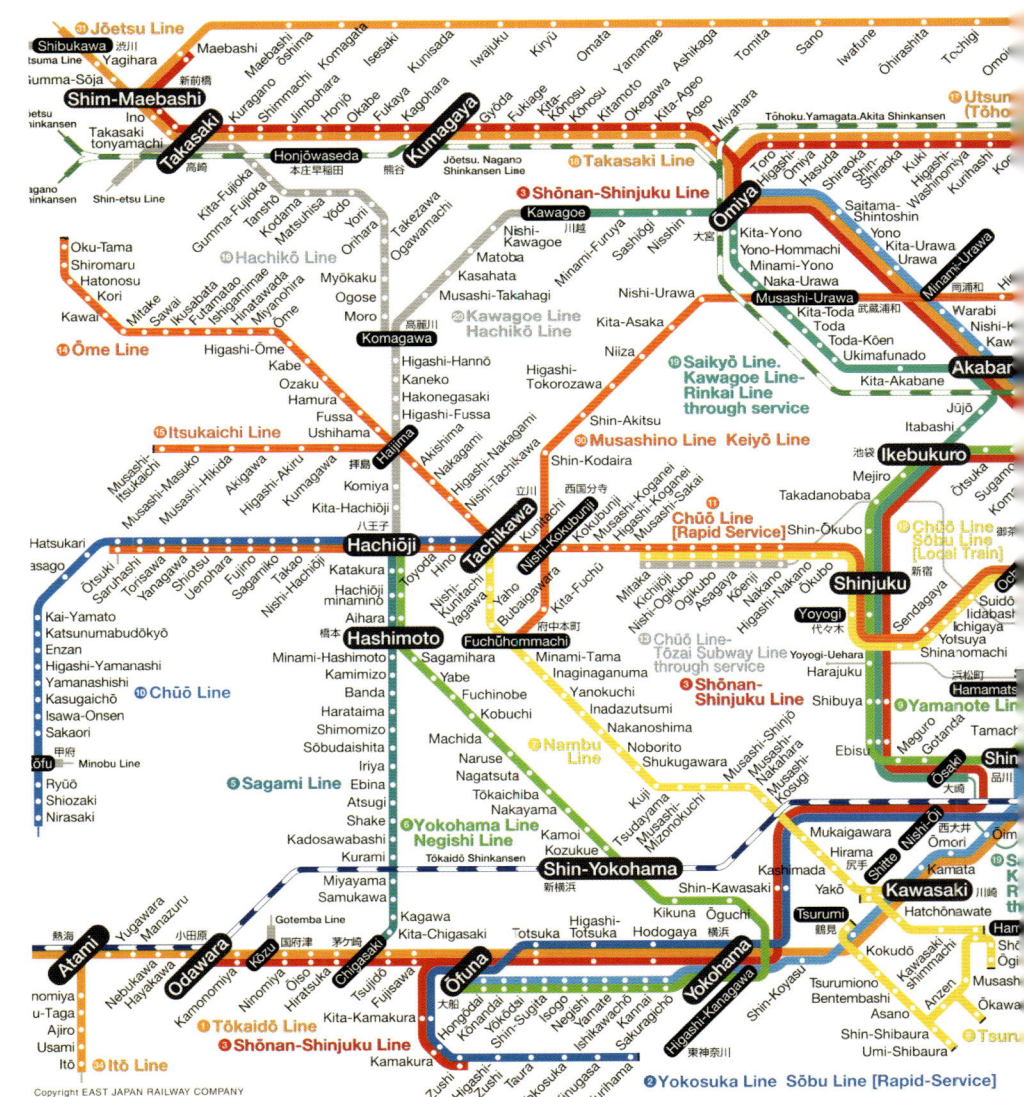

Copyright EAST JAPAN RAILWAY COMPANY

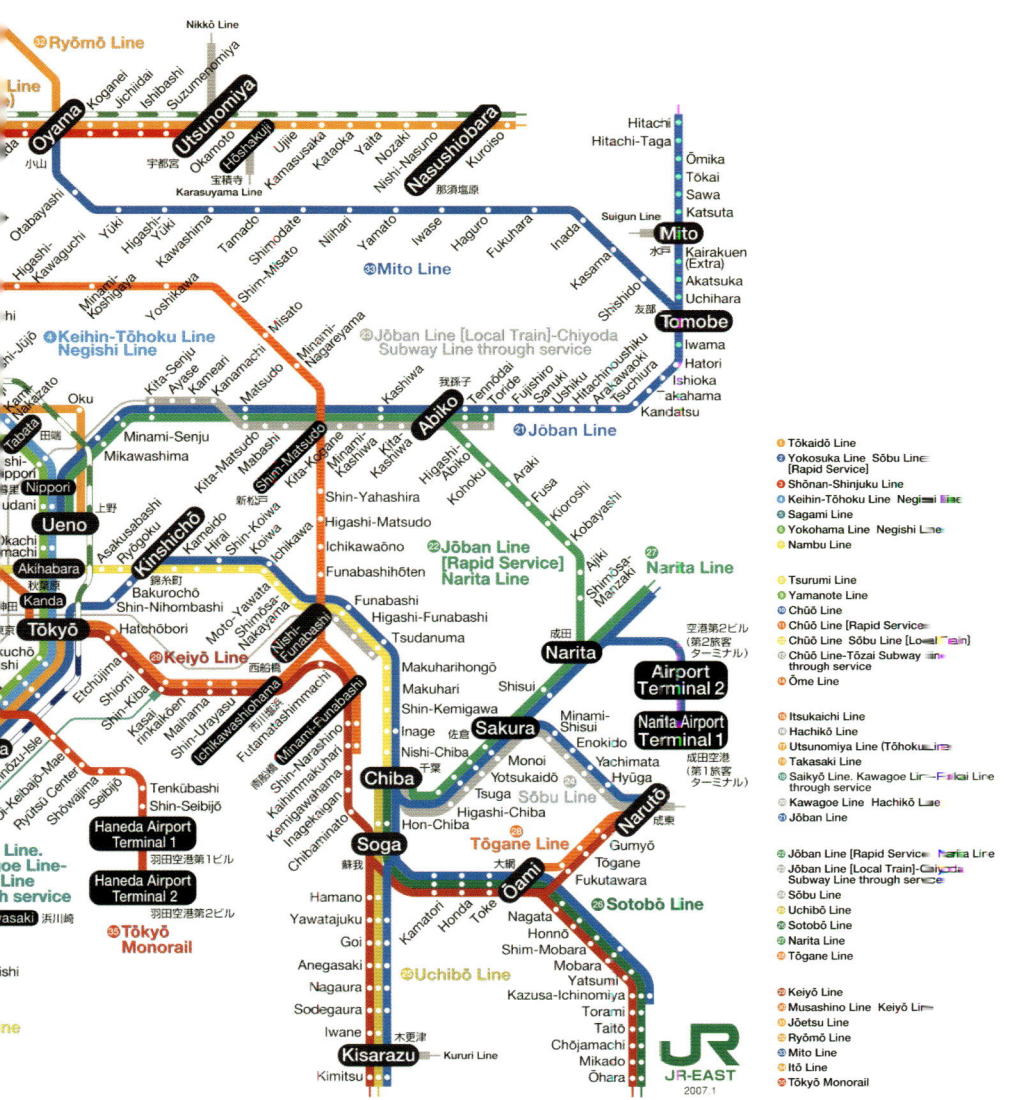

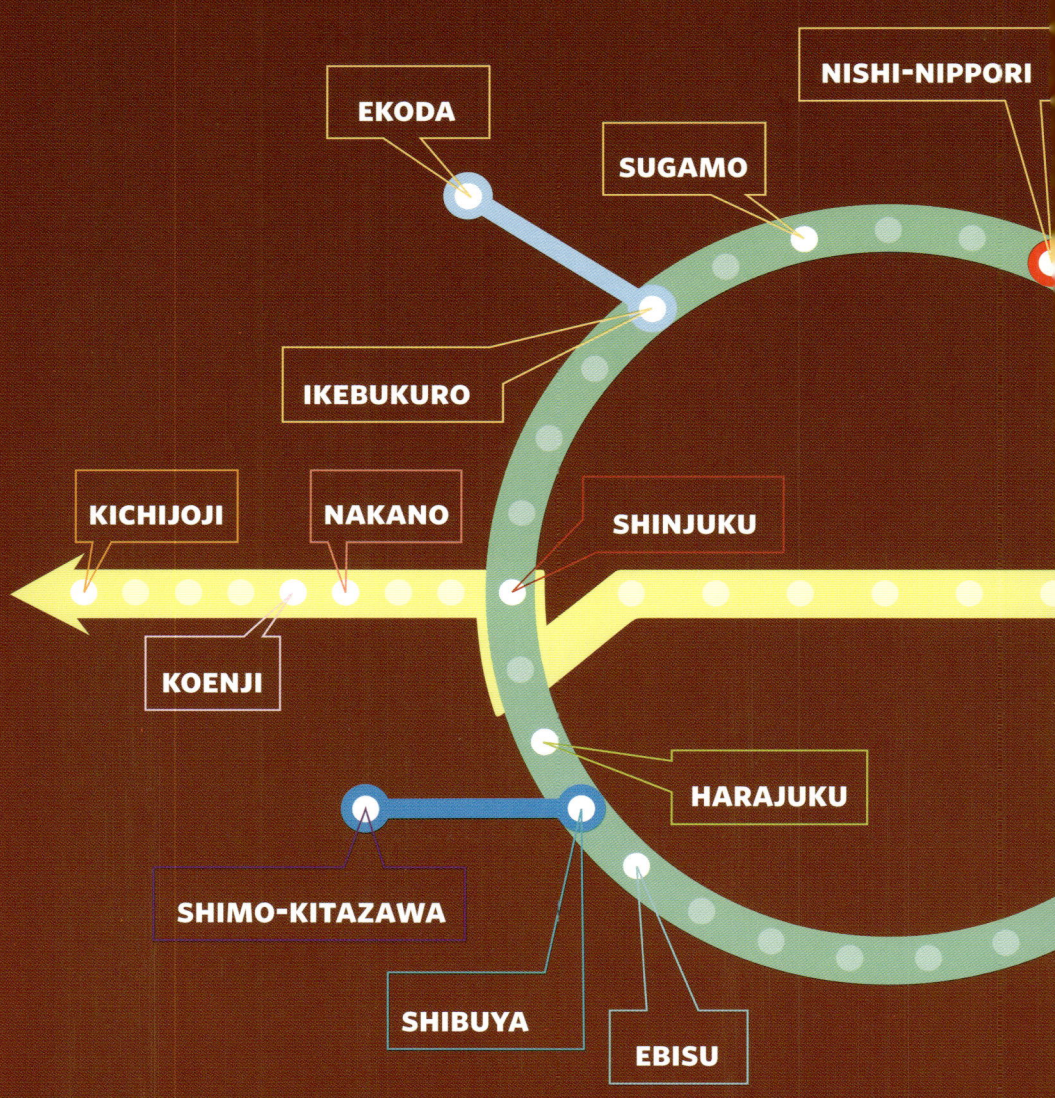

EKODA

SUGAMO

NISHI-NIPPORI

IKEBUKURO

KICHIJOJI

NAKANO

SHINJUKU

KOENJI

HARAJUKU

SHIMO-KITAZAWA

SHIBUYA

EBISU

TRANSIT

Feel free to ignore that giant map on the preceding pages. The only two trains you really need (for this book, at least) are the JR Yamanote (green) and the JR Sobu (yellow). The other four train lines shown here are for trips to single specific neighborhoods, and you will only use them once.

It's easy to get around town. The JR Yamanote goes in a circle, so you can always get back to where you came from. The JR Sobu is a straight west-to-east line that can drop you off inside or outside the Yamanote circle.

Now then, that wasn't so scary after all, was it?

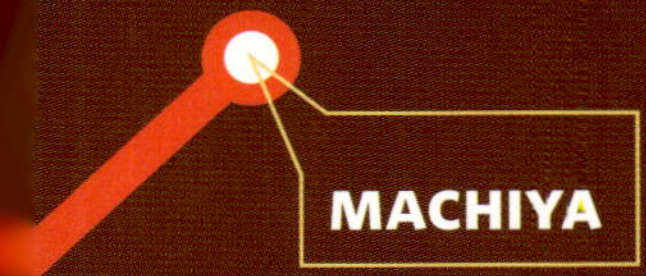

MACHIYA

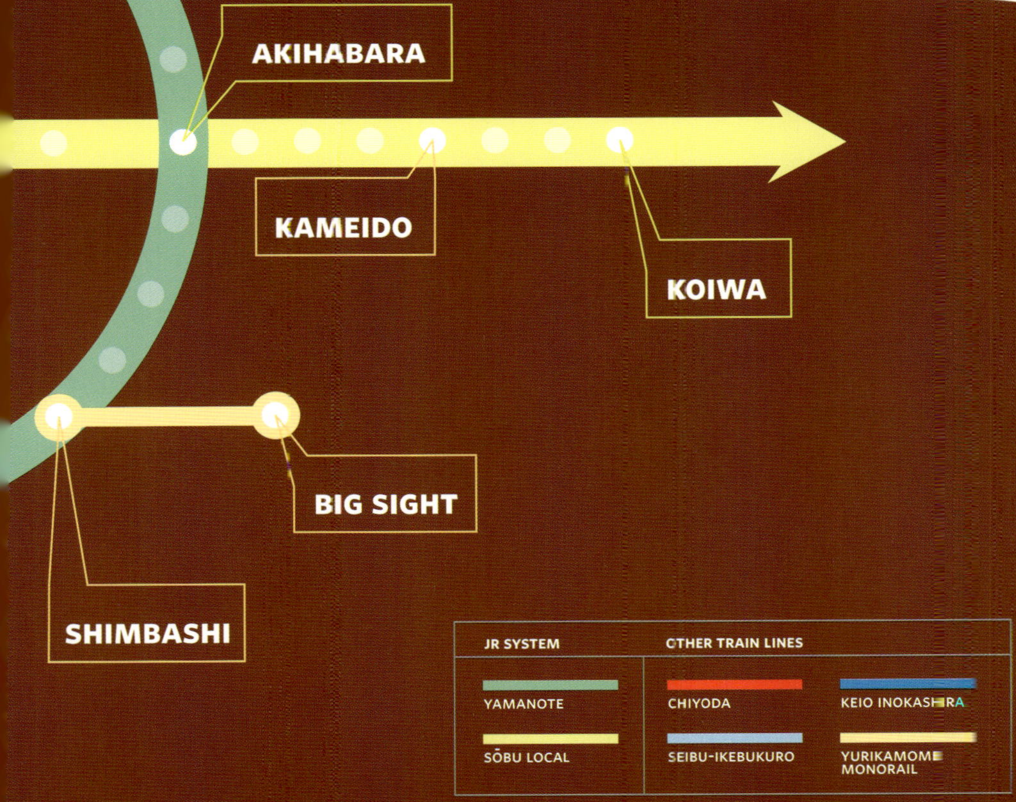

AKIHABARA

KAMEIDO

KOIWA

BIG SIGHT

SHIMBASHI

JR SYSTEM	OTHER TRAIN LINES	
YAMANOTE	CHIYODA	KEIO INOKASHIRA
SŌBU LOCAL	SEIBU-IKEBUKURO	YURIKAMOME MONORAIL

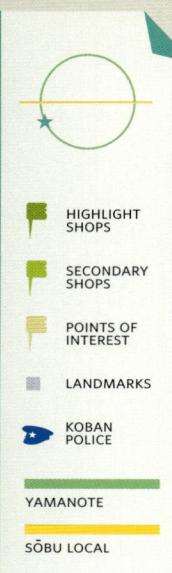

19

TOKYU
DEPT.
STORE

SHIBUYA

One of Tokyo's most famous shopping districts, Shibuya is
a must-stop for any traveler. Most famous for its two-minute
crosswalk, as seen in movies like *Lost in Translation*, it is one
of the most photographed locations in the entire city. With
abundant hotels, and access from the JR Yamanote line,
Tokyo Metro Subway system, and Keio train lines, Shibuya
never sleeps. Anchored by large department stores Parco,
0101, Tokyu, and variety store Tokyu Hands, its streets
are littered with boutiques large and small, offering a little
something for everyone.

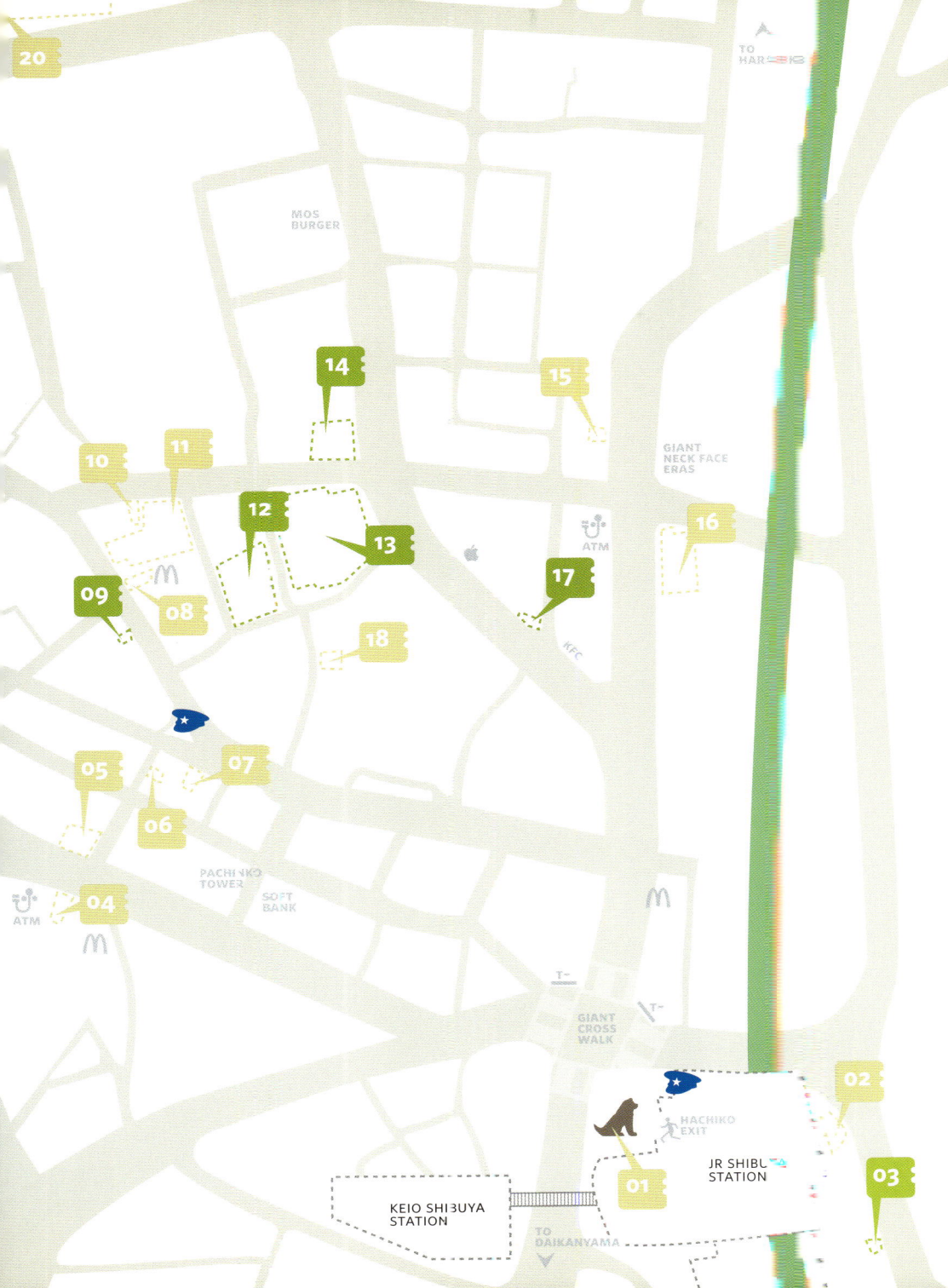

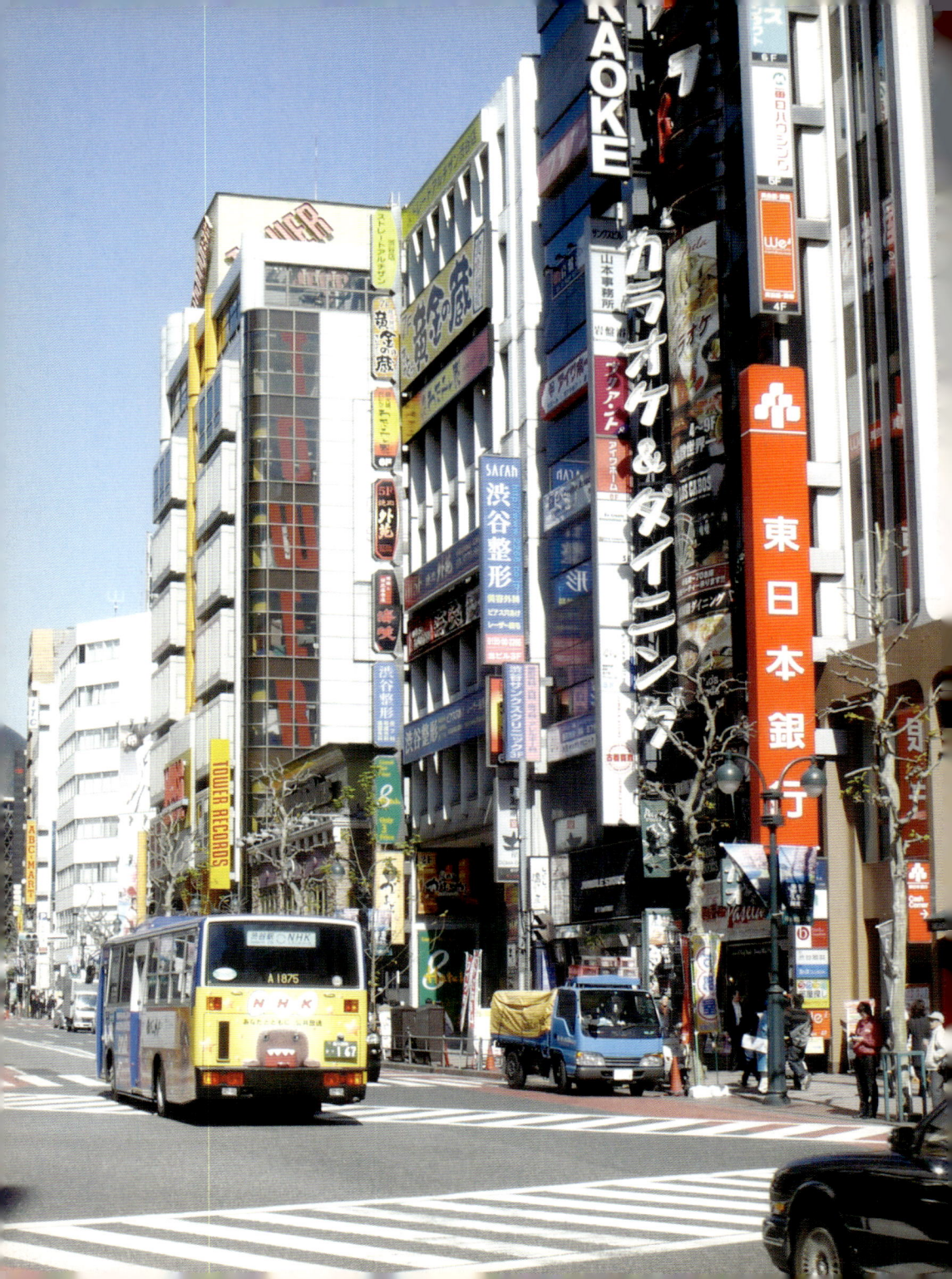

Shibuya is a great place to start your trip, as it offers you a taste of every stereotype you could hope to see in Tokyo.

If you are coming from the train station, look for signs leading you to the Hachiko exit at the north end of the station. As is true in most Tokyo train stations, you will see myriad exits, but Hachiko is the only one you need. As you exit the train station, the Koban (police box) will be on your right, and a crush of people will be in front of you. Across the plaza is a statue of Hachiko and a newly installed smoking area. Once you get your bearings, look for the giant television screens. The bigger of the two should be directly across the intersection, above the Starbucks. See, it's just like home. When the red lights come on and the walk sign lights up, you have the next two minutes to get across. All directions head at once, so like a salmon swimming upstream, make your way to any side you choose.

A conveniently located ATM is not far from the Shibuya station, so if you need to get some quick cash, this is a perfect time. Just past the McDonald's on the left is Citibank (04). If you ever feel a little lost and need to see another Western face, just wait here for a minute, and you're bound to see an expatriate popping out of the woodwork for a quick cash withdrawal.

For toy shops, Mandarake Shibuya (09), Project 1/6 (19), Blister (17), and Hobbit (03) cater to almost every collector coming to the area. To complete all your travel stories, you should plan a trip to hardware superstore Tokyu Hands (11), where you can find everything that you never knew you needed. Just around the corner is stationery store Picnic on Picnic (10), which always has the best journals, organizers, and stationery that you will never use, because you will be too scared to ruin it.

After loading up on paper goods, turn your attention to Parco 1 (13), 2 (14), and 3 (12). These three stores represent the best of boutique shopping in a department store setting. The Logos and Libro bookstores in the bottom of Parco 1 are our favorite bookstores in the city. The Tower bookstore (16), on the seventh floor of Tower Records, is a close second. Tower also sells CDs and, unlike their American counterpart, is still in business and has everything you're looking for. Design and magazine junkies will find Books First (05) and the twenty-four-hour bookstore (02) worth checking out as well.

Not far from Tower is designer t-shirt shop Graniph (15), selling affordable tees in constantly updated styles. Every American we know has become addicted to their "two tees for 4,000 yen" deal, a gateway drug to fabric crack. Along the way, keep your eyes peeled for a GIANT, Neck Face, and ERAS art piece that has been quietly occupying wall space just off the street for years now.

For quick eats or an early dinner, there are a couple of places you should try and many you should avoid (Shakey's, we're looking at you). If you like Indian, Curry Plaza (08) is easy to find, located between Tokyu Hands and Mandarake, while RAJ (06) is the neighborhood secret, squeezed in between a few floors of less reputable establishments. La Soffitta (18) is a dinnertime staple on every Super7 trip, and provides one English-language menu for your entire group of diners.

Other shops include Disc Union (07), which has a great punk record store on the fifth floor, and, at the opposite end of Shibuya, NHK Studios (20). For those of you familiar with Domokun, there's a gift store in the basement of NHK Studios that is the only place in Tokyo where you can still get Domokun items with any regularity.

From NHK, a short stroll past the stadium will lead you to Harajuku, if you are up for a leisurely walk. Otherwise, head back to the train station and proceed to the next stop.

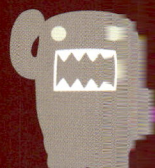

DOMOKUN:
THE FURRY, CHOCOLATE-COLORED WALL OF TEETH WAS TELEVISION STATION NHK'S MASCOT UNTIL JUST RECENTLY. THE ONLY WORD HE CAN SPEAK IS "DOMO," WHICH HE SAYS IN A MILLION DIFFERENT WAYS TO INDICATE EVERY NEED OR MOTION. HE LOVES TELEVISION. HIS FAVORITE BAND IS GUITAR WOLF, AND WHEN HE GETS NERVOUS HE PASSES GAS.

09

MANDARAKE
B2 31-2 UDAGAWACHO, SHIBUYA-KU
03-3477-0777, WWW.MANDARAKE.CO.JP/ENGLISH/SHOP/SBY.HTML
HOURS: 12:00 — 20:00

Easily the best-known toy shop in Japan, Mandarake is actually a chain of stores with shops spread all over the country. Mandarake specializes in secondhand goods, and the stock changes on literally a daily basis. The Shibuya Mandarake is no exception. Down two flights of stairs, covered in cavelike stucco and lit with seizure-inducing blinking lights, the store's descent is part of every visitor's tales of the city. Once you have safely arrived in the second-floor basement, there are rows and rows of manga, video games, mini-erasers, and, of course, toys. From vintage 1950s Tezuka *Astroboy* issues and original Marusan figures, all the way up to last week's Banda release or *Shonen Jump* issue, Mandarake has a plethora of items to choose from, usually at some of the best prices in the city. A must-stop for any traveler, just to marvel at the overwhelming nature of it all, or to buy some really great stuff you won't find anywhere else.

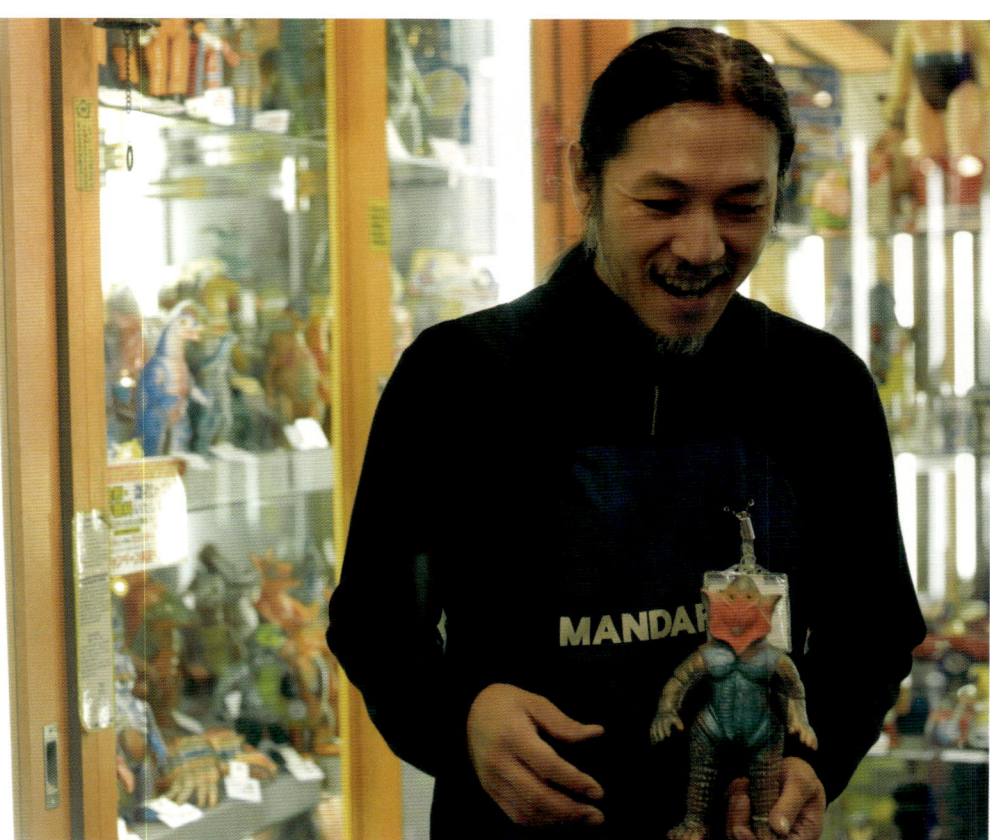

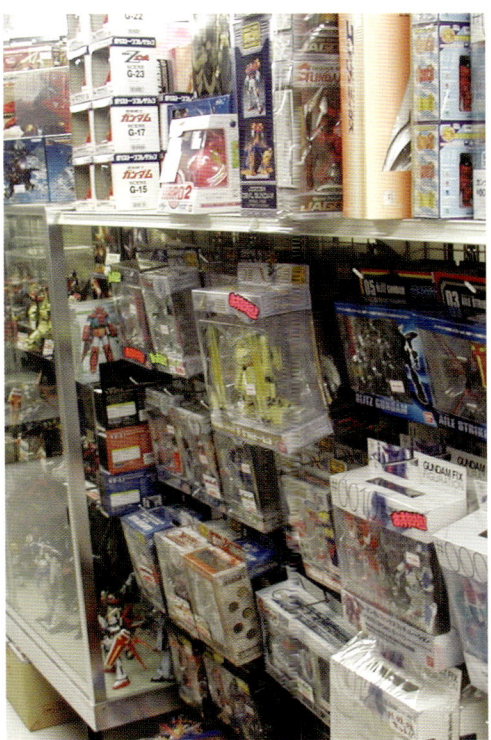

HACHIKO 01

The legend of Hachiko is amazing and depressing at the same time. The story goes that every day, a professor, Ueno Eizaburo, would walk with his dog, Hachiko, to the train station and go to work. Hachiko would then meet him at the end of the day to walk home together. One day, while at work the professor had a heart attack and died. That day Hachiko waited for the professor to come home on the train, which he never did. Hachiko returned to the train station, waiting for the professor to come home, every day for the rest of his life. Hachiko died nearly ten years later, along the way becoming a national hero for his loyalty and perseverance.

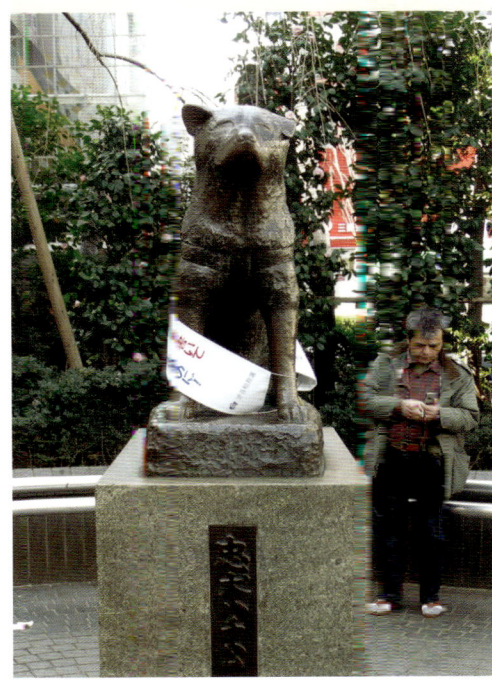

HOBBIT 03
3-18-12 KANE ICHI BUILDING 5F, SHIBUYA, SHIBUYA-KU
03-5468-2250, WWW.TOKYOHOBB1CO.JP
HOURS: 12:00 — 20:00

One of the several Hobbit shops found across Tokyo, Hobbit is a model-kit shop first and a toy store second. As a result, the toys they get are usually inexpensive. Hobbit always has a bizarre selection of new and old, and is always surprising and affordable.

17

BLISTER

SHIBUYA KOEN DORI BLDG., 1-20-6 JINNAN, SHIBUYA-KU
03-6415-3106, WWW.BLISTER.JP
HOURS: 10:30 — 20:30

For anyone remotely interested in anything action figure or Star Wars oriented, Blister should be your first stop. Stylishly designed and presented with panache, Blister has anything and everything you knew existed, as well as a steady stream of toy collaborations and unique products available only at their store. Most well known for their Star Wars specialty and exclusive items, Blister is the biggest single source of new-release action figure items in Tokyo, and possibly even in Japan. Named after the traditional action figure packaging style (a heavyweight printed "card" with a plastic "blister" attached to hold the figure), Blister is the antithesis of Mandarake, but just as fun and only a short walk away.

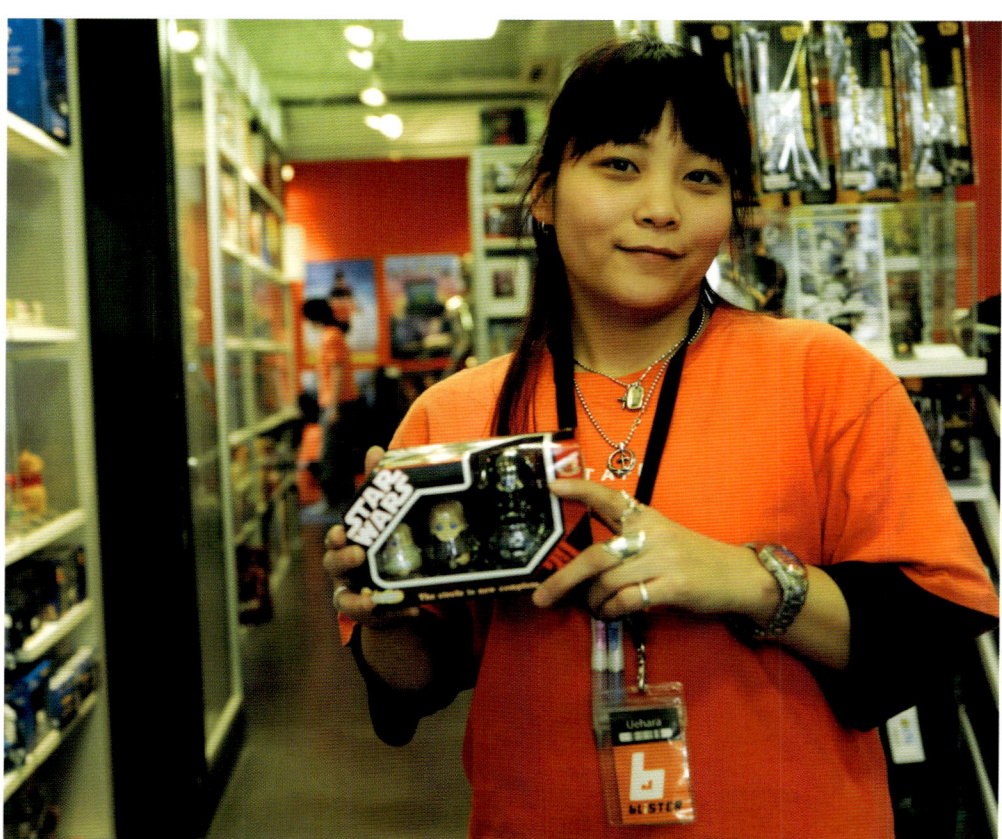

11

TOKYU HANDS

12-18 UDAGAWACHO, SHIBUYA-KU
03-5489-5111, WWW.TOKYU-HANDS.CO.JP/SHIBUYA.HTM
HOURS: 10:00 — 20:30

Rarely would anyone recommend a hardware store as a necessary stop, but Japan's Tokyu Hands is the exception to that rule. Stacked to the ceiling on eight staircase-filled floors (each featuring three sublevels), this retailer specializes in the unexpected. From stickers and stationery to trash cans and household appliances, from study aids and luggage to lumber and candy toys, you never know what you will find at this all-encompassing retailer. Affordably priced and showcasing the most extreme product juxtapositions from floor to floor, Tokyu Hands provides every traveler with a good story to share

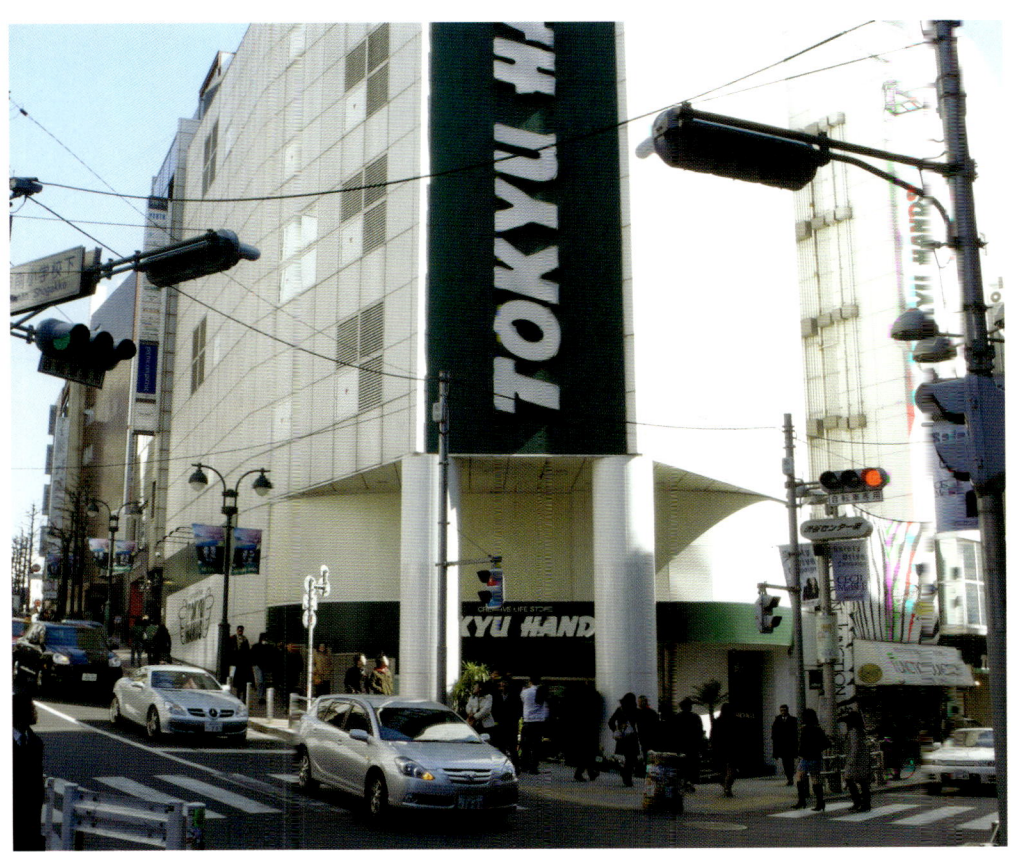

19

PROJECT 1/6

37-10 UDAGAWA, SHIBUYA-KU

03-3467-7676, WWW.MEDICOMTOY.CO.JP/INDEX_SHOPINFO.HTML

While not everyone may be familiar with the name Medicom, you probably know their products. Most famous for their ever-expanding line of Kubrick and Be@rbrick miniature figures, Medicom has been a toy staple in Japan for over a decade. Medicom originally began manufacturing hyper-detailed twelve-inch figures of comic, movie, and television characters, and has exploded ever since, becoming one of Japan's leading toy manufacturers. Project 1/6 is Medicom's flagship store, named after the scale ratio of their original twelve-inch figures. Nestled just off the main streets of Shibuya, it is worth dropping into to see the latest in Medicom goods, or any new store exclusives.

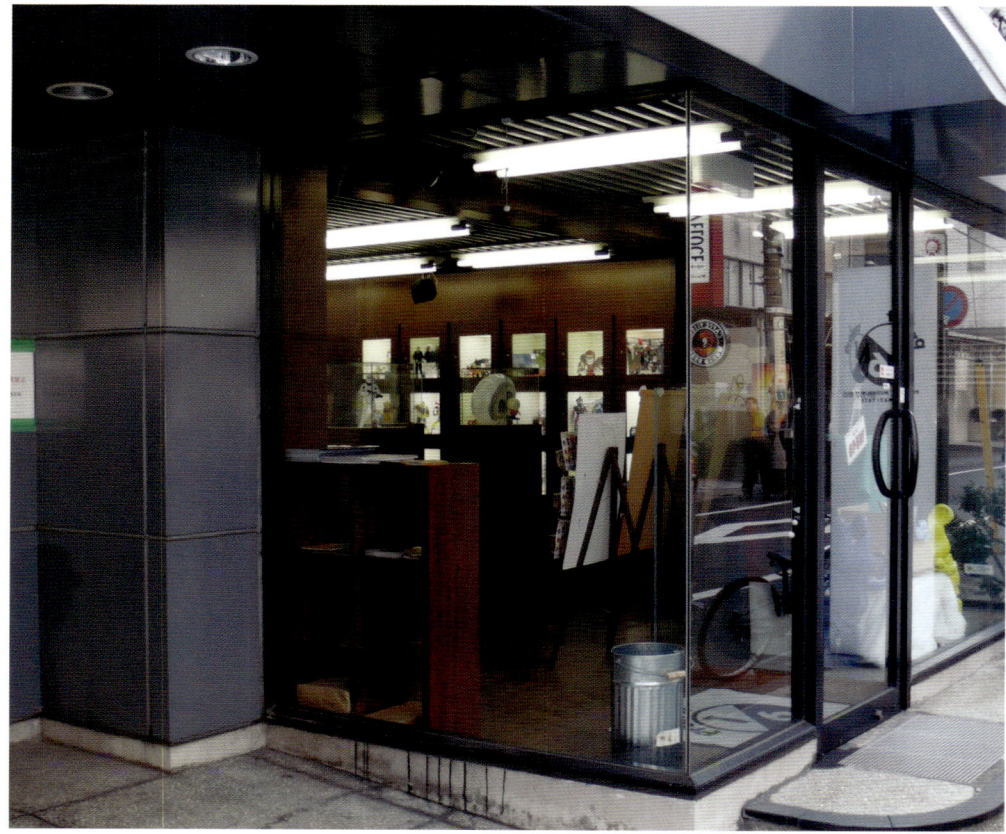

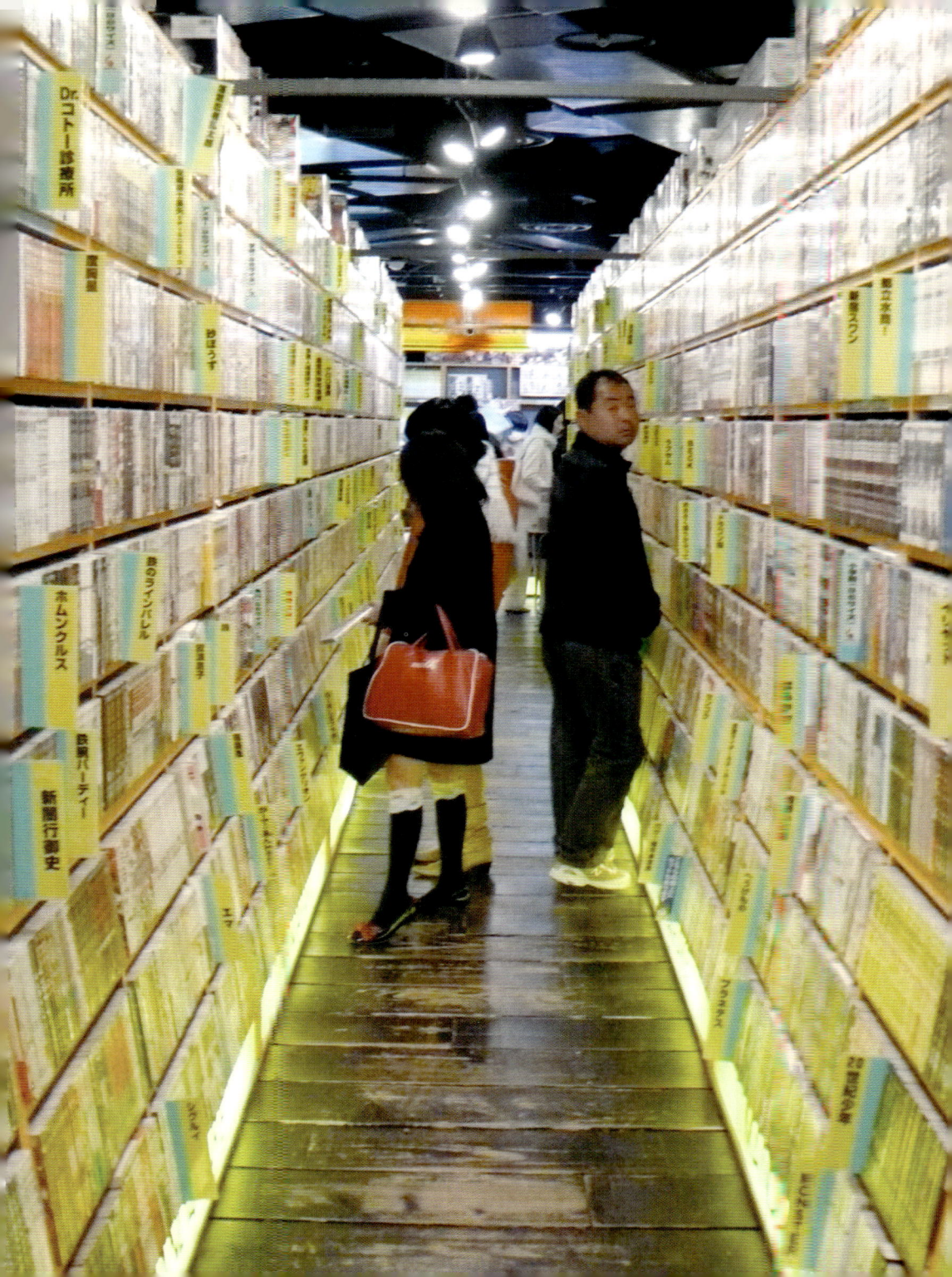

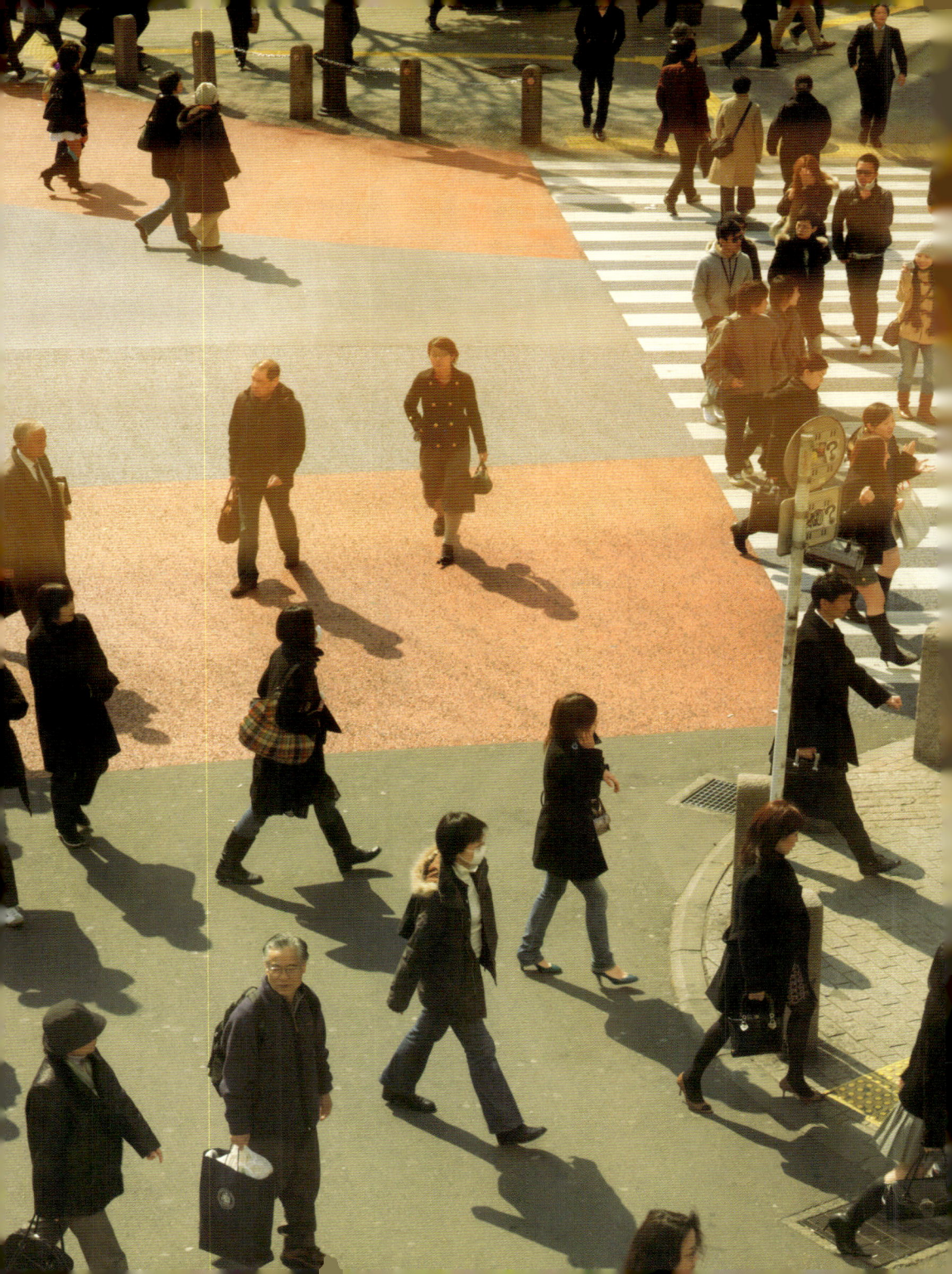

12, 13, 14

PARCO 1, 2, 3

15-1 UDAGAWA, SHIBUYA-KU
03-3464-5111, WWW.PARCO-SHIBUYA.COM
HOURS: 10:00 — 21:00

Shibuya's Parco department store is actually three entire buildings. Known as Parco 1, Parco 2, and Parco 3, this department store puts most others to shame within minutes. While most floors are devoted to the latest in boutique fashion the basement of Parco 1 is home to Delfonics, the Logos and Libro bookstores, a small gallery, and a few other specialty shops. Time and time again the bottom floor is full of books and design goods that exist seemingly nowhere else on earth. The café on the ground floor has good snack food for a quick bite, but falls short for a meal. The second floor of Parco 2 is home to housewares company Franc Franc, and well worth a stop if you are even remotely interested in stylish furnishings. Additionally, the basement level of Parco 3 features a constant rotation of new and interesting shops, while the seventh floor is home to a massive gallery that usually has world-class, can't-miss art shows.

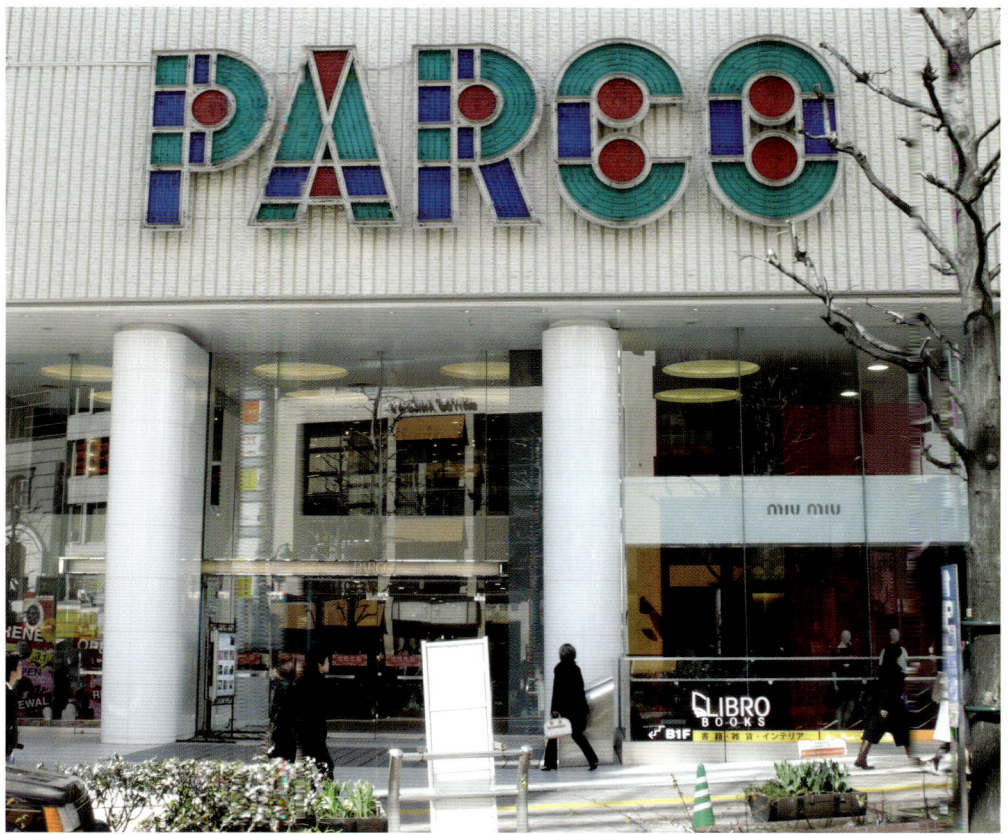

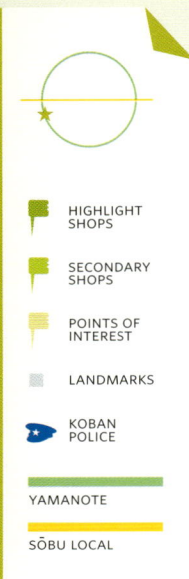

HIGHLIGHT
SHOPS

SECONDARY
SHOPS

POINTS OF
INTEREST

LANDMARKS

KOBAN
POLICE

YAMANOTE

SŌBU LOCAL

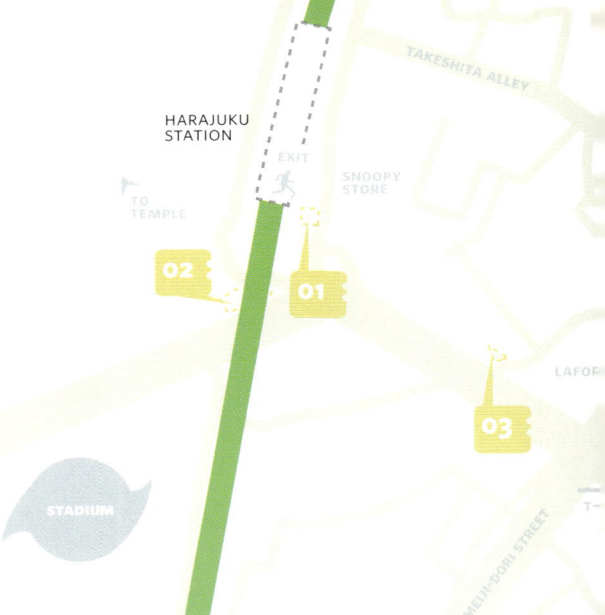

HARAJUKU STATION

TAKESHITA ALLEY

EXIT

SNOOPY STORE

TO TEMPLE

02

01

LAFOR

03

MEIJI-DORI STREET

T-

STADIUM

25

26

T-

TO SHIBUYA

HARAJUKU

Yet another of Tokyo's signature neighborhoods, Harajuku is best known for being both the birthplace and the cutting edge of current Japanese street fashion and culture. Weekends you'll see tiny shops with lines wrapped around the block for the latest shoe, denim, clothing, or toy release. Sundays are especially dramatic, with gothic Lolitas, 1950s rockabilly hounds, and homemade fashionistas dressing up to full effect and posing for pictures at the south end of the JR Yamanote Harajuku station.

01_ SUNDAY GOTH GIRL CRAZINESS **02_** ROCKABILLY DUDES **03_** MUJI **04_** PIZZA EXPRESS RESTAURANT **05_** KINETICS
06_ NEIGHBORHOOD BLACK FLAG SHOP **07_** ICE CREAM **08_** MADFOOT **09_** AIRSTREAM BURGER **10_** GRAVIS/REAL MAD HECTIC
11_ INVISIBLE MAN **12_** XLARGE/X-GIRL **13_** SUPREME **14_** BOUNTY HUNTER **15_** NIKE AIR FORCE 1, 25TH ANNIVERSARY SPACE
16_ GRANIPH **17_** BEAMS TEE **18_** SPIRAL TOY SHOP **19_** SECRET BASE **20_** EROSTIKA **21_** BAPE CAFÉ **22_** BAPE KIDS
23_ BAPE CUTS **24_** KIDDY LAND **25_** POOK ET KOOP **26_** ASTRO MIKE **27_** KUA 'AINA BURGER **28_** DOVER STREET MARKET
29_ GOOD DESIGN **30_** BLACK FLAG CORSO COMO **31_** ORIGINAL FAKE **32_** PRADA **33_** MIU MIU **34_** BAPE FLAGSHIP STORE
35_ HYSTERIC GLAMOUR FLAGSHIP STORE **36_** REED SPACE

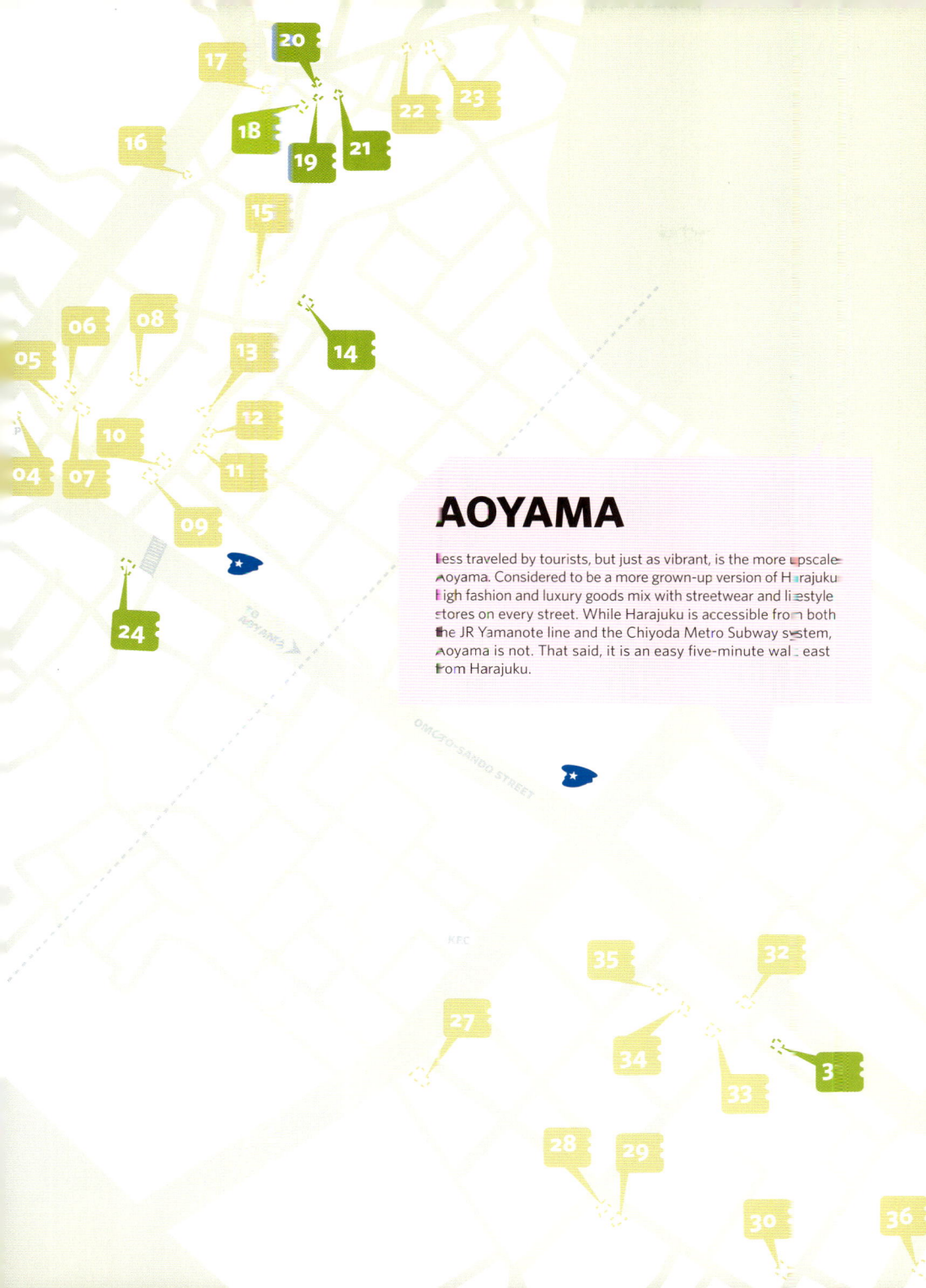

AOYAMA

Less traveled by tourists, but just as vibrant, is the more upscale Aoyama. Considered to be a more grown-up version of Harajuku. High fashion and luxury goods mix with streetwear and lifestyle stores on every street. While Harajuku is accessible from both the JR Yamanote line and the Chiyoda Metro Subway system, Aoyama is not. That said, it is an easy five-minute walk east from Harajuku.

19

SECRET BASE

MERC BLDG. B1, 3-27-17 JINGUUMAE, SHIBUYA-KU
3-3403-8188, WWW.SECRET-B.COM
HOURS: 12:00 — 20:00

Just down a narrow side alley, and down an even narrower set of steps, lies Secret Base, one of Japan's better-known manufacturers of modern vinyl. In a new location at the northern end of Harajuku, and with more than three hundred figure releases under their belt—as well as collaborations with Balzac, Pushead, Super7, Usugrow, Hiro-Grim, Saga-Chan, and Take-Shit, to name a few—this toy boutique has a loyal, almost cultish following. With new releases nearly every two weeks, chances are good that some limited figure will be available at any given moment. In spite of their relentless schedule, Secret Base remains in high demand, and most releases sell out quickly. When you do stop in, be sure to check out the locked pirate's case featuring one version of every figure Secret Base has released to date.

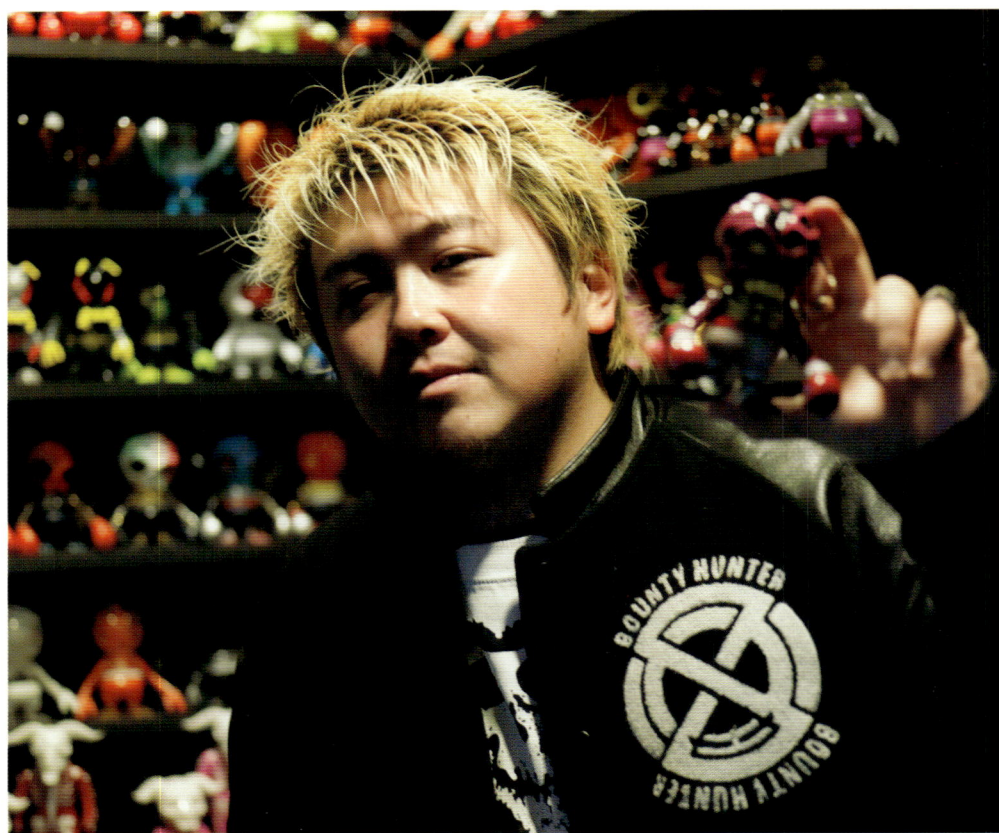

What can be said about Harajuku that hasn't been said before? Heck, even Gwen Stefani names songs and her backup dancers after these cool kids. To see Harajuku at its absolute craziest, stop by on a Sunday. At the south end of the station (01), the finest in homemade fashion will be on parade and ready for pictures. Dominated by gothic Lolitas and immortalized in books like *Fruits,* this Sunday afternoon fashion show puts Paris on notice and makes you wonder what these kids do for the rest of the week. Just across the bridge, at the entrance to the park, will be groups of retro rockabilly dudes (02) in full gear, dancing the afternoon away. Is it crazier that we are mentioning it, or that they are dead serious?

From one fashion extreme to another, head on over to Harajuku proper. Home to the latest in hipster streetwear from around the globe, and every type of sneaker imaginable, Harajuku is not for those with a light wallet or well-worn shoes. Some of the best local shops and brands sure to bump up your street cred, are Kinetics (05), Neighborhood (06), Madfoot (08), Real Mad Hectic (10), and Invisible Man (11), as well as American brands X-Large and X-girl (12), Supreme (13), and the Nike twenty-fifth anniversary Air Force 1 shop (15).

For art-lovers, we suggest stopping by the Real Mad Hectic shop (10) to see a large group of Phil Frost paintings, and the Bape Café (21) to see the original paintings of KAWS' *Kimpsons* preserved for eternity. Speaking of Bape, the worldwide domination of *Planet of the Apes* iconography has extended to both a kids' store (22) and a barbershop (23) located nearby, which have to be seen to be believed (who can imagine a playpen full of foam bananas?). Located next to the Bape triumvirate is artist Rockin' Jelly Bean's shop, Erostika (20), and just behind that lurks the lair of Secret Base (19), one of Tokyo's premier boutique toy manufacturers and ongoing collaborator with Pushead, Medicom, and Super7. Flanking Secret Base is toy shop Spiral (18), featuring a mix of old and new character goods.

As you make your way back to the main road, stop by the legendary Bounty Hunter (14). Known in Japan as a key fashion brand, Bounty Hunter is also known for helping kick off the entire designer toy movement in 1999 with their Kid Hunter figure, along with the Fink-Shit figure designed by Gocobat's Take-Shit.

Back on the main street, Omote-Sando, and on the other side of the bridge is the multiple-story new toy paradise known as Kiddy Land. Though it caters more to little ladies than to boys, Kiddy Land still has a bit of everything. For the toy-shop completist, a quick trip down the side alleys will take you to Pook et Koop (25) and Astro Mike (26), two shops specializing in newer, more affordable toys and knickknacks. Muji (03), renowned for its simplicity, has a decent-size shop just off the main street. Although it may not be as well stocked as its larger stores, there is always something worth picking up at this Japanese retailer.

AOYAMA
Just a short walk from Harajuku is the more upscale Aoyama. There, luxury brands rub shoulders with the streetwear elite and a few brands that manage to straddle the line.

For designer-toy hunters, the main point of a trip to Aoyama is to see the impressive Original Fake (31). With its giant anatomical study of the KAWS Companion guarding the entrance, KAWS' flagship store has housed almost every new KAWS release since its opening. Equally impressive in design, and worth seeing even if you care nothing for the brands, are Miu Miu (33), the Bape flagship store (34), the Hysteric Glamour flagship store (35) and Prada (32). Other shops worth browsing are Staple's Reed Space (just behind Marc Jacobs, and just off the map (36)), Black Flag (30), Dover Street (28), and, for the modernist houseware and furniture lover in you, Good Design (29). After all that walking, head over to Kua 'Aina (27) for a great burger or veggie sandwich direct from Hawaii, return to Harajuku for a burger at the Airstream trailer (09), or go one floor above the Gap for pizza and pasta from London's Pizza Express (04).

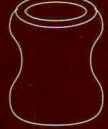

WRITING ON THE WALL:
BEST KNOWN FOR HIS CLEAN,
WAVY LINE WORK, KAMI'S ALTER
EGO PAINTS THESE LITTLE SHAPES
ALL AROUND THE CITY. WHEN YOU
SEE ONE, YOU KNOW THAT "KAMI
WAS HERE," JUST LIKE YOU ARE.
THEN YOU CAN TELL YOUR FRIENDS
YOU CROSSED PATHS WITH ONE OF
TOKYO'S FINEST ARTISTS.

21

BAPE CAFÉ
3-27-22 JINGUMAE, SHIBUYA-KU
03-5770-6560
HOURS: 10:30 — 20:00

While not an official retail store, the Bape Café is an easy place to grab a quick drink or snack while jetting around Harajuku. The real reason for its mention is not the food, but the artwork lining the walls. The entire bottom floor is ringed with the original KAWS *Kimpsons* paintings in perfect, single scale, with no character left unturned. For good measure, the giant *Kimpsons* Sergeant Pepper homage is the centerpiece of the second floor. This is a must-see for any KAWS or modern vinyl fan.

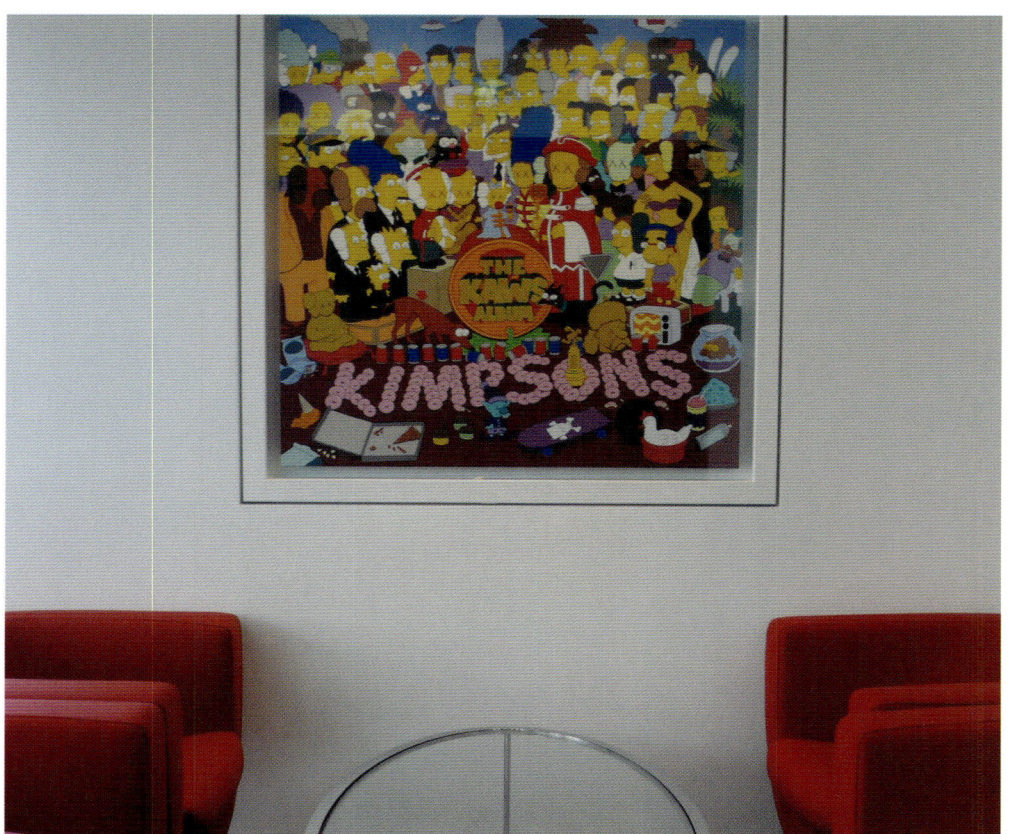

14

BOUNTY HUNTER
3-15-8 JINGUMAE, SHIBUYA-KU
3-3746-1044, WWW.BOUNTY-HUNTER.COM
HOURS: 12:00 — 20:00

Renowned as one of the innovators of Japanese punk rock street fashion, and considered one of the original vinyl toy manufacturers, Bounty Hunter has set countless trends that others try to follow. After releasing their genre-inducing Kid Hunter figure in 1999, Bounty Hunter was the first toy company to work with now-ingrained toy designers KAWS, Frank Kozik, and James Jarvis, while creating their own signature character, the Skull Kun. Named after founder Hikaru Iwanaga's obsession with the Star Wars bounty hunter Boba Fett, Bounty Hunter is always unafraid to do the unexpected. People go for the fashion, but Bounty Hunter's biggest claim to fame may be the toy movement they helped inspire.

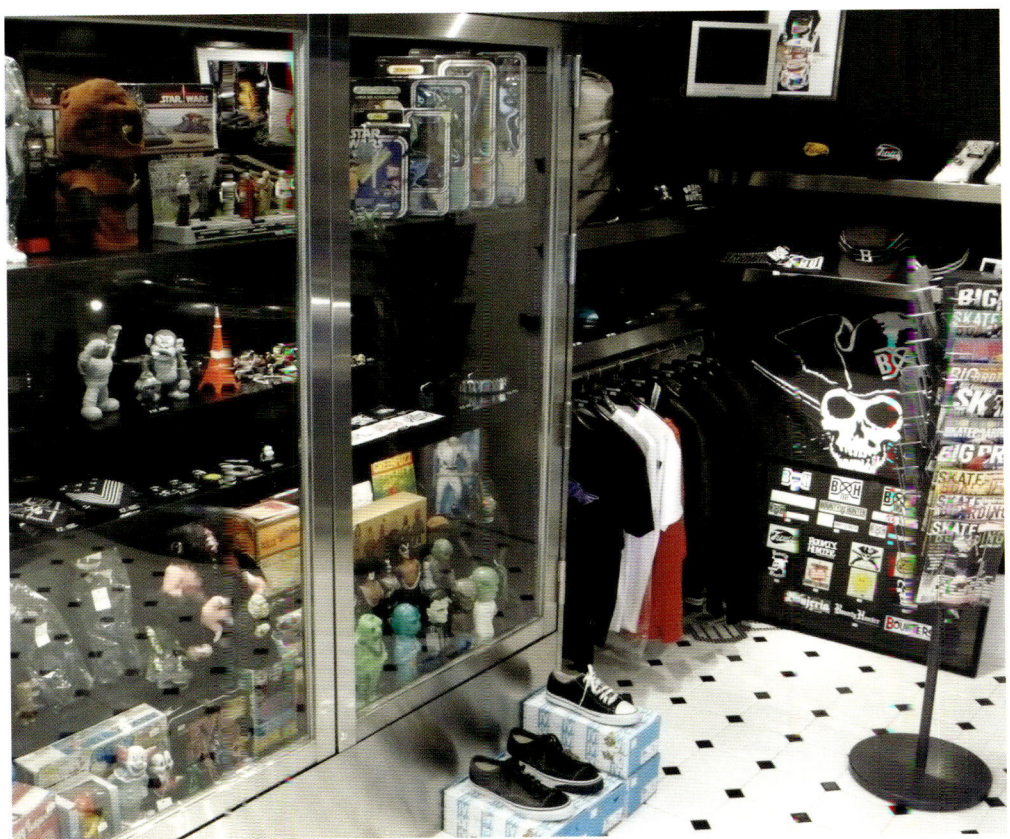

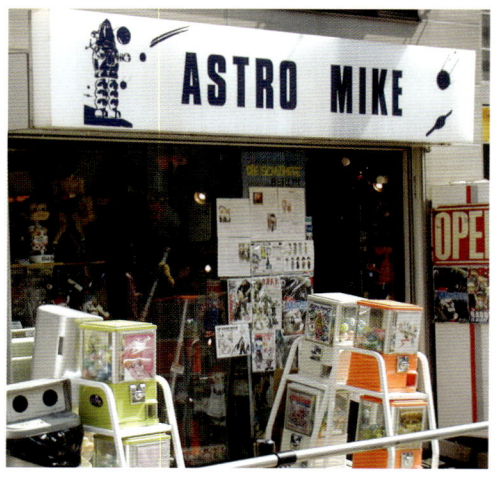

ASTRO MIKE   26
5-25-2 JINGUMAE, SHIBUYA-KU
03-3499-2588, WWW.MIKE-TOYS.COM
HOURS: 12:00 — 20:00

Offering a heavy selection of American action figure toys, along with knickknacks and lots of classic science fiction novelties, Astro Mike is a wide net of inexpensive toy trinkets that could best be summarized as "new retro."

POOK ET KOOP   25
6-15-9 JINGUMAE, SHIBUYA-KU
03-5466-8504, WWW.POOK.CO.JP, POOK.EASY-MAGIC.COM
HOURS: 11:30 — 20:00

A hybrid toy store and novelty store, Pook et Koop has a mix of newer toys, Kubricks/Be@rbricks, character goods, Disneyana, Rat Fink, action figures, and cheap tin reproductions. In short, all manner of new, affordable, and somewhat collectible toys and gifts fills this store.

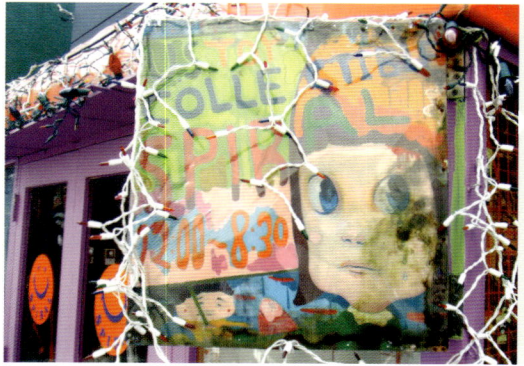

SPIRAL TOY SHOP   18
A-1 NAGATA BLDG, 3-27-17 JINGUMAE, SHIBUYA-KU
03-3479-1262, WWW.SPIRAL-TOY.COM
HOURS: 12:00 — 20:30

A small shop tucked out of the way and across from Secret Base, Spiral's newer toys and characters span a broad spectrum. Focusing more on lines like The Nightmare Before Christmas or Dr. Seuss, the shop can appear novelty driven at times.

20

EROSTIKA

3-27-21-B1F, JINGUMAE, SHIBUYA-KU
03-5775-0924, WWW.EROSTIKA.NET
HOURS: 11:00 — 20:00

Best known for his voluptuous, retro artwork for rock posters and album covers, and for maintaining an impeccable personal appearance with stylish suits and custom wrestling masks, Rockin' Jelly Bean has managed to simultaneously keep his identity a secret and boost his public image. At his custom shop, Erostika, you can find a wide variety of t-shirts, posters, buttons, and prints embellished with the artist's signature work. On special events, Rockin' Jelly Bean has collaborated with Japanese vinyl company Rumble Monsters to create multiple colorways of Pharaohs and Damnedron that are exclusive to this shop. With a fun, outgoing staff, Erostika is worth the daring trip down the white stairs to the space beneath.

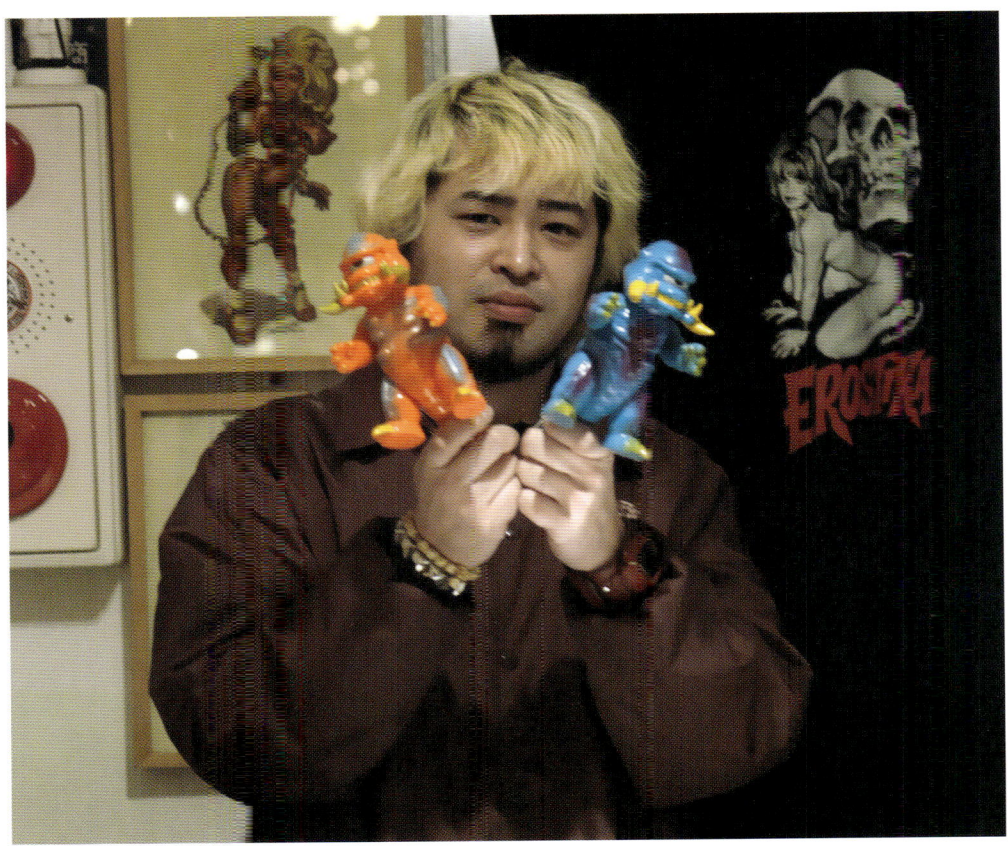

24

KIDDY LAND

6-1-9 JINGUMAE, SHIBUYA-KU
03-3409-3431, WWW.KIDDYLAND.CO.JP
HOURS: 10:00 — 18:00, CLOSED THE THIRD TUESDAY

Another of Tokyo's well-known toy stores, Kiddy Land is actually a new toy store with a heavy emphasis on cuteness. Most interesting for tourists seems to be the fact that the store is six stories tall, with something different on each floor. With Gundam, Godzilla, and boy toys located near the top, Kiddy Land is the perfect place to find gifts, from affordable to outrageous, for the kid or adult on your list. Kiddy Land is also a bit of a cultural landmark, even appearing in the *Megazone 23* anime.

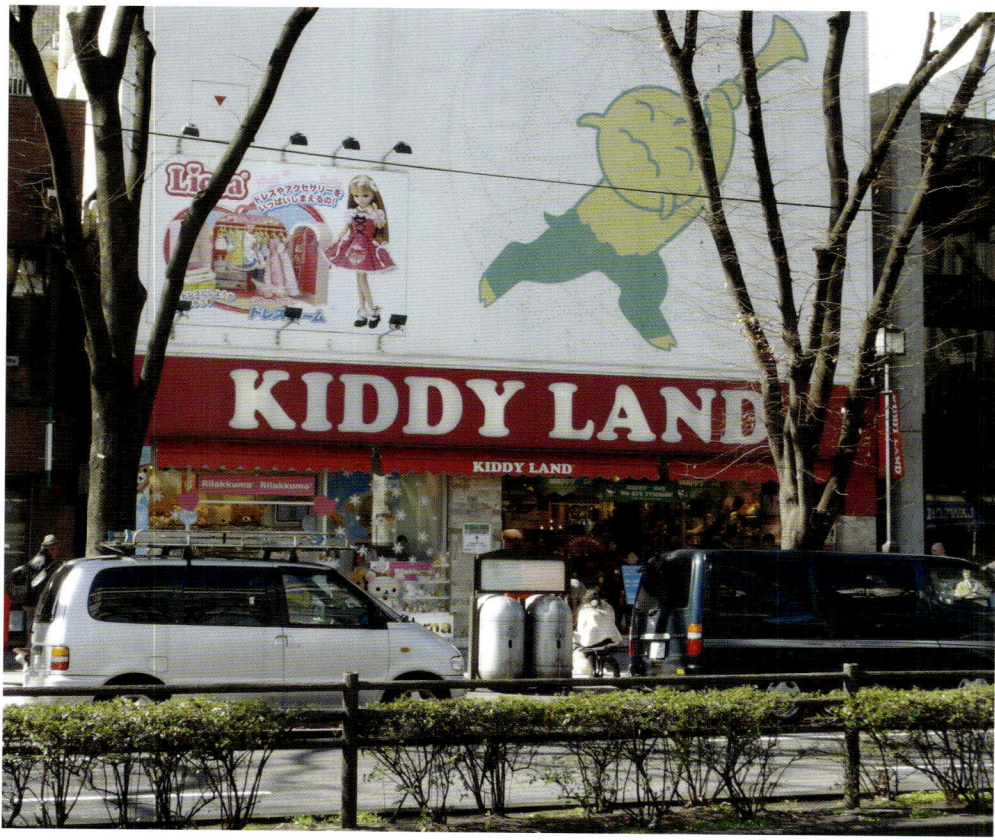

31

ORIGINAL FAKE

OH BLDG., B1F, 5-3-25 MINAMIAOYAMA, MINATO-KU
3-3499-3333, WWW.ORIGINALFAKE.COM
HOURS: 12:00 — 20:00

No detail was left untouched in this Aoyama shop, one of the most aesthetically stunning spaces in all of Tokyo. With a larger-than-life anatomical Companion standing guard at its entrance, Original Fake is the flagship store for the artist KAWS. With both sides of a bisected shop lined in glazed or unglazed custom ceramic tile, and nearly invisible glass cases, Original Fake is a boutique first and a toy store second. Since opening in 2006, Original Fake has become the first (and usually only) place to get the latest KAWS figures and clothes. With clothing and toy prices reflecting ultra-limited availability and impeccable attention to detail, lines form early in the morning (or even the night before) for every new release.

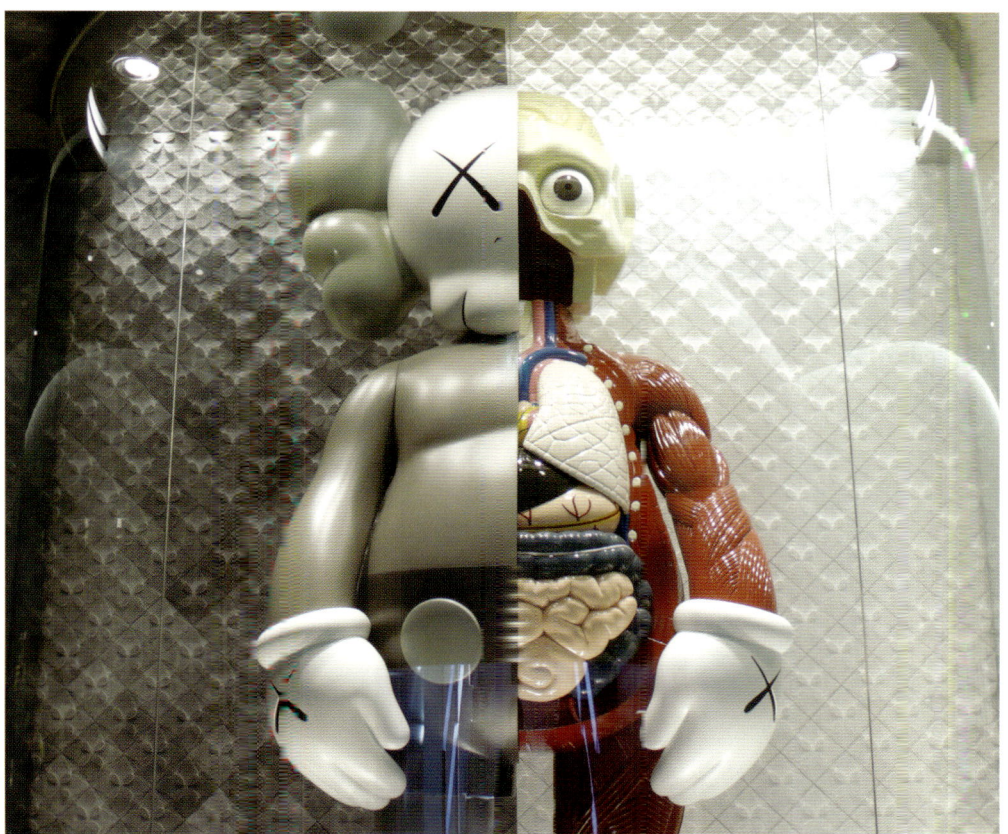

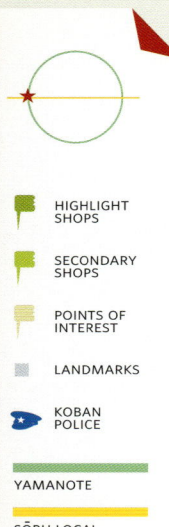

SHINJUKU

Famous for its high rises, hotels, shopping, and massive train station, Shinjuku has a few toy stores worth stopping into as well. Take the east exit for Kabukicho, which will put you in front of a small plaza, directly across from a large television screen. From here, cross the plaza, take a right, and head down one short block to the Kinokuniya building (01), which is next door to one of the two Citibank (08b) locations in Shinjuku.

From here you can walk either around the block or through the Kinokuniya building to get to Forest Comic and DVD (02), as well as Sakuraya Hobby (03). Always full of new and late-season toys, Sakuraya's second floor has a large variety of new toys and candy toys.

Hidden down the side streets from here is the Stüssy store (04) and the designer toy store Few Many (05). Japanese vinyl manufacturer Wonderwall's signature shop, the product mix is a surprising blend of their own products and select outside brands. Just around the corner is housewares shop Franc Franc (06) and the Shinjkuku Disc Union punk shop (07).

On the opposite side of the station is superstore Yodobashi (09), with a basement full of brand new toys at discount prices. Both a Citibank (08a) and a post office are nearby in case you need to make a cash withdrawal. Last, little shop Hobbit (10) is at the upper end of Shinjuku, and, like its sister stores in Shibuya and Akihabara, it boasts a healthy model kit selection with a varying array of vintage toys.

POST
OFFICE

09

08^

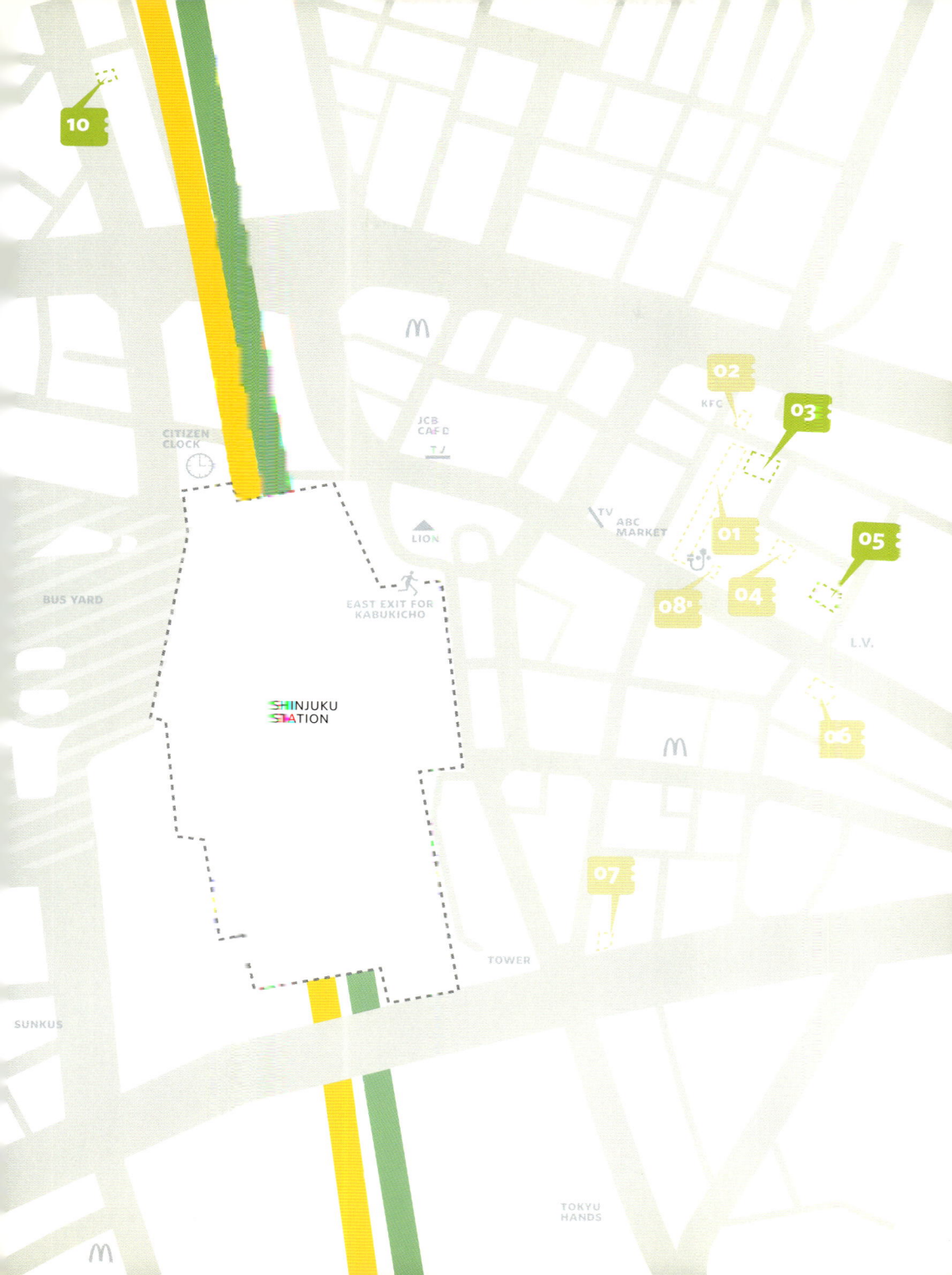

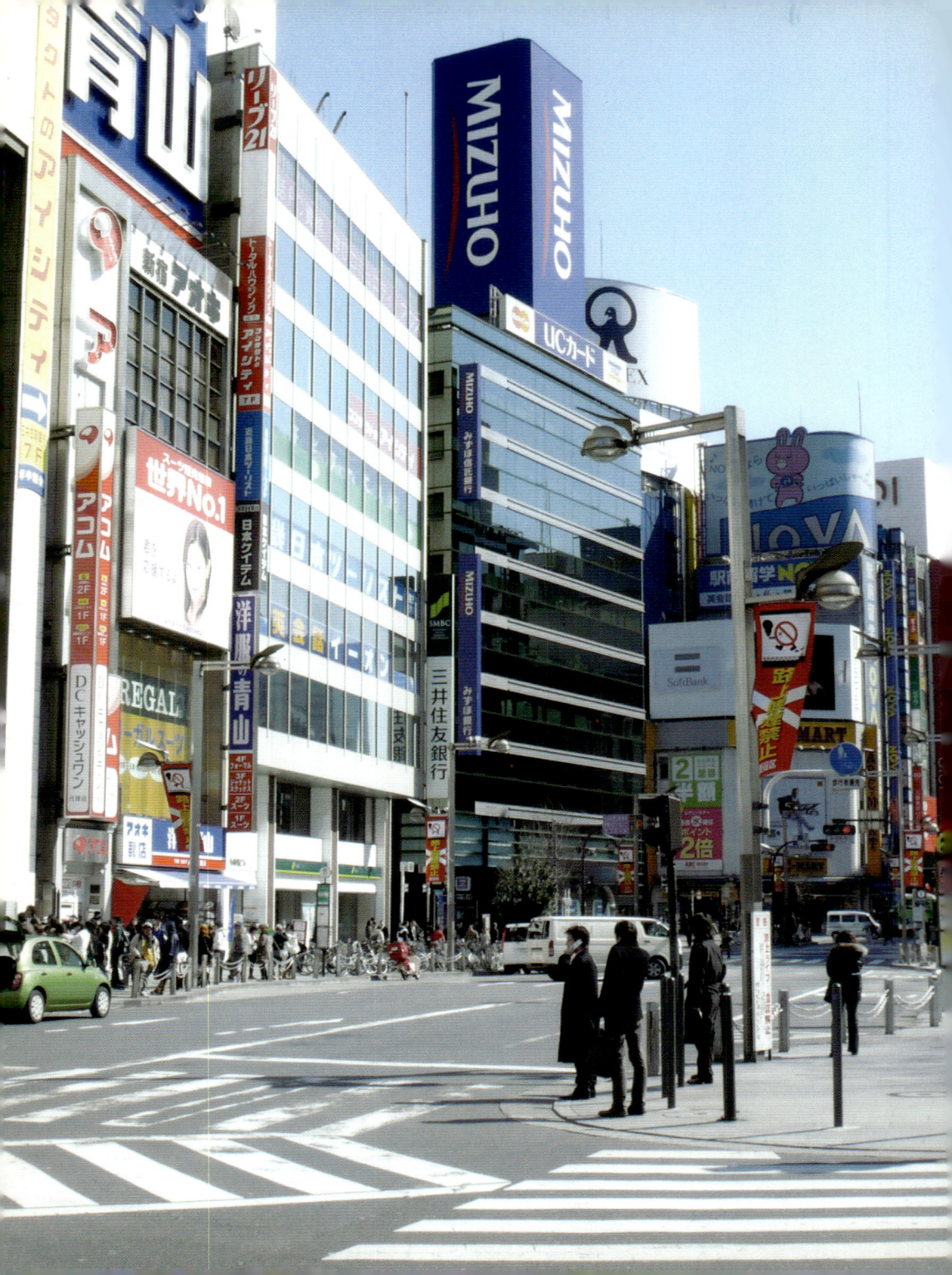

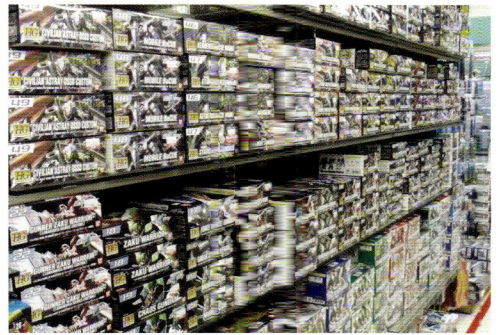

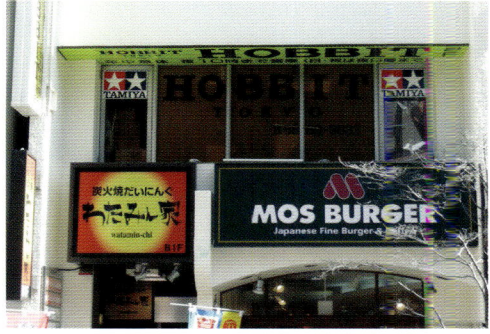

SAKURAYA HOBBY   03
3-17-17 SHINJUKU, SHINJUKU-
03-3226-6868, WWW.SAKURAYA.CO.JP/SHOP/SHI_HOBY.HTML
HOURS: 10:00 — 21:00

Another of the electronic/video game/toy crossover stores, Sakuraya has a good selection of toys on the second floor, emphasizing new or last season's toys at a deep discount. The selection varies and can never be predicted, but the shelves are always full.

HOBBIT   10
7-1-8 2F NISHI-SHINJUKU, SHINJUKU-KU
03-5389-3933, WWW.TOKYOHOBBIT.CO.JP

Just above the Mos Burger is the little shop with the little name, Hobbit. With a decent model kit selection and a thin but ever-revolving selection of used die-cast and vinyl, toys are priced to move, sometimes absurdly so.

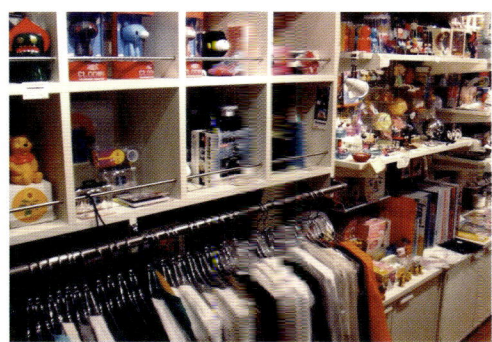

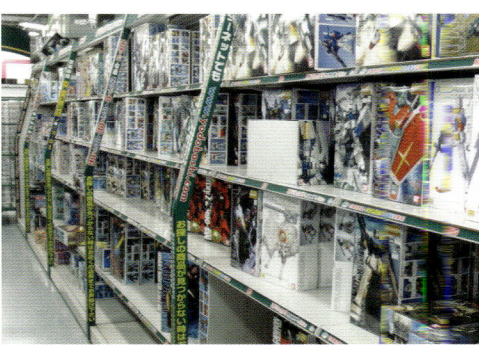

FEW MANY   05
3-17-21 SHINJUKU, SHINJUKU-
03-3353-2532, WWW.FEWMANY.COM
HOURS: 12:00 — 20:00

Hiding in an unassuming side alley is designer toy store Few Many. In this home shop for Wonderwall, collaboration toys, tees, and other gifts share shelf space with a curated stock of cult idle brands. Rare shop-only releases and an eclectic selection make every trip to Few Many different from the last.

YODOBASHI   09
1-11-1 NISHI-SHINJUKU, SHINJUKU-KU
03-3346-1010, WWW.YODOBASHI.COM
HOURS: 9:30 — 22:00

Well known for its varied selection of anything electronic, the Shinjuku Yodobashi store has a wide selection of toys hidden in their basement. From model kits and Kamen Rider to video games and infant toys, everything is usually priced 10 to 20 percent below retail. This is a hot spot for super robot, sentai, and chogokin collectors.

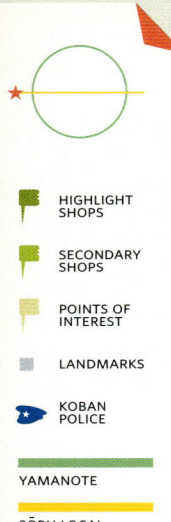

NAKANO

If the Tokyo toy community had a nerve center, Nakano would be it. Home to the highest density of toy shops in the entire city, this little residential neighborhood is much more than meets the eye.

Take the north exit from the train station, and across the plaza, you should see the scalloped entrance to the Sun Mall, an open-air mall with a covered ceiling. Walk the length of the mall, past the shoe, t-shirt, and pantyhose dealers and McDonald's. Go all the way to the end of the mall; even when you second-guess yourself and think you have gone too far, just keep going. You may not even notice when you exit the Sun Mall and enter the Broadway Mall, but when you do, there will be an escalator and a set of stairs to your right. The escalator goes to the third floor, while the stairs go to all floors. We suggest taking the stairs. Sixty-four toy stores are spread across the second, third, and fourth floors, and visiting them all will take hours.

For those of you who do notice the Broadway Mall demarcation, take a quick left, and about thirty feet down is a set of stairs on the right leading up to one of Nakano's best shops, Moda-Yu (01).

Besides the plentiful Mandarake shops, the Broadway Mall is filled with shops, both great and not so great, covering every conceivable aspect of toy collecting. Our favorites include the Robot Robot case shops on the third floor (46 and 47), Bow Wow case shop (15), Toy Shop Rough (11 and 12), and the Antique Toy Shop (24). Any store can have amazing stock on any given day, so we generally spend about four hours checking them all out.

SECOND
FLOOR

02-64

NAKANO
BROADWAY
MALL

01

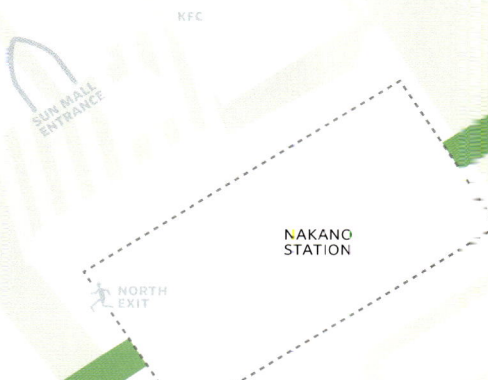

TWIN
PLAZA

SUN MALL
ENTRANCE

KFC

BIKE
GARAGE

NORTH
EXIT

NAKANO
STATION

01

MODA-YU-Q-TE
SEE MAP ON PAGES 62–63
03-5380-3512

The only shop in Nakano not actually located inside the Broadway Mall, Moda-Yu is also one of the neighborhood's finest. Moda-Yu is located about thirty feet to the left of the main mall entrance, and up one narrow flight of stairs. Inside you will find a deep stock of a wide variety of toys, from vintage vinyl and die-cast to new capsule figures. The store is jam-packed to the ceiling and the walls are bulging with toys, so leave your backpack and bags by the door to avoid inadvertently knocking something over. Moda-Yu's pleasant staff and reasonable prices ensure that everyone can enjoy a stop here.

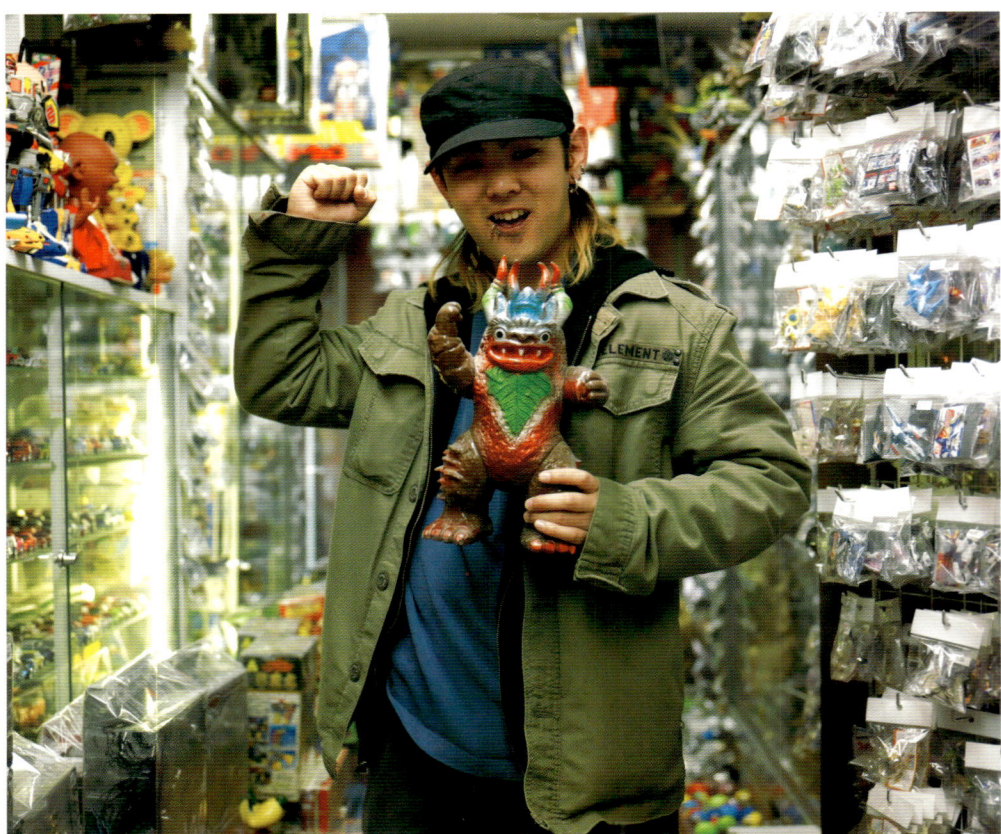

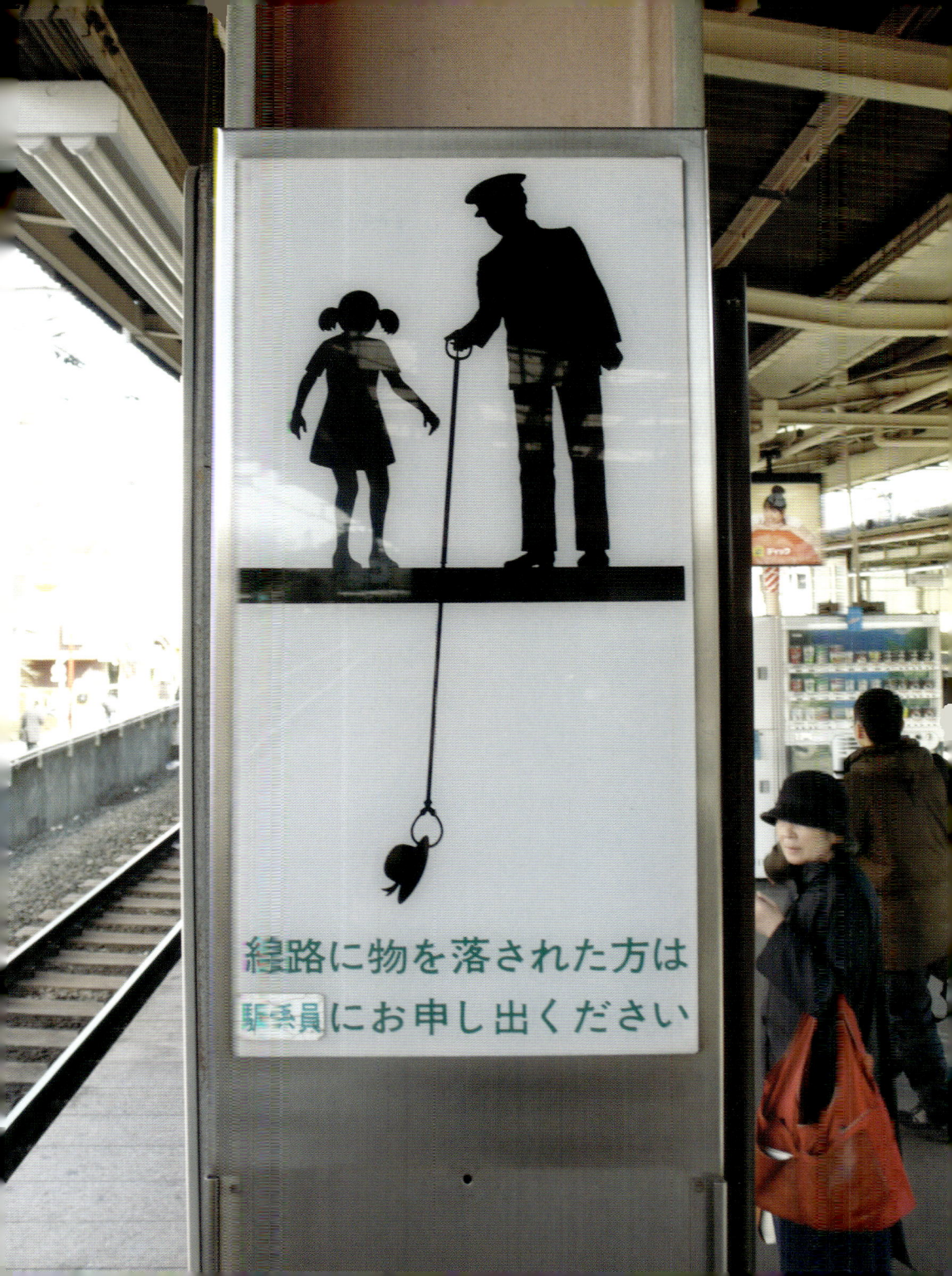

01, 08, 14, 19, 20, 22, 23, 25–27, 29, 33–38, 54, 57–60, 62

MANDARAKE
5-52-15 NAKANO, NAKANO-KU
03-3228-0007, WWW.MANDARAKE.CO.JP/ENGLISH/SHOP/NKN.HTML
HOURS: 12:00 — 20:00

Distributed liberally over three floors and twenty-three locations in the Broadway Mall, Mandarake has one of almost everything. With shops devoted to mini-erasers, manga, R/C cars, and cosplay, Mandarake covers the spectrum like no one else can. Mandarake's most prominent shop, New Special, is nothing that the name implies. Guarded by a larger-than-life Tetsujin-28, the shop is home to all vintage toys, jumbos, die-cast, or vinyls that have not been pulled for their semiannual auction. Other prominent Mandarake stores include Special 3, on the third floor, which specializes in secondhand current toys, and a tin and advertising display shop on the fourth floor. Describing Mandarake's complete inventory is impossible, but you can discover that for yourself as you walk the halls of the Broadway Mall.

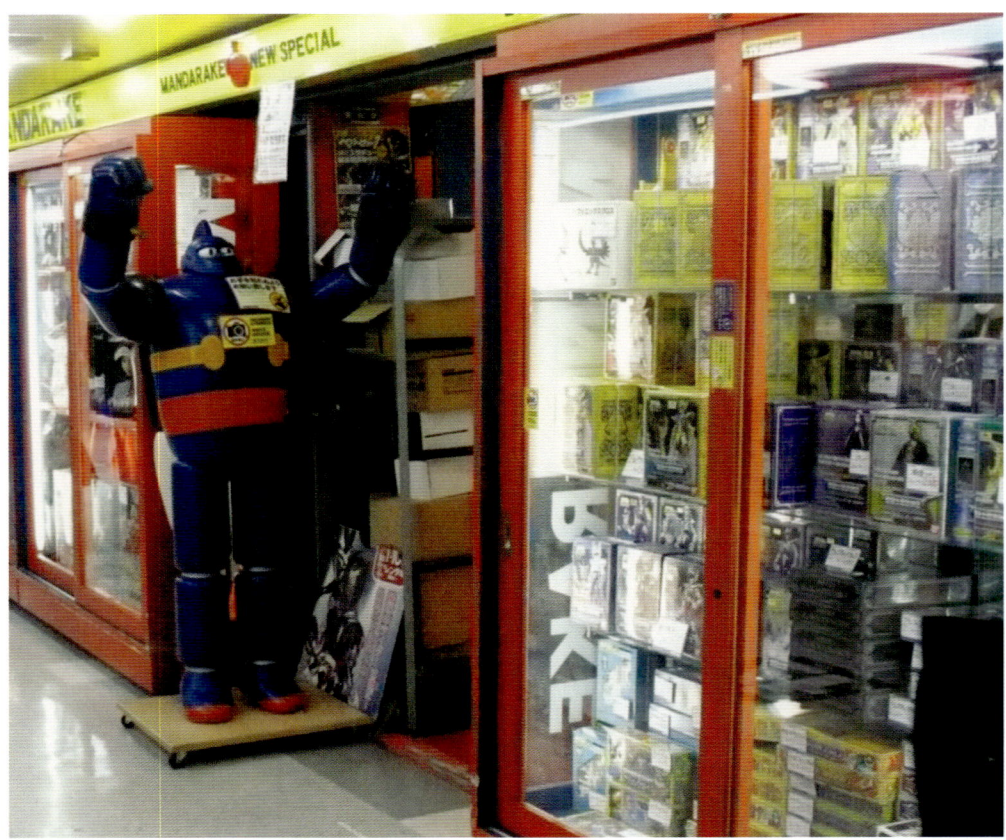

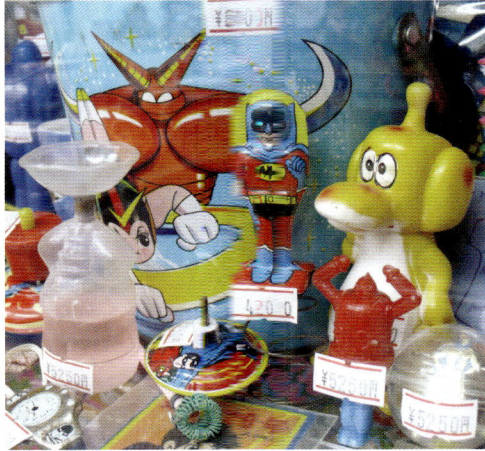

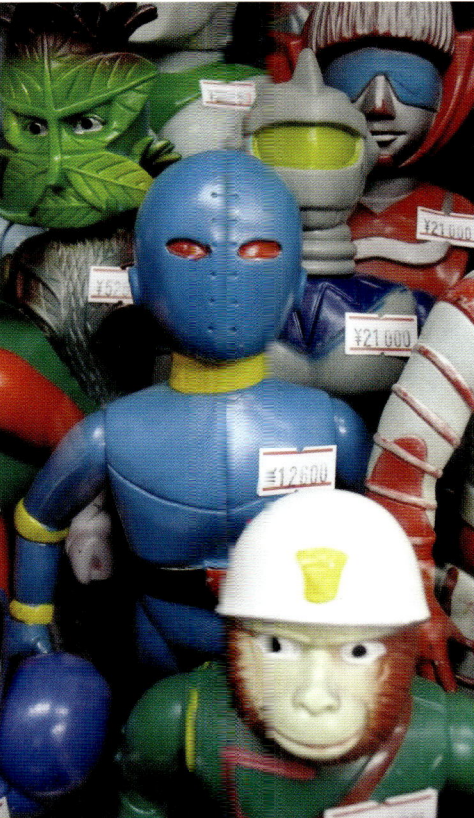

SECOND FLOOR

01_ MANDARAKE NEW SPECIAL (VINTAGE STORE)
02_ CASE SHOP
03_ HIGH-GRADE SHOP
04/05/06_ CASE SHOPS
07_ BOX KEY CASE SHOP
08_ MANDARAKE AMAZING (AMERICAN TOYS)
09/10_ CUBE STYLE CASE SHOPS
11/12_ TOY SHOPS ROUGH CASE SHOPS
13_ CASE SHOP
14_ MANDARAKE DRAWING
15_ BOW WOW CASE SHOP
16_ CAR SHOP
17_ GAMES WORKSHOP
18_ CASE SHOP
19_ MANDARAKE GACHA TEN
20_ MANDARAKE CARS
21_ A. BARTH (MISC. TOYS)
22_ MANDARAKE LIVE
23_ MANDARAKE GALAXY
24_ ANTIQUE TOYS
25_ MANDARAKE UFO 2
26_ MANDARAKE GIRLS' SHOP
27_ MANDARAKE UFO CASE
28_ CASE SHOP
29_ MANDARAKE UFO CASE
     (NOW FILLED WITH VINYL)

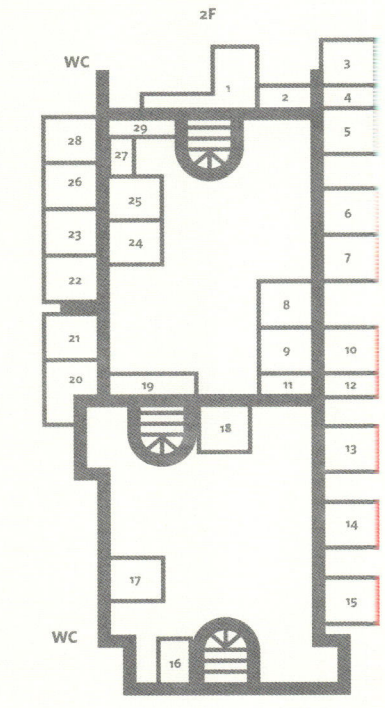

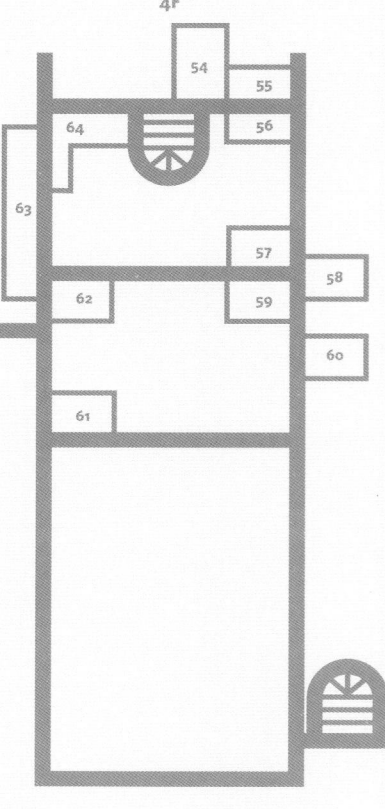

4F

WC   3F

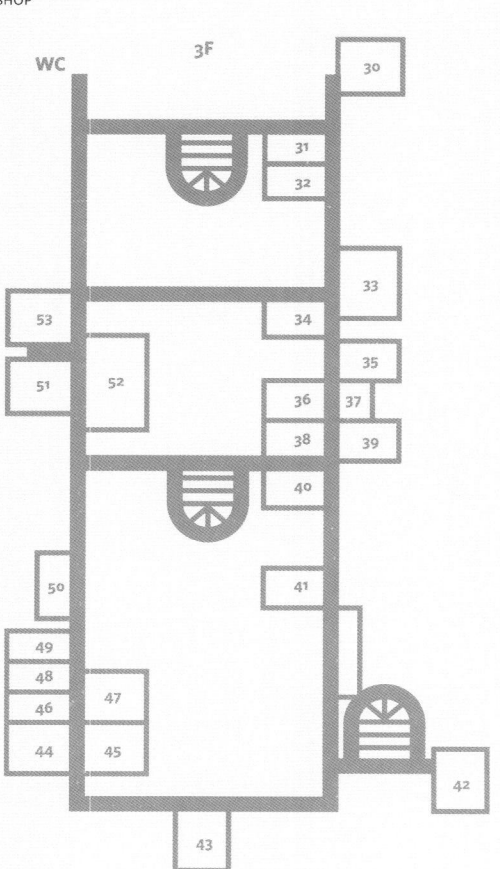

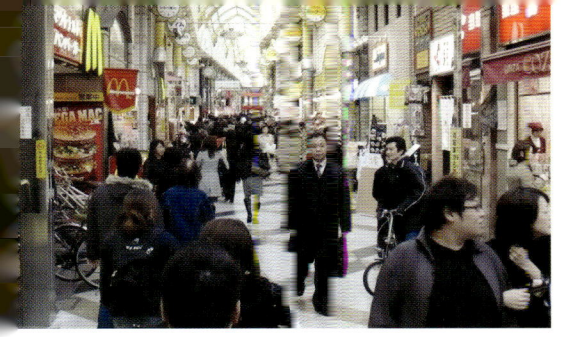

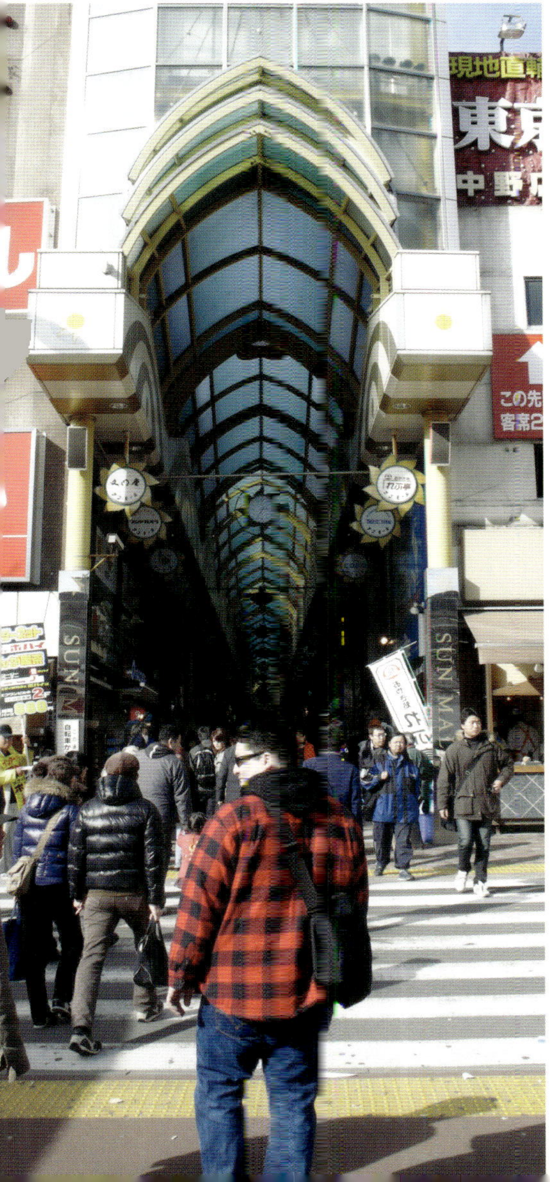

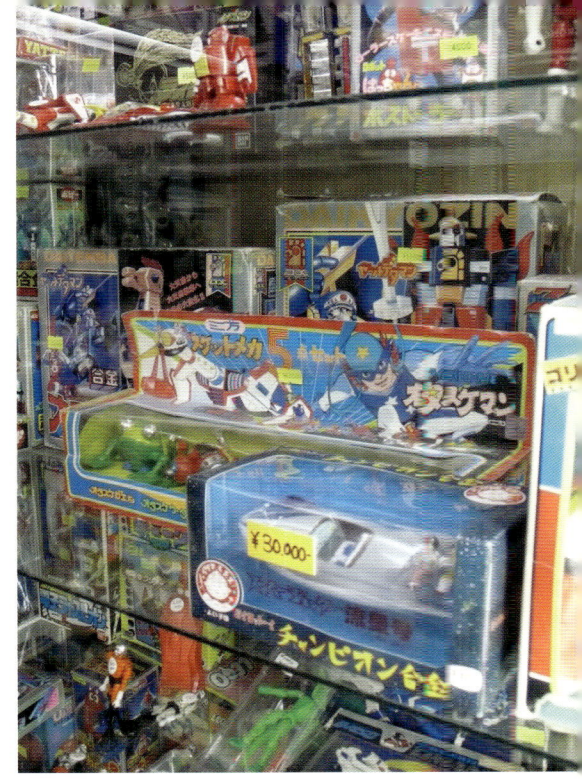

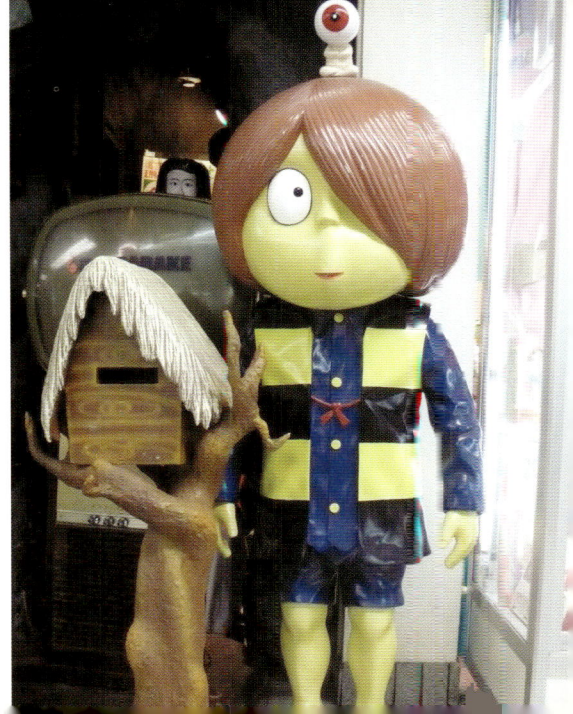

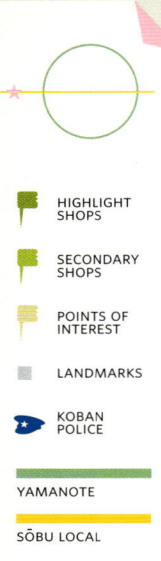

KOENJI

Just a single short stop on the Sobu line from Nakano is the neighborhood of Koenji. A local area with a vibrant mix of used record, vintage clothing, and toy stores, Koenji is Nakano's punk rock or heavy metal older brother. Rarely traversed by the average tourist, Koenji feels like a modern neighborhood, with few traditional buildings but simple, functional architecture. Slower paced than some of the larger neighborhoods, Koenji is home to several great vintage shops, as well as Gargamel's Thrash Out flagship store and Boy Records, one of Tokyo's oldest punk record stores.

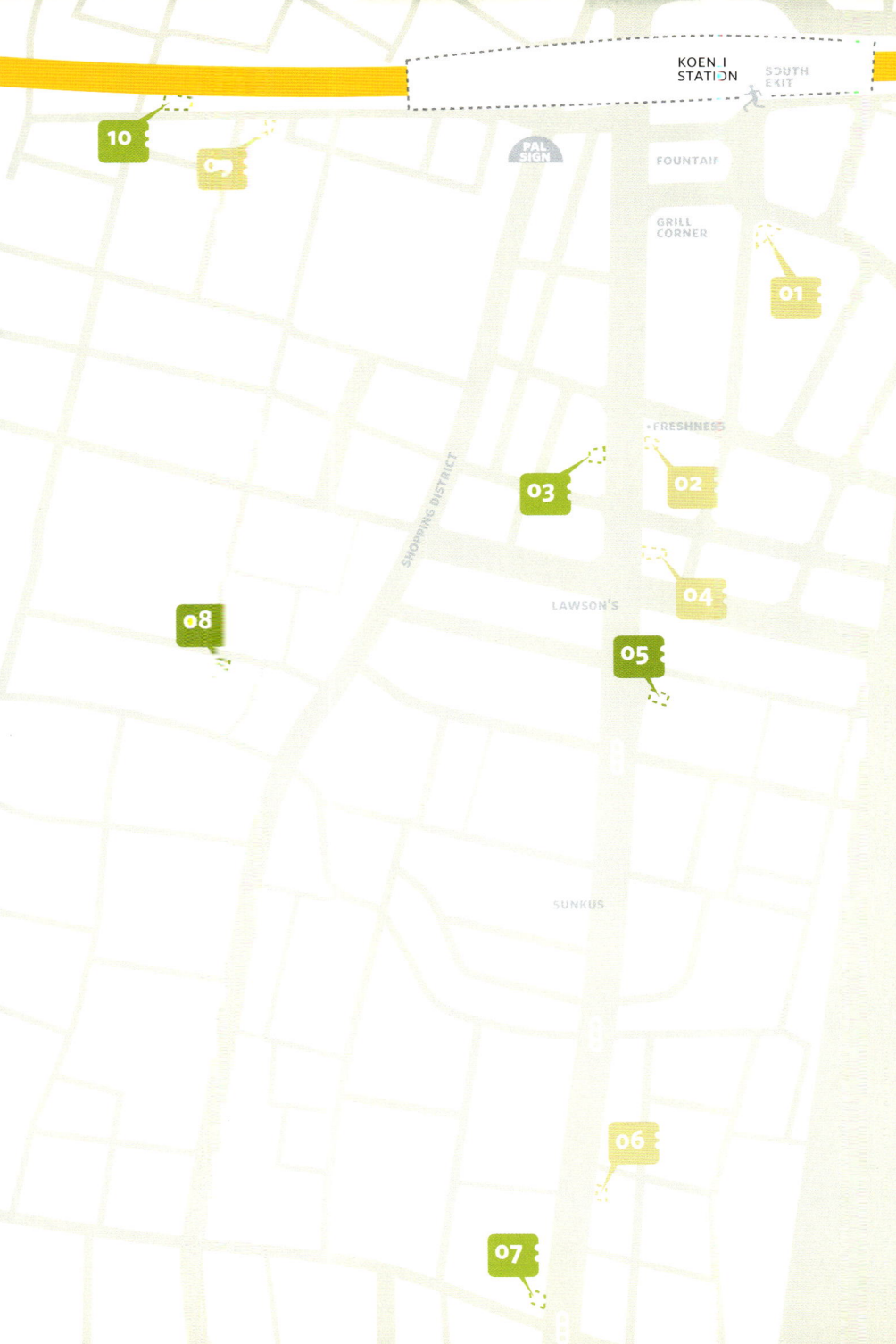

When you arrive in Koenji, there is only one exit from the station, but immediately after exiting, you will need to take a right and go to the south side of the station. When you emerge from the station, to your right you should see a small fountain and an abstract metal structure. Just across the plaza you will see a corner with grills of skewers. (Regardless of the apparent popularity of the grill, we have always heard that it's not very good.) Along the main street, you will pass Bone Bag (02, 2F) and Record Shop Base (02, 3F) on your left and Hobby Toy (03) on your right. Both Bone Bag and Record Shop Base have a good selection of new and used records, while Hobby Toy is a new toy and model store that occasionally has a few late-model toys worth picking up that may no longer be available at larger stores.

Another two and a half quick blocks down is Thrash Out (05), vinyl toy manufacturer Gargamel's flagship store. Just look for the small light-up sign and the gachapon machine full of giant toys, and then head up the stairs to Gargamel's wood-trimmed hideout. After picking up the latest shop exclusives, you can continue down the same road to Well Rounded (07), which is a Hot Wheels shop, or cross the street to Ichiban-Boshi (08), which offers plenty to buy and even more to see. From there, it's a quick jaunt up the back streets or main streets to the train tracks. Following the tracks west, you will pass Boy Records (09) on the left. Look out for the small white sandwich board out front, because it's easy to miss. In a dark wood building with a narrow staircase leading up to the second floor, Boy is one of Tokyo's oldest punk record stores, specializing in crust, hardcore, and political punk but including a nice sampling of other subgenres, as well as plenty of rare, out-of-print records. Be warned: Boy only accepts cash payments, so credit cards won't work here.

Just past Boy Records is Godzilla-Ya (10). One of Tokyo's older shops, Godzilla-Ya is just up yet another narrow set of stairs, and on the left-hand side. Filled wall to wall with vinyl, die-cast, jumbos, and more, Godzilla-Ya can at times feel more like a garage sale than a toy shop. You never know what you can find here.

Heading back to the station, feel free to wander the side streets and PAL Shopping Arcade for other miscellaneous shops. If you need a snack, the second-floor Yanchome Café (01) offers a wide variety of food, while the aptly titled Good-Fellas (04) is a neighborhood pizza and pasta restaurant. Farther away is Planet 3rd (06), which is more of a coffeehouse/restaurant/Internet café with quick snacks, a bizarre form of tacos, and iMacs available for anyone in need of an email or Yahoo! Auctions fix.

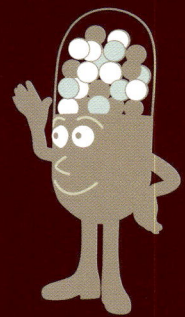

MR. CONTACT:
POSSESSING TWICE THE
PERSONALITY OF ANY OTHER
OVER-THE-COUNTER DRUG,
MR. CONTACT IS A LIVING PILL
READY TO BATTLE THE ILLS
OF THE WORLD. IF ONLY OUR
COLD REMEDIES WERE
THIS EXCITING.

05

THRASH OUT/GARGAMEL

2-51-9 2F KOENJI, SUGINAMI-KU
03-3315-6570, WWW.GARGAMEL.JP, /THRASHOUT
HOURS: 13:00 — 21:00, CLOSE WEDNESDAY

A hefty combination of heavy metal and dark wood will entice you at the top of the stairs at Thrash Out. Home to one of Japan's finest new toy companies, Gargamel, Thrash Out is their signature store. The founders, three longtime friends named Taguchi, Kiyoka, and Cha-Man, pay homage to Japan's lesser-known kaiju and recreate them in new ways, much to the delight of their fans. The store has a visual history of Gargamel's figural friends, as well as a few key vintage and newer vinyl toys. Thanks to exclusive collaborations with Tim Biskup, Bwana Spoons, and Super7, stock often goes fast, so don't wait if you hear of a new release.

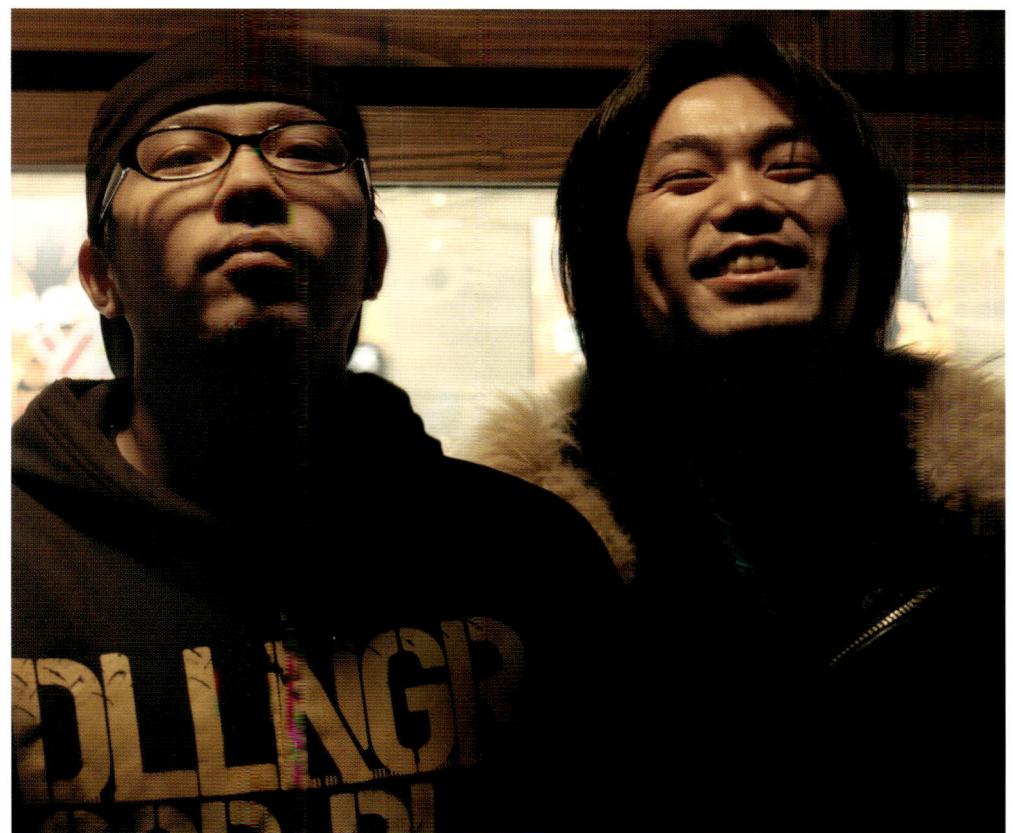

08

ICHIBAN-BOSHI
3-37-19 MINAMI, SUGINAMI KOENJI
03-3313-8025, WWW.1BAN-BOSHI.COM
HOURS: 14:00 — 20:00

A great vintage store just off the beaten path, Ichiban-Boshi has a huge selection of toys for almost all collectors. Cases of rare vintage vinyls mix freely with new figures and reproductions, while quality die-cast and Jumbo Machinders make a stand in the side cases. Formerly located in Shinjuku, Ichiban-Boshi relocated to Koenji in late 2005 and has helped make the area a collectors' destination. Prices are generally reasonable across the board, but some of the rare pieces are priced accordingly. Another interesting component of Ichiban-Boshi is their custom figure of Ryusei Ninja, developed as a collaboration with RealxHead. In addition to a friendly staff, store-only releases of their figure offer extra incentive to pay this shop a visit.

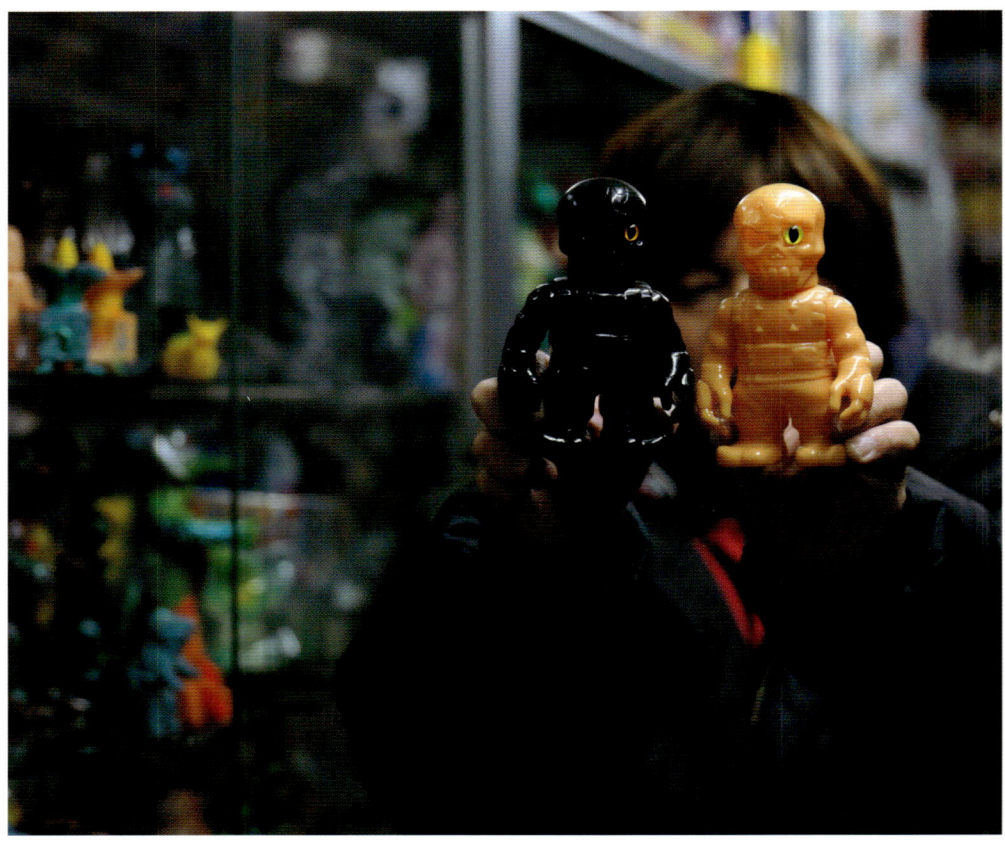

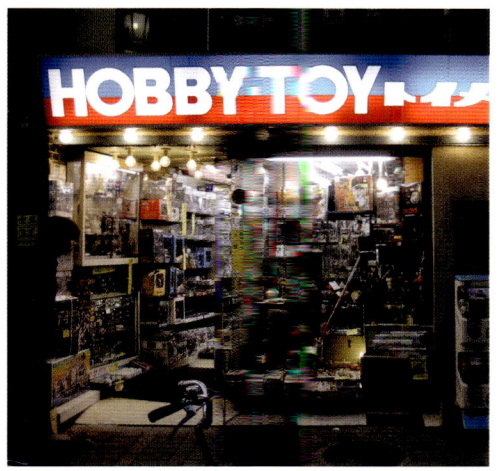

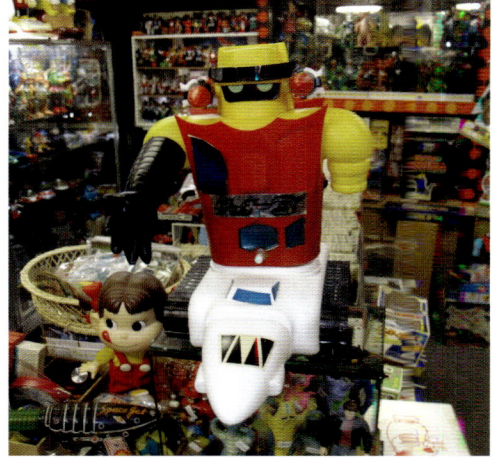

HOBBY TOY   **03**
4-24-1 KOENJI, SUGINAMI-KU
03-3314-5021

A classic example of a neighborhood toy shop. Hobby Toy is a perfect place to get a sense of what it must have been like to grow up buying Japanese toys your entire life. With a smattering of everything from model kits to kaiju, you never know exactly what they will have, but they will have a couple of whatever it is for sure.

GODZILLA-YA   **10**
3-67-1 KOENJI, SUGINAMI-KU
03-3336-3178, WWW.PLALA.OR.JP/GODZILLAYA
HOURS: 14:00 — 21:00, CLOSED WEDNESDAY

A rare holdover from the heyday of Japanese toy collecting, Godzilla-Ya is a true institution. While it is packed to the gills with nearly every kind of toy imaginable, Godzilla-Ya is a hit-or-miss kind of store. Upon first impression it can appear a bit junky, but there is a method to Godzilla-Ya's madness, and if you look in just the right place, you may strike toy gold. Prices fluctuate wildly, and seem to be a little more beat down than usual, but so does the merchandise, so condition-sensitive completists be warned. Regardless, shops like this paved the way for many others, so stop and show your respect.

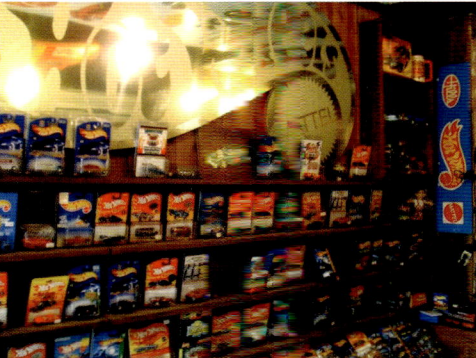

WELL ROUNDED   **07**
2-24-23 MINAMI, SUGINAMI KOENJI
03-3317-2242

A Hot Wheels and car collectors' destination, Well Rounded is a fun shop at the south end of Koenji. Very serious about their miniature machines, the staff are always ready to talk cars. If you collect any of the above, make sure to stop by.

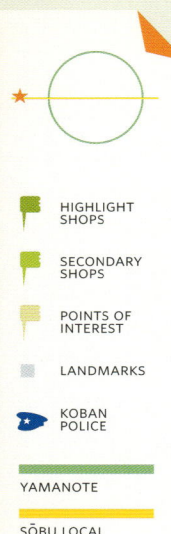

KICHIJOJI

Kichijoji is a large neighborhood on the west side of Tokyo that is home to a surprising number of Western expatriates. The immediate area outside the north exit of the train station is a fairly typical concentration of large and small shops, with two international ATMs nearby, at either the post office or Citibank. Just behind the area's main façade is a large gachapon parlor called At First (01), design t-shirt shop Graniph (02), and a wide range of books at Books Ruhe (03). Around the corner, you will see the gigantic and always humorous DOG WIZ sign, which leads you to the main road through this section of Kichijoji. Just before you reach the T-shaped intersection, in the basement to your right is Tonkatsu (04), a restaurant shrouded in mystery, highly guarded from the public by generations of shadowy, international toy purists. Could we be more vague?

If you turn right at the T-shaped intersection, Wave Be-J (06) is located three blocks down the road on the left-hand side. Full of new toys, from gachapon to chogokin to action figures, they carry a tantalizing sampling of everything. From there, go back one street, over one block, and down the side street. Before you hit Hotel Aland is Toy Cats Showcase (05), hidden in the basement of the building. Toy Cats Showcase specializes in new and old Star Wars items, and features an interesting assortment of newer used items and vintage toys in the showcases.

When you return to the train station, check out the department store Yuzawa (07), located on the south side, which has a good selection of new toys on the eighth floor.

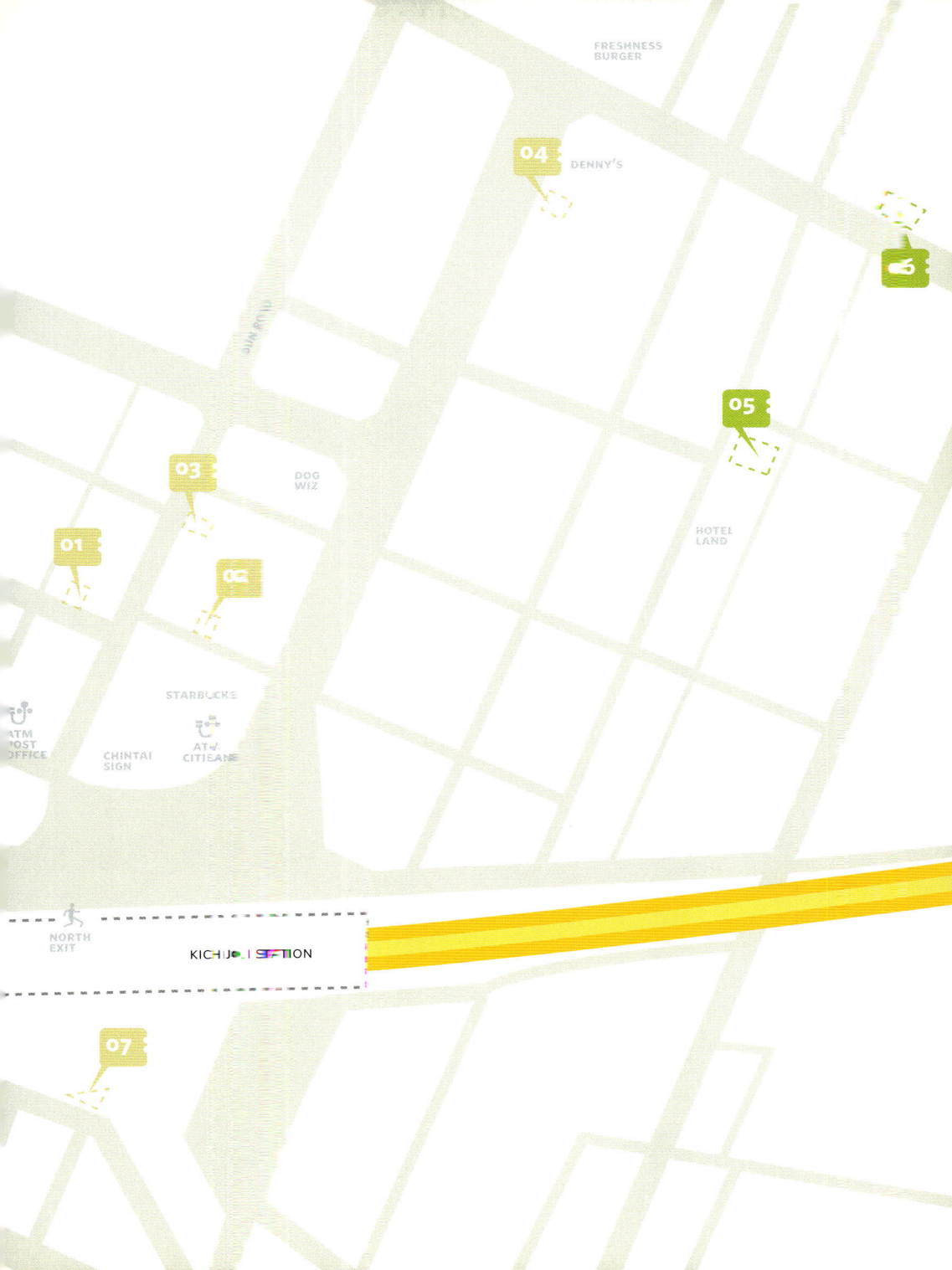

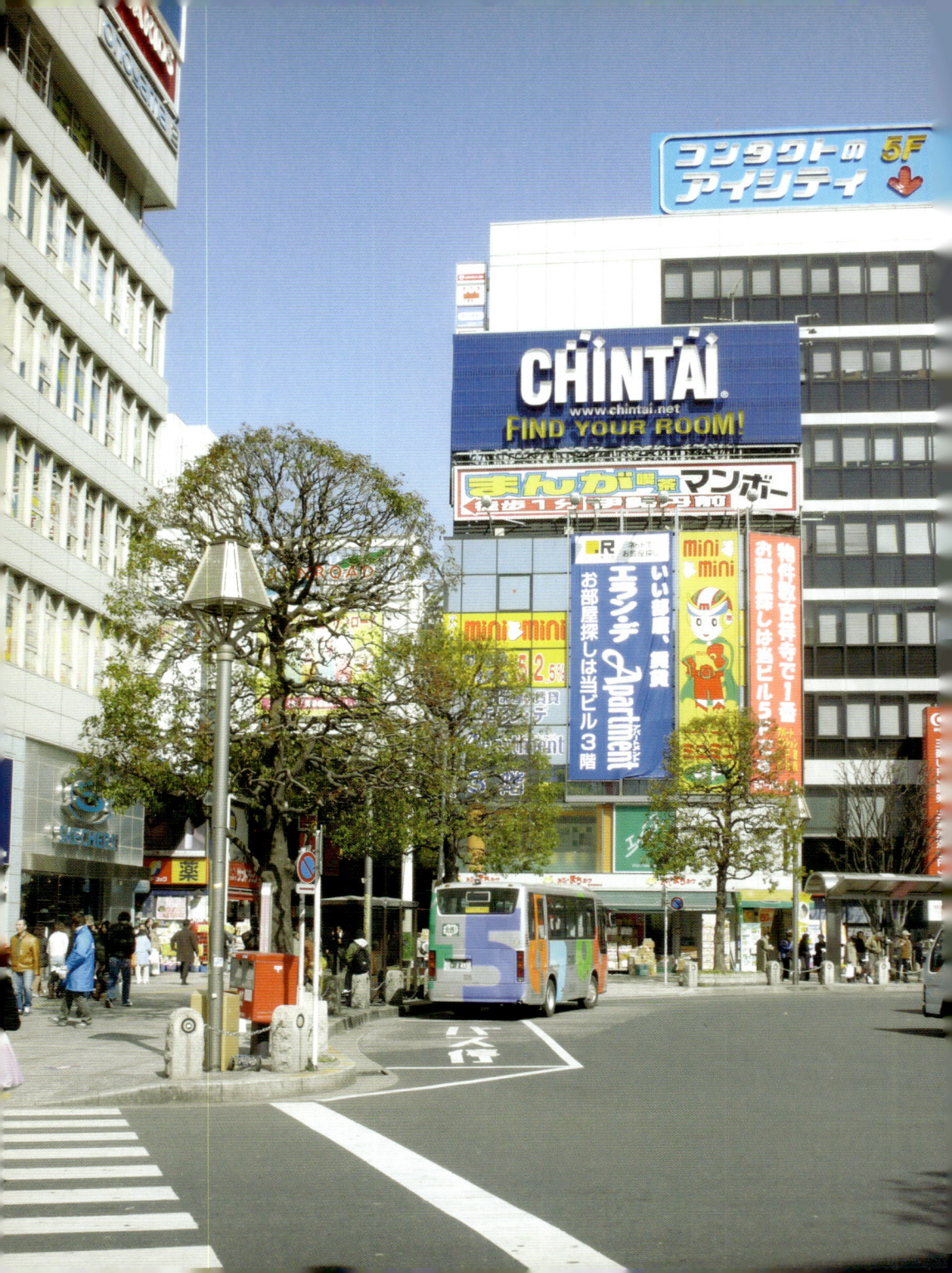

RIGHT:
UPON LEAVING THE NORTH EXIT IN
KICHIJOJI, THIS WILL BE YOUR VIEW
FROM HERE, IT IS A SHORT WALK
TO ANY OF THE SHOPS IN KICHIJOJI

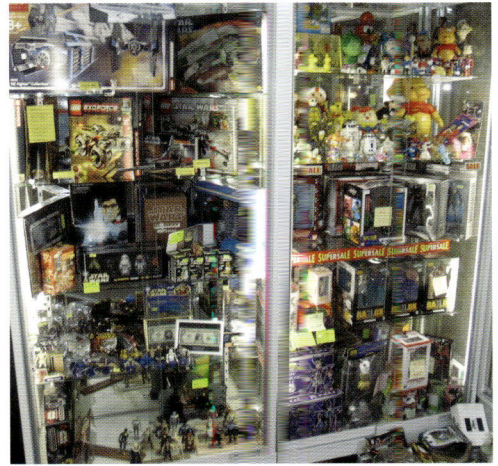

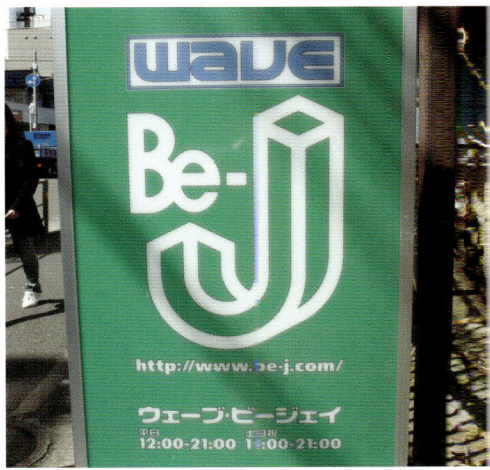

TOY CATS SHOWCASE 05

1-26-4 HORIUCHI BLDG. B1, KICHIJOJI HOMMACHI, MUSASHINO-KU
04-2223-1055, WWW.TOYCATS.NET/INDEX.HTML
HOURS: 12:00 — 20:00

In a less obvious location that is well worth the hunt, Toy
Cats Showcase has a large selection of Star Wars toys,
consignment toys, and a few nice vintage pieces. With
a friendly staff and friendly prices, Toy Cats Showcase
is always a fun shop to visit.

WAVE BE-J 06

1-11-20 KICHIJOJI EAST, MUSASHINO-KU
04-2221-0733, WWW.BE-J.COM
HOURS: WEEKDAYS 12:00 — 23:00, WEEKENDS 11:00 — 23:00

A comprehensive toy and hobby store, Wave Be-J has
all the latest Gundam and chogokin action figures,
gachapon, and model kits. There are no vintage toys,
and prices range from standard retail to slightly
expensive, but not offensive.

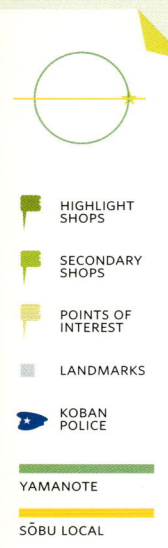

HIGHLIGHT SHOPS

SECONDARY SHOPS

POINTS OF INTEREST

LANDMARKS

KOBAN POLICE

YAMANOTE

SŌBU LOCAL

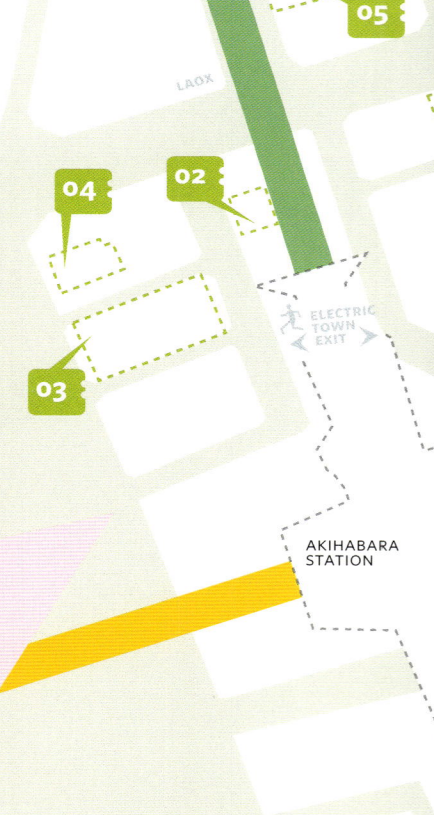

AKIHABARA

"Bright Lights, Big City of Dreams"—This might as well be the theme song of Akihabara, which boasts more neon and signage than most other places in Tokyo, but the area is usually referred to simply as "Electric Town." Just beneath its glowing veneer, Akihabara is also home to the otaku. The term may conjure up annoying mental images of older, single, overweight men with glasses who play video games and watch animation all night, but in Akihabara you can find the alpha of this stereotype, as well as a million evolutionary offshoots.

For most anime, robot, or sentai series fans, Akihabara is your primary destination. The streets are littered with toy shops, ranging from new to old, small to large, and carrying just about anything you can imagine, as well as a few things you shouldn't. Along the way, just about any electronics gadget you never knew you needed is also available, so stock up on digital cameras, video games, and cell phones that are far too advanced to be compatible with Western technology.

01_ YODOBASHI-AKIBA **02_** GAMERS **03_** RADIO KAIKAN **04_** ASOBIT CITY HOBBY **05_** HOBBIT **06_** ASOBIT CITY CHARA **07_** YELLOW SUBMARINE **08_** YANIGAWA SOFT **09_** MANDARAKE **10_** CREPE STAND **11_** HOBBY SHOP KOTOBUKIYA **12_** ROBOT-HEROKAN **13_** COLLECTABLES TOKYO **14_** LIBERTY 7 **15_** HOBBY FIGURE **16_** LIBERTY 9 **17_** TOYS GOLDEN AGE **18_** CHIOCCIO@PIZZERIA

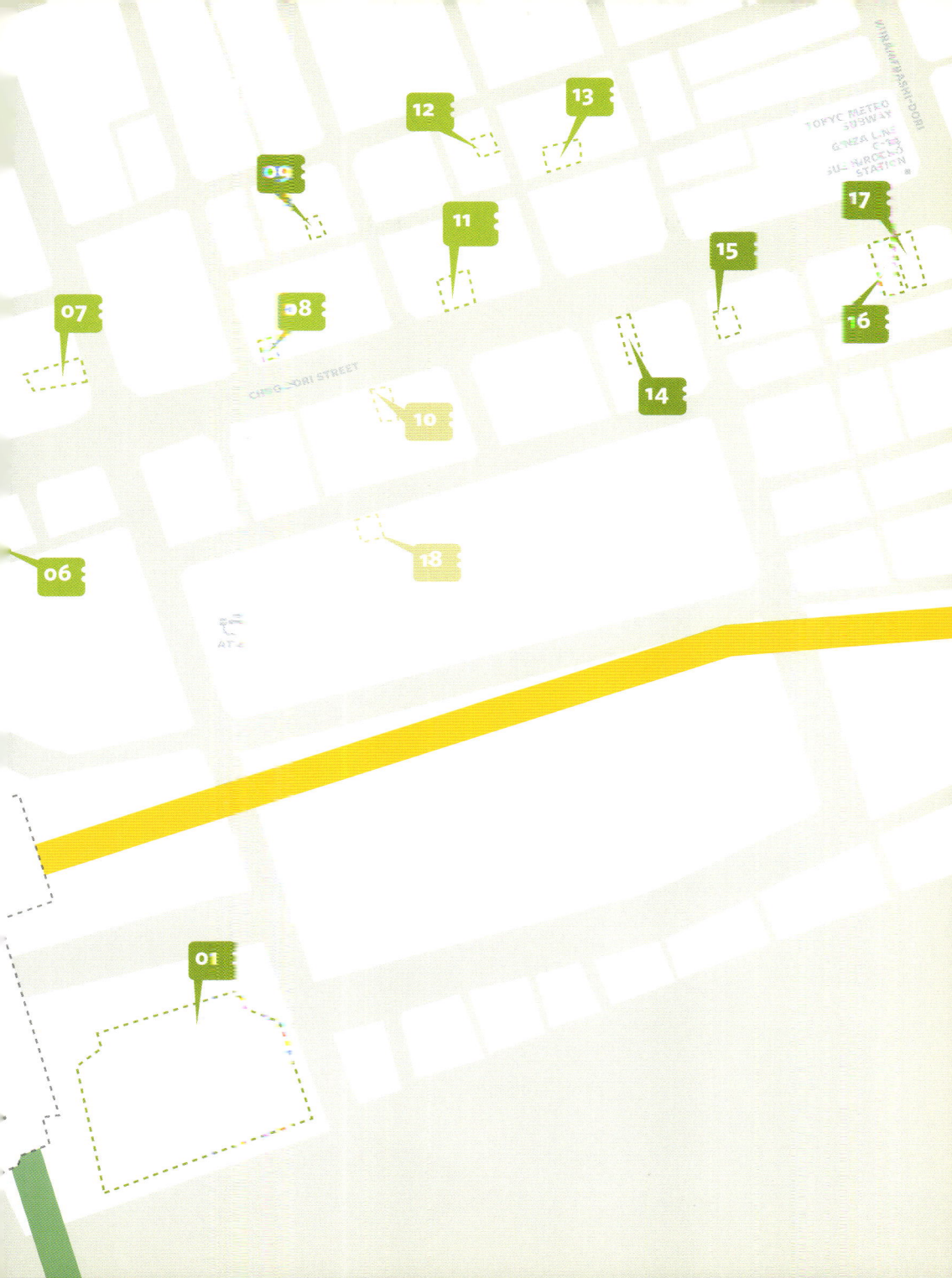

01

YODOBASHI – AKIBA

1-1 SOTOKANDA, CHIYODA-KU
03-5209-1010, WWW.YODOBASHI-AKIBA.COM
HOURS: 9:30 — 22:00

Yodobashi is an electronics superstore with floors devoted to almost every object that can be operated with a power or USB cord. Interestingly enough, the sixth floor is home to a wide variety of video games, but an even wider variety of toys. Like all great superstores, they carry it all—from toddler toys and Apanman squeakies to the latest in sentai superheroes and scale model kits. In addition to their broad selection, Yodobashi's other great allure is their prices, which are usually 20 percent below conventional retail. It's not unusual to see a first-time visitor going wild on Yodobashi prices and filling bags' worth of toy gold for the trip home. Additionally, Yodobashi has the largest gachapon aisle you will find in Akihabara (or anywhere else, for that matter) for all the mini-size collectors looking for the latest releases. As Yodobashi is open later than most collector shops, we recommend saving it for last, unless you want to carry your haul for the rest of the day.

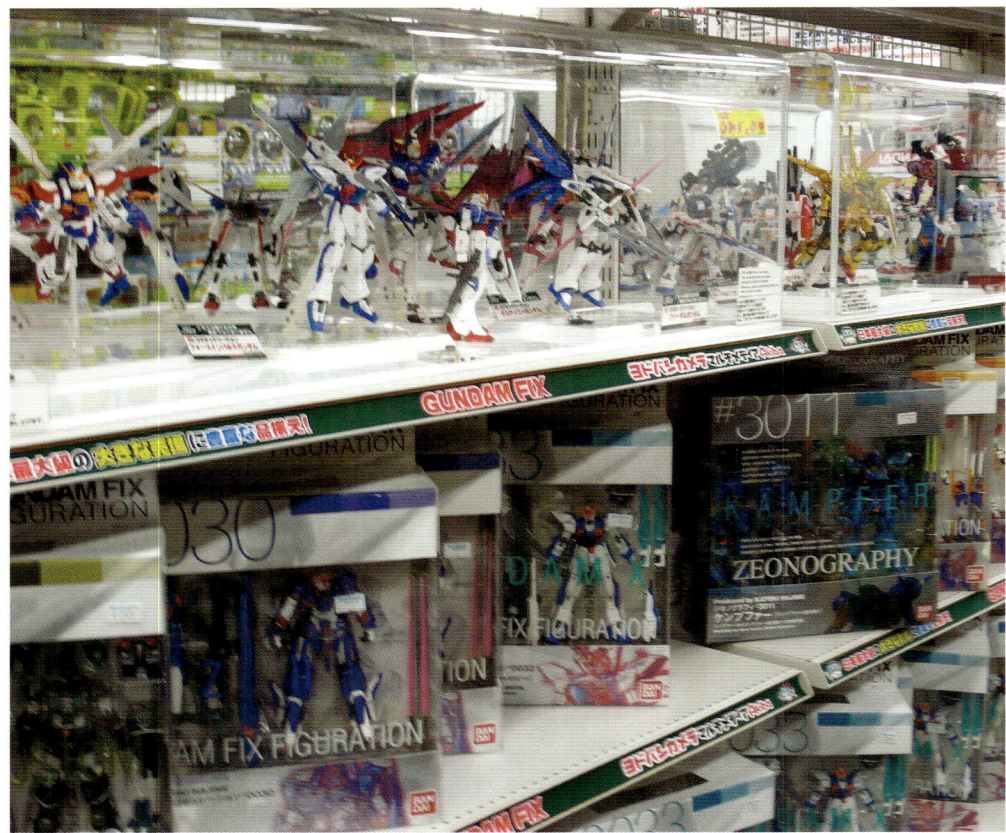

Welcome to Akihabara, home to the second-largest group of toy shops in Tokyo (behind Nakano) and the largest group of otaku in all their various and uncomfortable forms. As you get off the Sobu or Yamanote train, head for the Electric Town exit. Upon exiting the turnstiles, take a left, which should put you on a side street facing just to the left of Radio Kaikan (03) and Asobit City Hobby (04). Though they occupy separate buildings, the overlapping signage makes the distinction between buildings slightly less obvious. Both buildings are full of various case shops, small consignment shops, and a general toy store carrying Star Wars and character goods. On the same side of the street as the train tracks is Gamers (02), a general store of all things otaku. Just past this is the main street of Akihabara, Chuo-Dori (Just look for the LAOX sign if you get turned around.)

Take your time as you travel down Chuo-Dori, stopping in a wide array of toy stores. We suggest walking down one side of the street, and coming back on the other. As happens in Nakano, you can experience toy burnout in Akihabara, so pace yourself or come back for more later.

The north side of the street is home to the area's smaller shops. Hobbit (05) has a nice selection of everything on the fourth floor, with models on the third floor and RPG cards on the fifth. Asobit City Chara (06) is across the street, and has six floors full of character goods, but the volume of quality stores nearby prevents it from being a highly trafficked destination. Yellow Submarine (07) has toys on the fourth floor and RPG cards on the seventh. Yanigawa Soft (08) is an electronics store with a plentiful supply of chogokin and robot series toys on the second floor. Tucked discreetly in the alley behind it is Mandarake Akihabara (09), which is miniscule compared to its Shibuya and Nakano brethren. The fifth floor is all toys; the sixth floor is full of manga and anime.

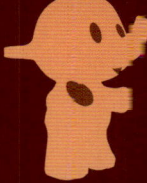

Hobby Shop Kotobukiya (11) is the first of the multi-story toy stores in the area, with each floor devoted to a single style and a Kotobukiya specialty shop on the seventh floor. One block behind Hobby Shop Kotobukiya is Robot-Herokan (12), a small but nicely maintained vintage store specializing in chogokin, and Collectables Tokyo (13), a new shop full of Kubrick and gacha-pon toys.

Cross the street at the intersection of Chuo-Dori and Kuramaebashi-Dori, and you'll begin to enter the big toy stores that anchor Akihabara's reputation. First up is the overstuffed Toys Golden Age (17), which is one step away from being a crime scene, and is literally bursting at the seams with toys. Right next door is Liberty 9 (16), an eight-floor toy store with something for everyone. The polar opposite of Toys Golden Age, Liberty 9 arranges its displays so carefully as to never miss create too much space. Next up is Hobby Figure (15), just off Chuo-Dori to the south. Part of the same Liberty family as Liberty 9, it is another multi-story shop with a very similar layout, and even more stock. To make it even more complicated, Liberty 7 (14) is the third of these megastores. You can burn out easily if you visit all three of the Liberty shops in a row.

On your way back to the train station, there is a great crepe stand (10) to the left, or, if you're in the mood for more than a snack, try Chioccio@Pizzeria (18) at the base of the building one block back. There is also an ATM in this building around the corner.

Now that you have seen everything else in Akihabara, it's time to hit Yodobashi-Akiba (01). Lots of people make this their first stop in Akihabara, but unless you want to carry these bags the whole time, we recommend saving it for last (its late closing time makes this easy to do). Yodobashi is a giant department store, and the sixth floor is stocked to the brim with toys and video games. Everything is brand new and priced 10 to 20 percent below retail. All fans of chogokin, model kits, Transformers, video games, or anything new toy-wise owe it to themselves to stop in, as no one leaves empty handed.

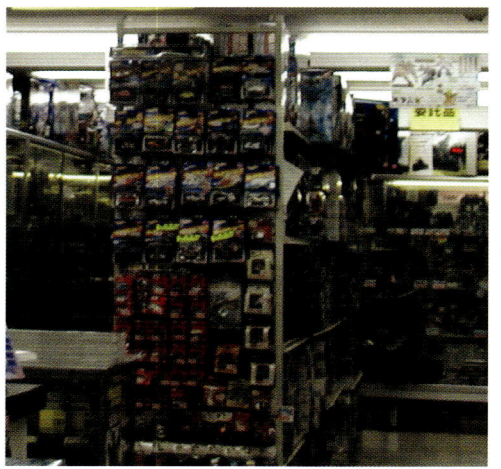

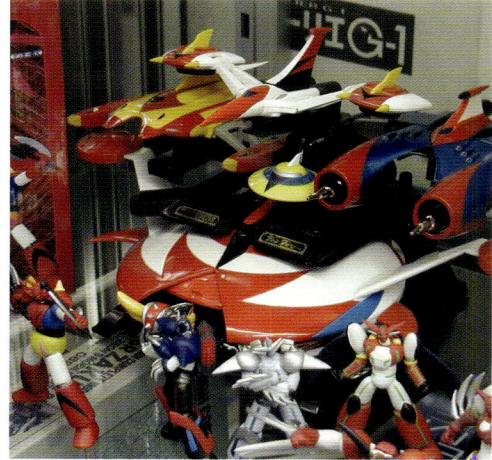

ASOBIT CITY HOBBY 04
1-15-18 SOTOKANDA, CHIYODA-KU
03-5298-3581, WWW.AKIBAASOBIT.JP
HOURS: 10:00 — 22:00

ASOBIT CITY CHARA 06
1-13-2 SOTOKANDA, CHIYODA-KU
03-3251-3100, WWW.AKIBAASOBIT.JP
HOURS: 10:00 — 22:00

Six and seven floors, respectively, the Asobit stores are multi-level monsters stocked with every kind of new toy, video game, character good, or hobby item you could want. However, their average retail pricing and apparent lack of enthusiasm mean that you will probably end up shopping elsewhere, and have a better time doing it.

YELLOW SUBMARINE G-SHOP 2 07
03-5289-5400
WWW.YELLOWSUBMARINE.CO.JP/MAIN3.HTM
HOURS: 11:00 — 20:00

Yellow Submarine is a surprisingly varied store with a heavy emphasis on super robots, model kits, and chogokin. They even have some vintage thrown around the store, and it is usually priced to sell. A nice shop, and not as well known as some of the bigger shops in the area.

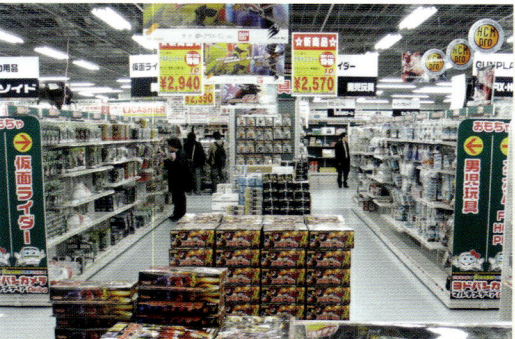

YANIGAWA SOFT 08
SEE MAP FOR DIRECTIONS

Yanigawa Soft is one of the typical video game/electronics and toy retailers that you can find all over Akihabara, as well as Tokyo at large. The second floor of Yanigawa Soft has a good selection of robot and chogokin toys.

17

TOYS GOLDEN AGE

4-7-2 KOBAYASHI, CHIYODA-KU
03-5256-0012, WWW.GEOCITIES.JP: CYCLONE_0999/ANNAI.JPG
HOURS: 11:30 — 21:00

The last shop on the main Akihabara drag, Toys Golden Age is also one of the best. While many of the other shops have divided their stock on numerous floors, Toys Golden Age has stuffed it all into a single level. Toys are literally stacked two or three deep in front of showcases and behind the counter, so picking out individual items can be a test of your visual stamina. Take your time, drop your bags at the door, and get to searching—rarities, common items, and obscurities from just about every genre are hidden here, but you may have to work a bit for them. The staff are happy to move and rearrange things to get to hidden gems, but do not speak any English, so employ your best version of toy sign language for your archeological adventure.

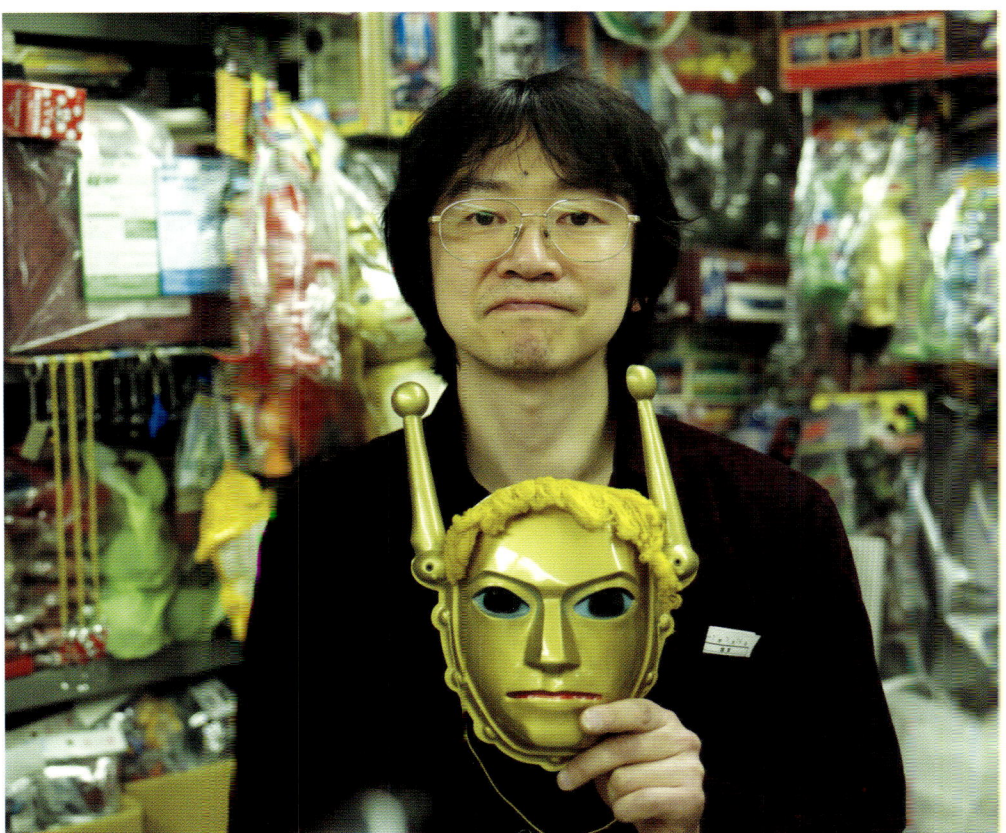

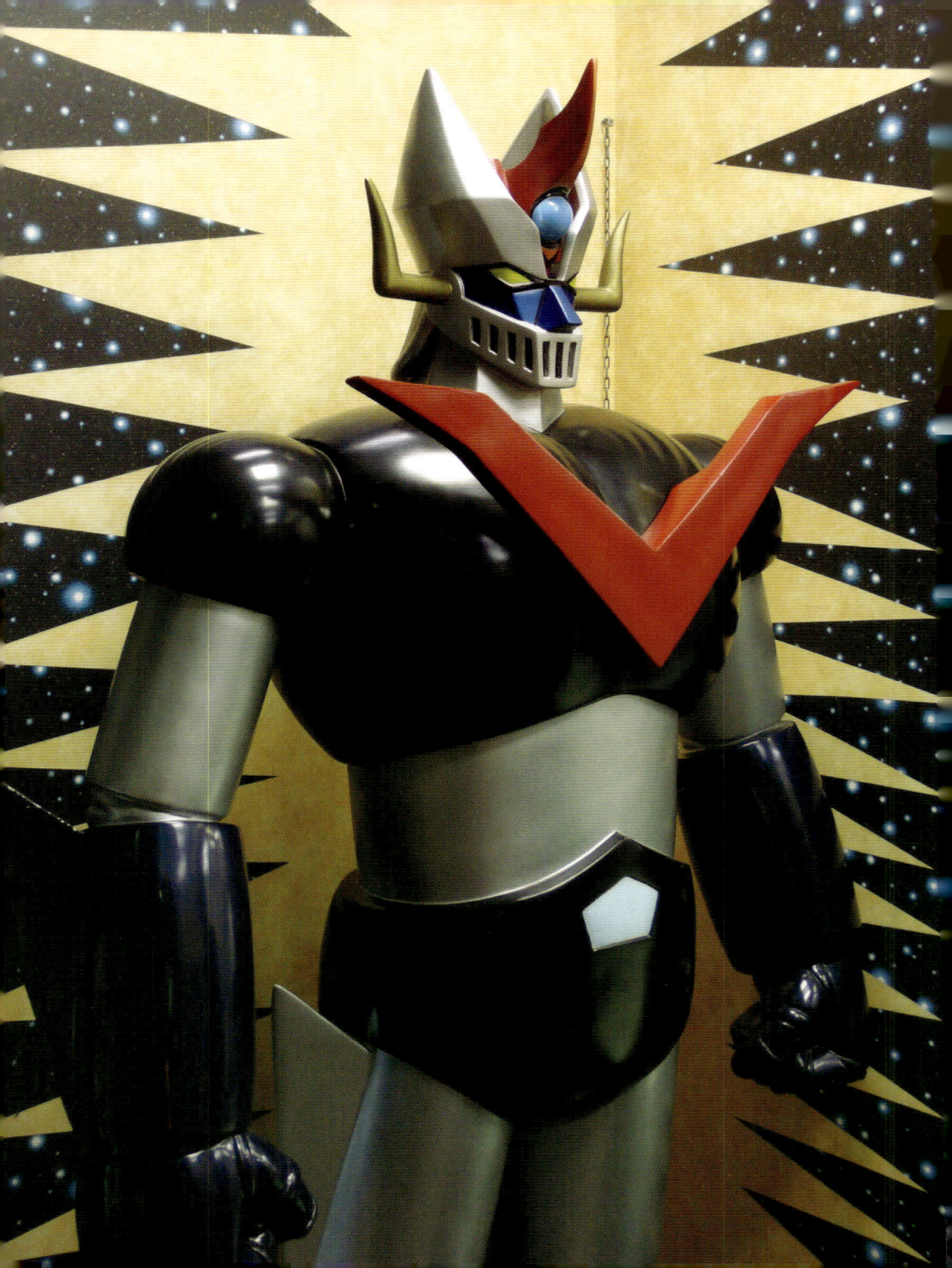

14, 15, 16

LIBERTY 7, HOBBY FIGURE LIBERTY 9

WWW.LIBERTY-SHOP.CO.JP/AKIBA/AKIBA_CHIZU.HTML
WWW.LIBERTY-SHOP.CO.JP
HOURS: 11:00 — 20:00

These three stores, all part of the Liberty group of stores and the anchors of the Akihabara toy scene, are almost identical in setup and point of view. All are multi-story shops with floors dedicated to particular genres of collecting. The bottom floors are generally all chogokin and super robot related, with other floors dedicated to gachapon figures, anime, military, RPG, action figures, Disney and other character goods. Vinyl of any sort is few and far between, and all stock is secondhand, yet the latest releases are always here. Prices are usually quite good on anything considered out of date or only marginally popular, while the hot new releases make up for any savings you may find on the older items.

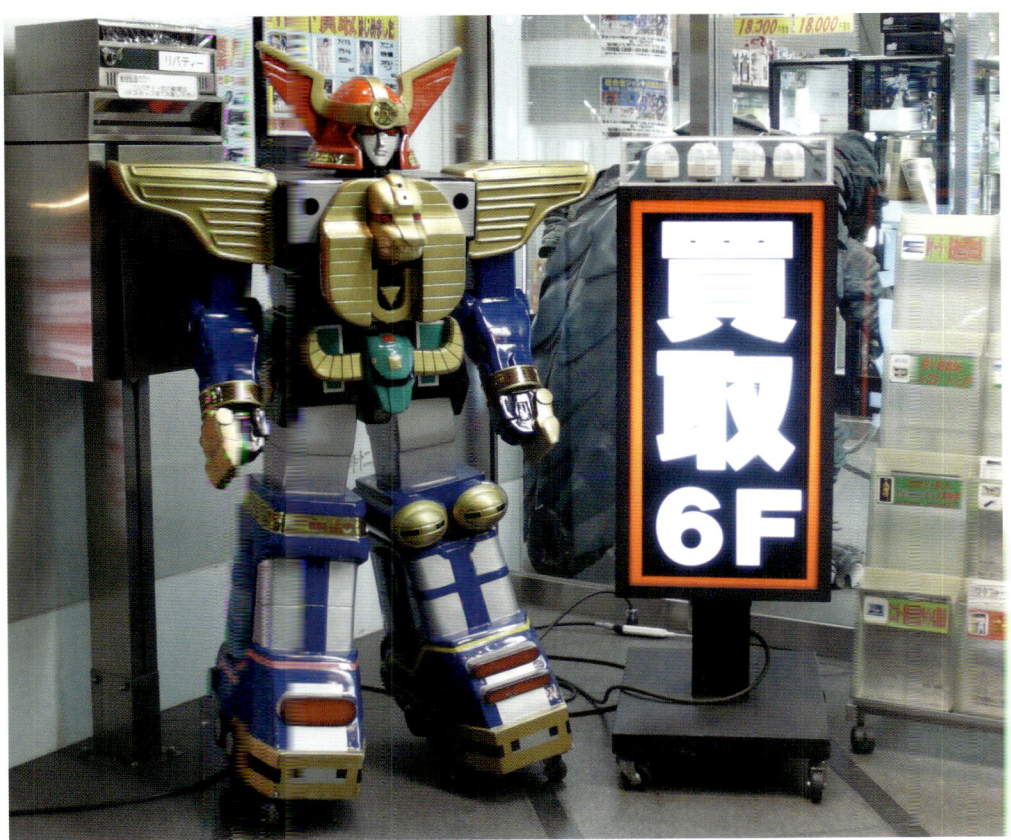

09

MANDARAKE AKIHABARA

3-11-2 6F SOTOKANDA, CHIYODA-KU
03-3252-7007, WWW.MANDARAKE.CO.JP/ENGLISH/SHOP/AKB.HTML
HOURS: 11:00 — 20:30

The smallest of all the Mandarake stores, the Akihabara version is easy to miss. Inconspicuously located on the fifth and sixth floors of a seemingly generic building, this version pales in comparison to Shibuya and Nakano. That said, the store's diminutive size and selection can sometimes bring you luck, as other collectors often pass it over en route to the larger shops in the area. The toys are located on the fifth floor, with manga and anime on the sixth.

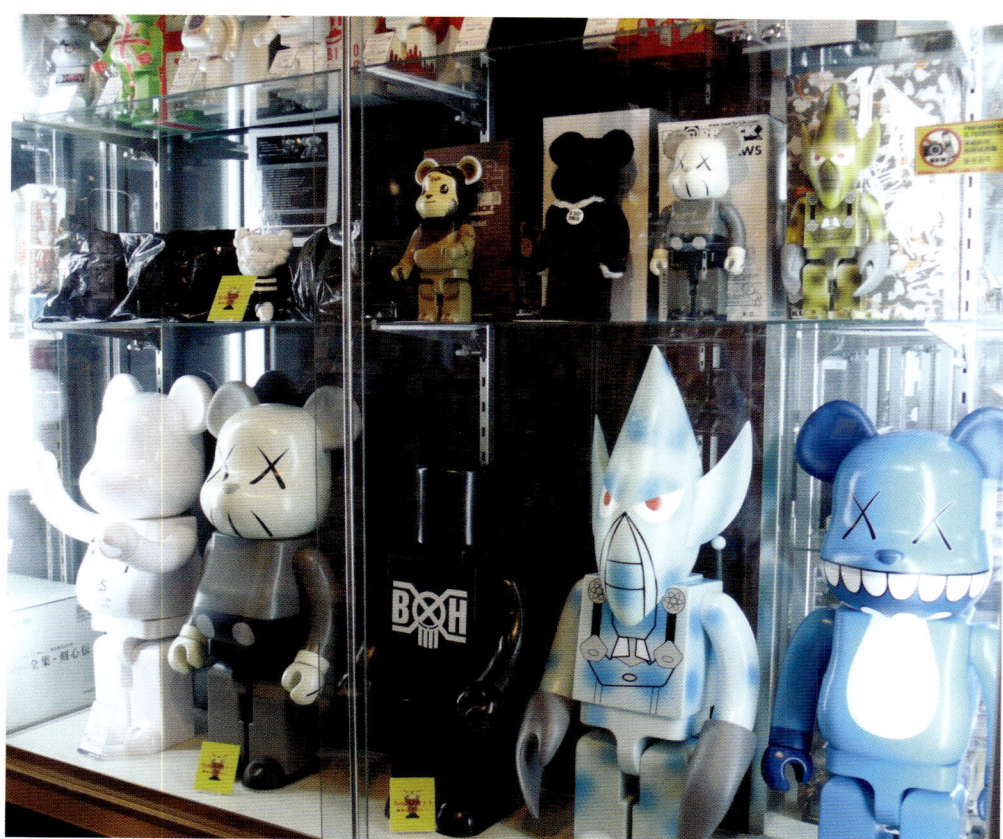

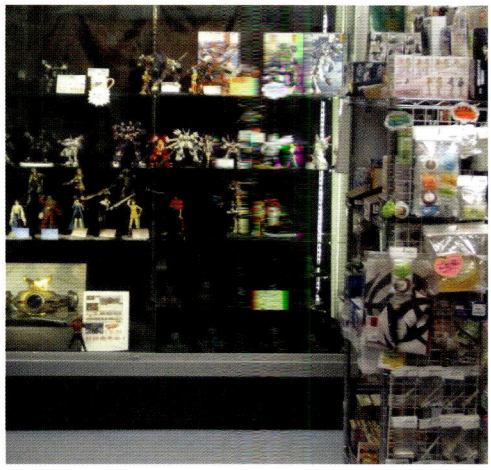

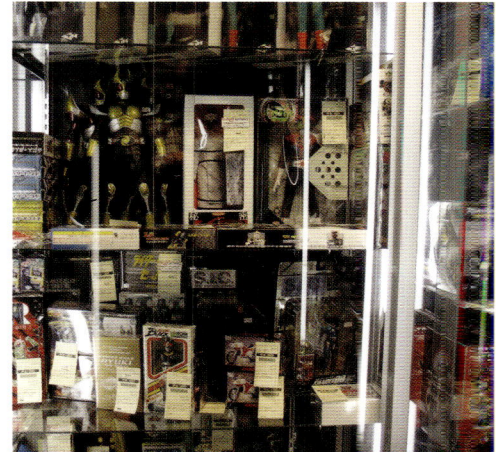

HOBBY SHOP KOTOBUKIYA   11

3-14-9 SOTOKANDA, CHIYODA-KU
03-3257-2360, WWW.KOTOBUKIYA.CO.JP/KOTOBUKIYASHOP
HOURS: 10:30 — 20:00

Hobby Shop Kotobukiya is a seven-floor toy shop
divided into categories. What sets this venue apart
from others is that the seventh floor is a flagship shop
for the Kotobukiya brand. Once known for their model
kits, the store's realistic, affordable Star Wars figures
have garnered them new prominence among
American collectors.

ROBOT-HEROKAN   12

3-10-6 MARUWA BLDG.-B1F SOTOKANDA, CHIYODA-KU
0120-135-163
HOURS: 11:00 — 20:00

A small shop selling used toys, Robot Herokan focuses
on Transformers, Gundam, Tokusatsu, and sentai, with a
few vinyl toys thrown in for good measure. The prices are
good and the shop owner is friendly, but more than three
people can turn this tiny space into a claustrophobic's
worst nightmare.

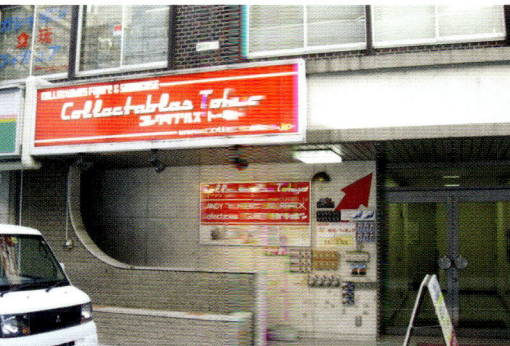

COLLECTABLES TOKYO   13

3-9-8 SOTOKANDA CHIYODA-KU
03-5294-6171, WWW.COLLECTABLES.JP
HOURS: 11:00 — 20:00, SUNDAYS & HOLIDAYS 11:00 — 19:00

Following all the latest trends in micro-collecting,
Collectables Tokyo is full of all the latest candy toys,
Kubricks, Be@bricks, and anything else you can think
of that is three inches tall or smaller. Unless you are a
candy-toy completist, you can skip this store.

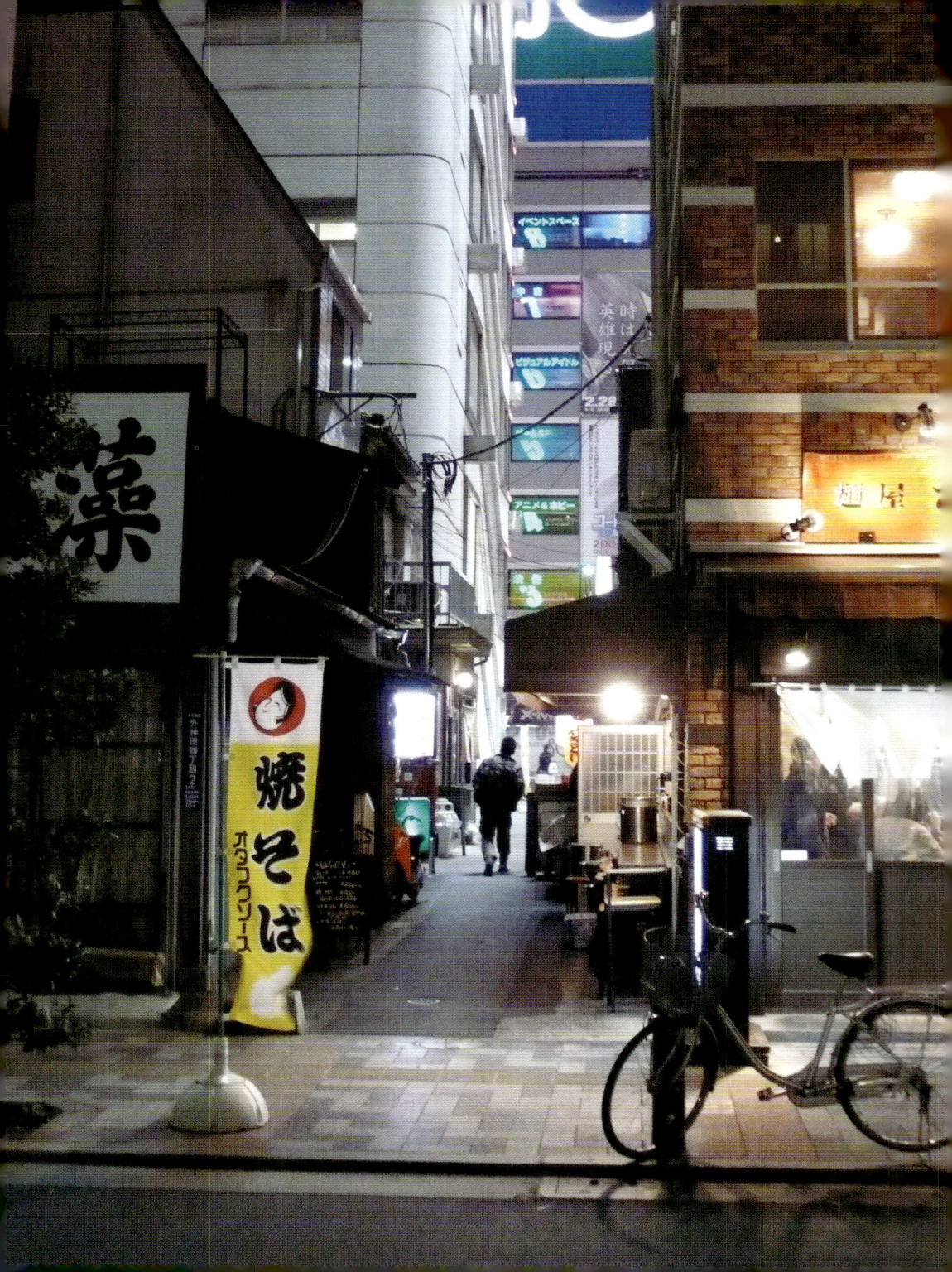

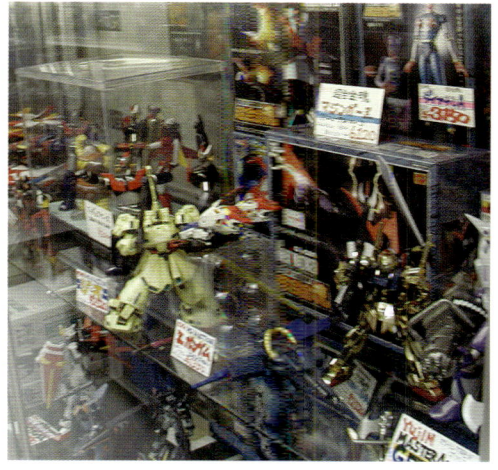

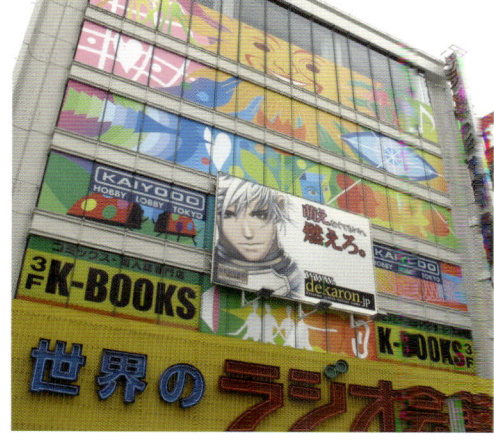

HOBBIT **05**

1-10-11 4F SOTOKANDA, CHIYODA-KU
03-5209-4111, WWW.TOKYOHOBBIT.CO.JP
HOURS: 12:00 — 20:00

Another of Tokyo's Hobbit stores, this version occupies
the third, fourth, and fifth floors of its building, with
model kits on the third floor, toys on the fourth, RPG
cards on the fifth. It's heavily focused on new chogokin
and robot action figures, but there are a few vinyls as
well. Prices are always inexpensive, and the selection is
chaotically diverse.

RADIO KAIKAN **03**

1-15-16 SOTOKANDA, CHIYODA-KU
03-3251-3711, WWW.RADIOKAIKAN.ORG
HOURS: 10:00 — 21:00

Filled with toys, anime, and manga shops, Radio Kaikan
can be a thrilling and scary place. K-Books, on the third
floor, is a famous manga bookstore, and floors four,
five, and six are home to a wide variety of shops. But be
warned—this is the first of many buildings with a variety
of dubious adult content, hentai, and eyebrow-lifting
items right next to traditional toy sellers.

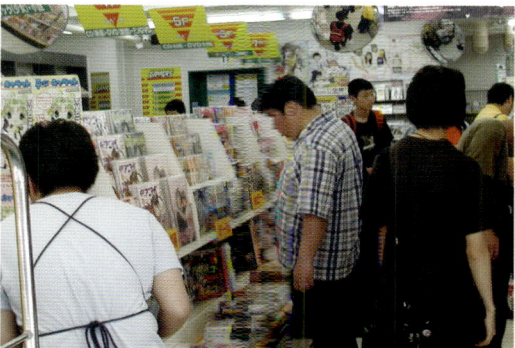

GAMERS **02**

1-14-7 SOTOKANDA, CHIYODA-KU
03-5298-8720, WWW.BROCCOLI.CO.JP/GAMERS
HOURS: 11:00 — 21:00

A one-stop haven for all things otaku, you either love or
hate Gamers. Each floor is tailored to a different kind of
fanaticism; toys and models are on the seventh floor.

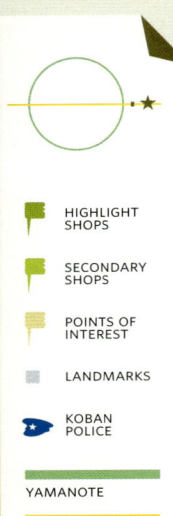

HIGHLIGHT
SHOPS

SECONDARY
SHOPS

POINTS OF
INTEREST

LANDMARKS

KOBAN
POLICE

YAMANOTE

SŌBU LOCAL

KOIWA/KAMEIDO

Koiwa is a small neighborhood closer to the outskirts of Tokyo. A forty-five-minute train ride from Shibuya on the Sobu local, Koiwa is very residential and free of tourists, other than those few daring souls coming to shop for toys.

Down to only two stores now (a third has since moved to Nakano), Koiwa is home to one of the most famous shops in all of Tokyo — Third Uncle/Characters (02). All that remains of the original Third Uncle family of shops, Characters is densely packed, full of more rare toys than any other shop in Tokyo, and more expensive than all the other shops combined.

When you arrive at the Koiwa station, take the main exit, then turn right as you pass the turnstiles. This should put you in front of department store Ito-Yokado, which has a few new toys on the sixth floor, and a few candy toys in the basement.

Taking the road on the left side of Ito-Yokado will get you to the main road of Kuramaebashi-Dori. On a side note, you will pass Three Cousin (01), which is artist Pushead's favorite negima in the area.

After you are through at Characters, go back to Kuramaebashi-Dori, heading west for four blocks and taking a left turn down a neighborhood side street, to visit Manga Beya (03). A truly vintage toy store, it is stocked with all sorts of tin toys and advertising characters from a time before must of us were born.

03

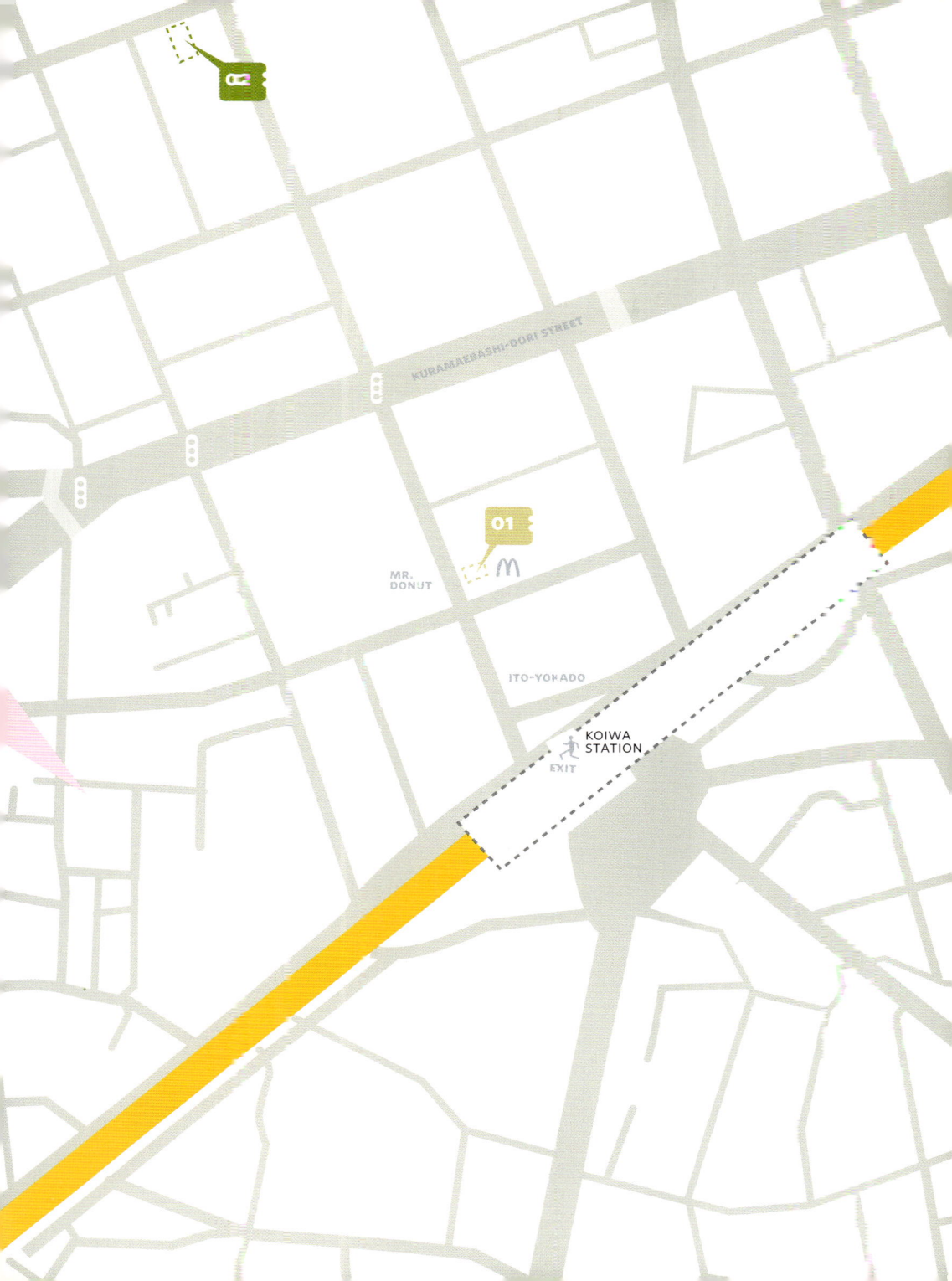

KURAMAEBASHI-DORI STREET

02

01

MR.
DONUT

ITO-YOKADO

KOIWA
STATION

EXIT

02

THIRD UNCLE/CHARACTERS

3-34-8 NISHI-KOIWA, EDOGAWA-KU
03-3659-5545, WWW.THIRD-UNCLE.COM
HOURS: 13:00 — 21:00, CLOSED MONDAY

One of Tokyo's best-known shops, Characters houses the crème de la crème of toy stock for every collector, with a selection so rare as to stop even the most jaded aficionados in their tracks. One of the original trifecta of dominant toy shops (like Forest Gangu and the original Third Uncle), Characters carries on their original legacy to this day. Beyond their impressive selection, Characters' other legacy may well be their prices. Never afraid to aim for the sky, Characters may have all the toys your heart desires, but your wallet may not be able to handle it. A must-see for any first-time or serious toy collector.

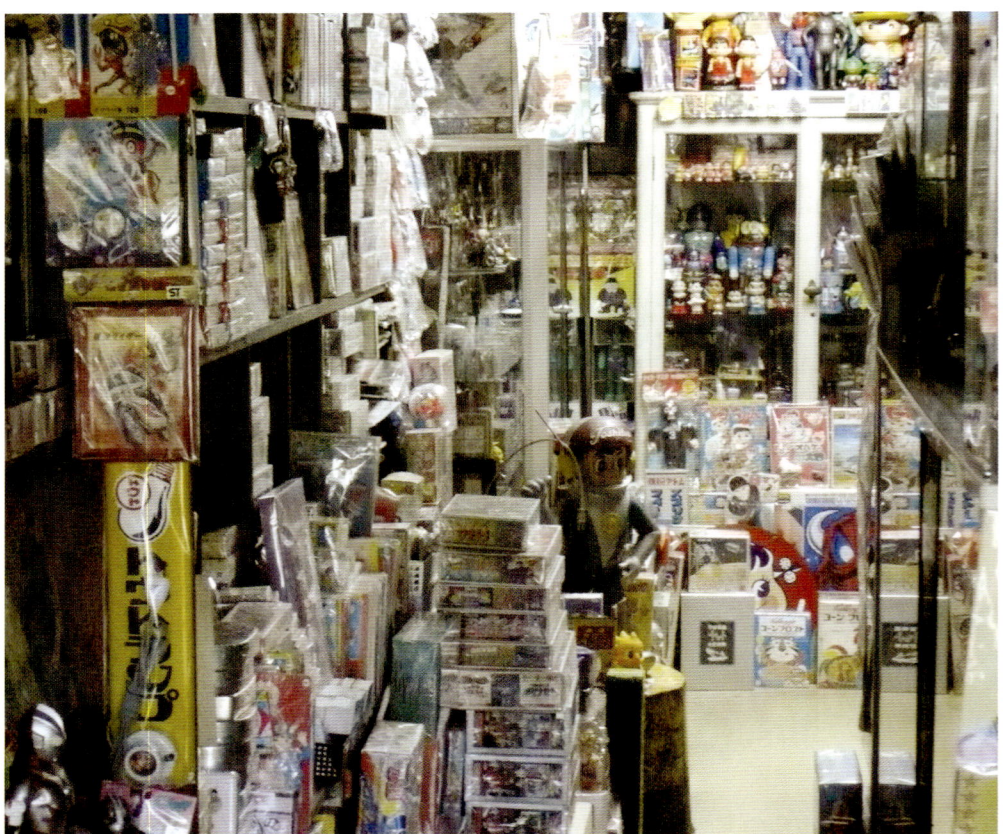

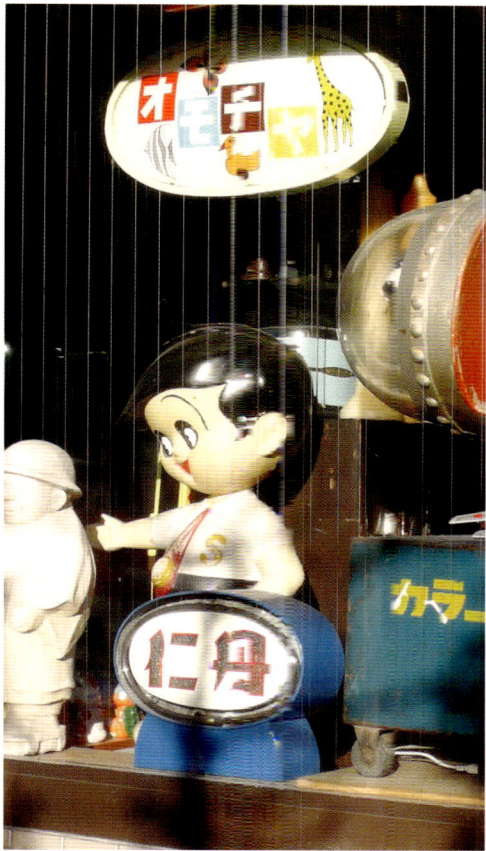

KAMEIDO

For those of you interested in shopping for new toys, there is a Toys-R-Us located close by in the neighborhood of Kameido. Located four stops past Akihabara, and three stops before you get to Koiwa, Kameido is an easy stop for anyone headed to Koiwa. The Toys-R-Us is actually one of the best in the city, as it's rarely visited by tourists and is usually well stocked. To get there, exit the Sobu line at Kameido (which is on the north side of the tracks), and walk around the station to the south side. You will see the shopping center with Toys-R-Us just down the road running parallel to the train tracks. The Toys-R-Us is at the back of the mall area, and like most malls, there are several somewhat questionable food choices as well. While there is surely something else worth mentioning about Kameido, we are not familiar with it, so let us know if you find anything.

MANGA BEYA
FOLLOW MAP FOR DIRECTIONS

03

As more of a tin toy and vintage advertising and display store, Manga Beya is what you imagine toy stores must have looked like in years past. Seemingly stuck in a time warp, Manga Beya is a fun stop for anyone who appreciates older toys, even if you don't collect them.

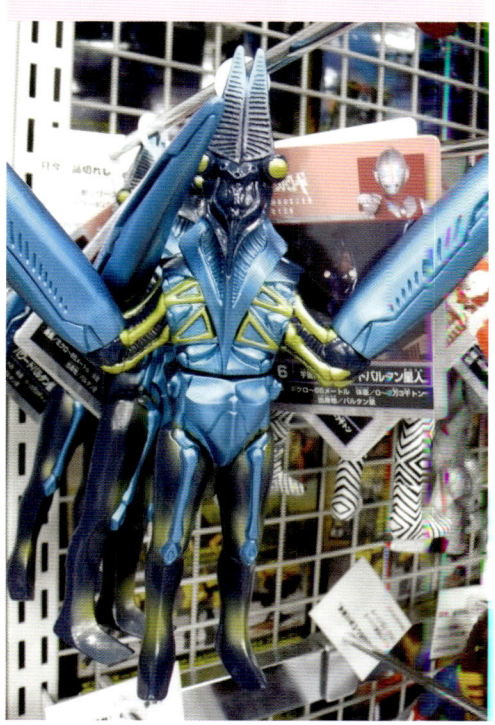

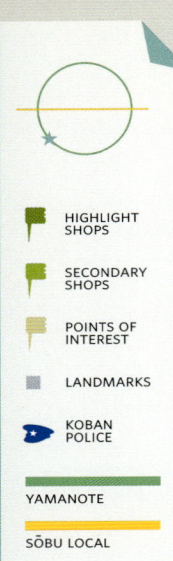

HIGHLIGHT
SHOPS

SECONDARY
SHOPS

POINTS OF
INTEREST

LANDMARKS

KOBAN
POLICE

YAMANOTE

SŌBU LOCAL

EBISU/
DAIKANYAMA

Ebisu and Daikanyama are two adjacent neighborhoods that
butt up against Shibuya's south side, but neither one of these
neighborhoods is a stop for the majority of our readers. Ebisu
has two stores, Mr. Craft and Monster Japan, both of which
specialize in American and Star Wars toys, with Mr. Craft
selling new toys, and Monster Japan selling vintage toys.

As you walk into Daikanyama, this area was originally supposed
to be the next Harajuku, as hip streetwear brands moved here
to avoid the oversaturation of Harajuku. Over the last few years,
however, the idea has not taken hold, and many shops have
either closed, relocated, or, in the case of Supreme, opened
up another store in Harajuku as well. For those interested in
streetwear, Daikanyama is still worth exploring, but it might
be worth leaving for last. For toy collectors, particularly fans
of Blythe and other big-eyed fashion dolls, Daikanyama is
ground zero, home to Junie Moon, the CWC flagship store. This
shop epitomizes how one type of toy can be highly sought
after by some collectors, and completely ignored by others.

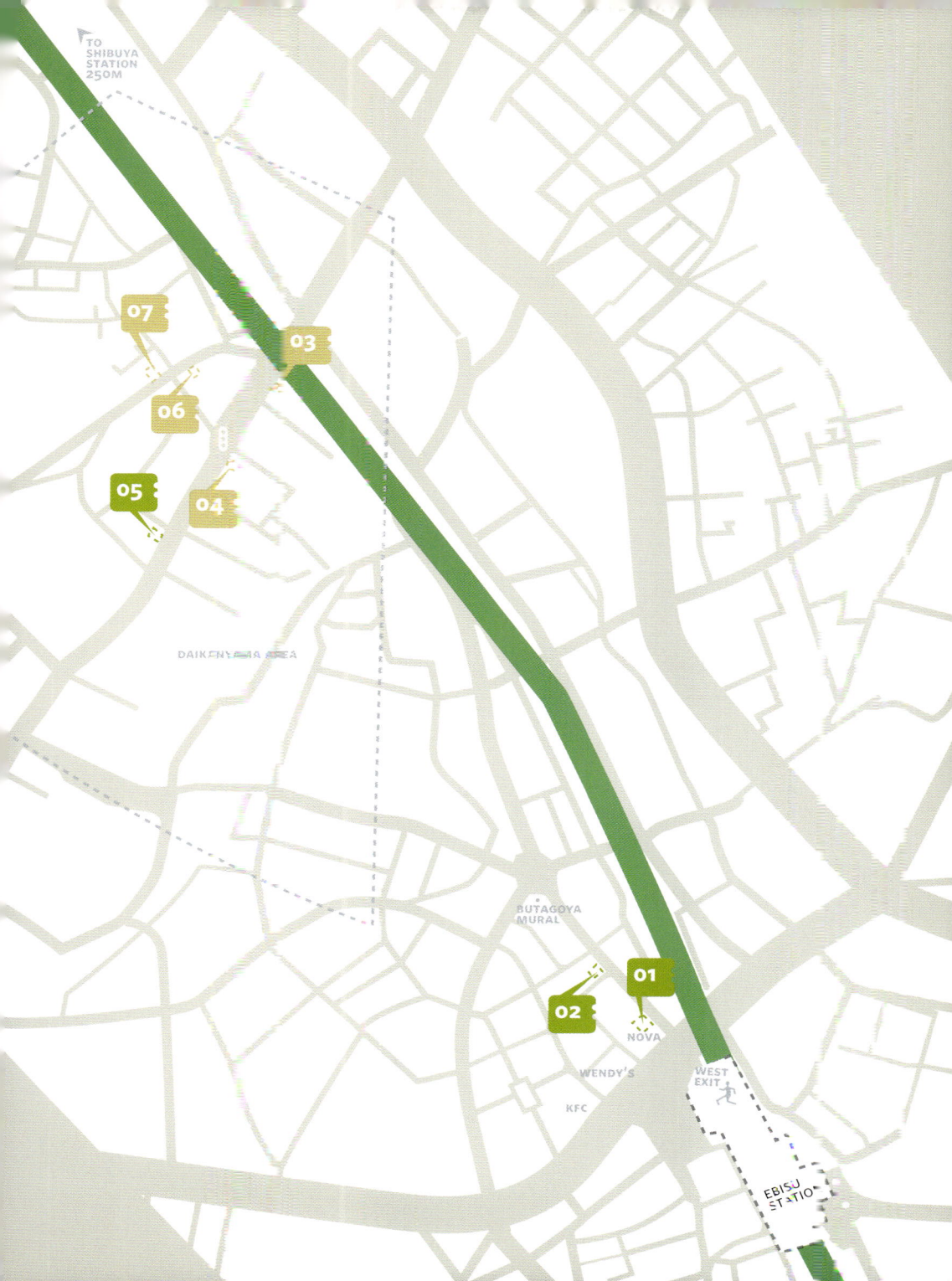

TO
SHIBUYA
STATION
250M

07

03

06

05   **04**

DAIKENYAMA AREA

BUTAGOYA
MURAL

01

02

NOVA

WENDY'S   WEST
EXIT

KFC

EBISU
STATION

Upon arriving at Ebisu, take the west exit, which will put you in a large courtyard. Directly across the street, you should see a large Nova sign, which has an interesting metal sculpture of the god Ebisu on the left side, above the first floor.

Immediately around the corner on the right-hand side is Mr. Craft (01). In this six-story building of shops, the main store on the bottom floor is full of new character toys, especially Star Wars figures. The remaining floors are mostly full of mini R/C cars, with some consignment cases on the fifth floor. Just one quick block up is Monster Japan (02), another toy store devoted to Western character toys. Specializing more in monsters and Star Wars, they have a diverse array of new and old figures and a surprisingly high quantity of prototypes and test shots from *Star Wars*.

At the large intersection two blocks ahead, you'll see a pork restaurant on the left called Butagoya. Having never eaten there, we can't recommend the food, but they do have an amazing mural that wraps around the top of the building.

To see more of the neighborhood, it is easiest to follow the tracks. Pass under an elevated railway and proceed one more block to an overpass road. The route along the way used to be covered in amazing graffiti by artists from all over the world, but most has been painted over, although KAMI and SASU recently painted the underside of the train bridge.

When you arrive at the elevated roadway, take the steps to your left, and you should be directly in front of hipster skate shop Supreme (03). A block and a half down from that is the English brand Silas (04). Across the street and another block down is big-eyed-doll heaven in the form of the shop Junie Moon (05), the CWC shop, which is home to the original big-eyed doll, Blythe.

From there, take some time to wander around the area, as there are lots of little shops along many of the narrow streets. Frames Café (06) is good for a quick bite, and Stendig Design (07) is a neat little modern furniture store. From here, it is easy to wander down the side streets and train tracks to the south side of the Shibuya station, where you can board a train to your next destination.

THIS LITTLE PIGGY:
THE LARGE WRAPAROUND MURAL ABOVE BUTAGOYA IS A FUN AND HUMOROUS COLLECTION OF SCENES THAT SPANS THE ENTIRE FRONT OF THE BUILDING. PAINTED BY YUZZA IN 2006, IT IS A RECENT ADDITION TO THE EBISU WALKING TOUR.

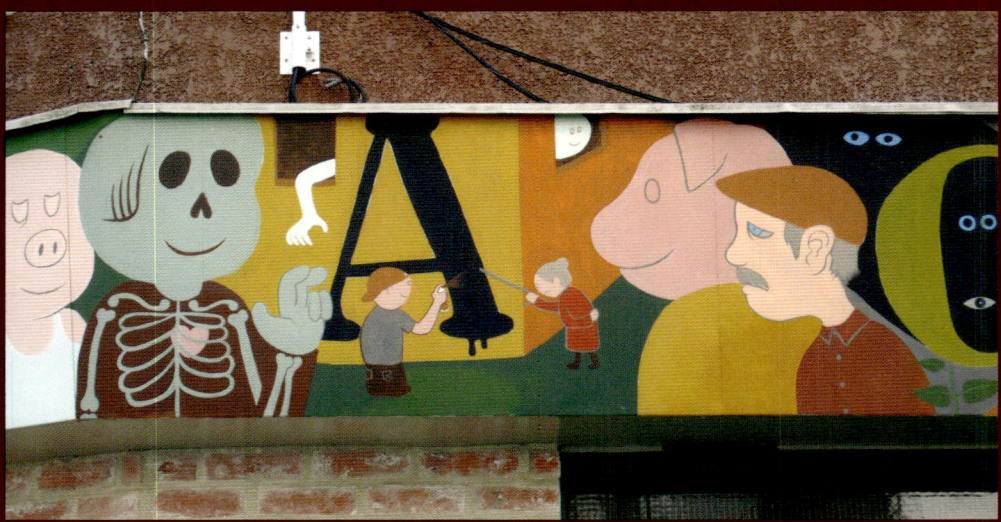

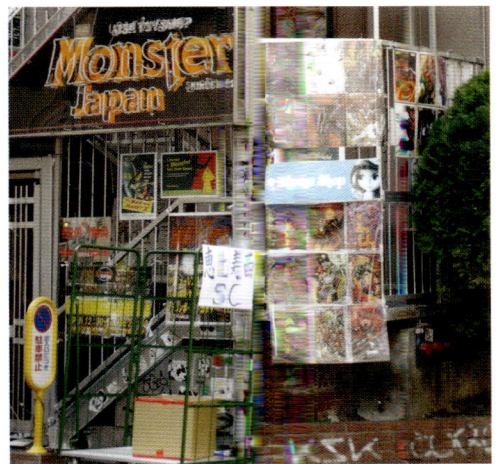

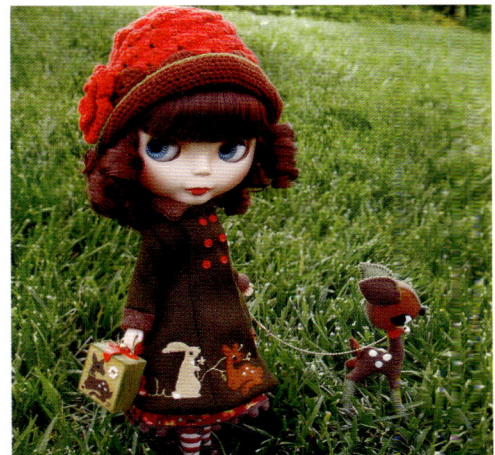

MONSTER JAPAN   02
1-6-1 3F EBISU WEST, SHIBUYA-KU
03-3463-3555, WWW.MONSTER-JAPAN.CO.JP
HOURS: 13:00 — 20:30

For the Star Wars or American movie monster enthusiast,
Monster Japan is a great shop. Surrounded by new and
vintage Western action figure-style toys, and vintage
Universal Monsters, Aliens, and American sci-fi items,
you'll be surprised that you can't find similar stores
stateside. Monster Japan's sizable stash of Hasbro
prototypes means you can obtain unique items here
that you won't find in other shops.

JUNIE MOON   05
4-3, 1F, SARUGAKU-CHO, SHIBUYA-KU
WWW.JUNIEMOON.JP/INDEX.E.CGI
HOURS: TUE.–SAT. 12 — 20:00, SUN. 12 — 18:00; CLOSED MON

Who knew that a big-eyed doll with changing eye color
could become so popular? Nearly forty years after her
introduction, Blythe has a loyal and fanatical following
of collectors and customizers like few other dolls.
Official Blythe licenser CWC shows off the latest in
Blythe style and fashion at their Junie Moon shop,
so that everyone can get a chance to buy these
sought-after dolls.

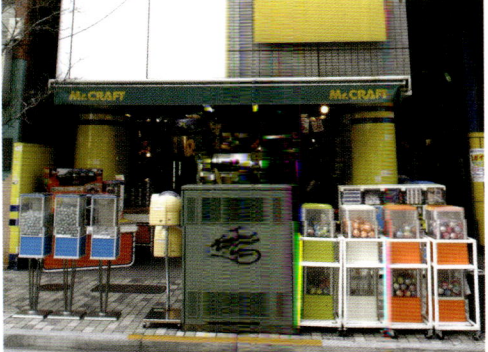

MR. CRAFT   01
1-7-4 EBISU WEST
03-3461-2665, WWW.MRCRAFT.COM
HOURS: WEEKDAYS 12:00 — 22:00, WEEKENDS 11:00 — 22:00

A six-story toy store, Mr. Craft's bottom floor is chock
full of action figures and a wide range of Star Wars items.
There are showcases on the fifth floor, and the rest of
the floors are devoted to R/C mini-cars, with racing
tracks on the sixth floor.

Mr. Craft floor list: **1F** new toys, **2F** F1 race cars,
3F mini-cars, **4F** events, **5F** showcase shop, **6F** racing
paradise Ebisu (www.banproject.com).

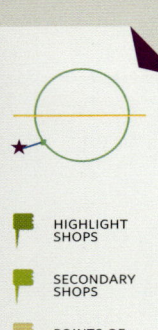

15

HIGHLIGHT
SHOPS

SECONDARY
SHOPS

POINTS OF
INTEREST

LANDMARKS

KOBAN
POLICE

YAMANOTE

KEIO-INAKASHIRA
LINE

SHIMOKITAZAWA

Shimokitazawa is off the beaten path, yet somehow is mysteriously filled with Western tourists, who are most likely not here to see the toy shops. Both sides of the station are filled with small new and used shops, most focusing on clothing, and the occasional sneaker shop, with a little bit of everything else thrown in for good measure. It can be difficult to get your bearings at first in Shimokitazawa, a confusing maze of small, windy streets, with two intersecting train lines making it even trickier.

With its eclectic mix of shops, Shimokitazawa is a fun destination for a leisurely afternoon of walking, but visitors in a hurry will not benefit from it, as you will be conveniently located next to absolutely nothing while here.

To reach Shimokitazawa, located just four quick stops from Shibuya on the private Keio-Inakashira line, you will need to exit the JR train station at Shibuya and follow the signs over the footbridge to the Keio lines across from the train station. (See the Shibuya map on page 39 for more details.) More advanced travelers can also take the private Odakyu line six stops from Shinjuku, but navigating that train station is up to you. Departing from Shibuya makes it easy, because the train line terminates there, so there is no possibility of boarding a train going in the wrong direction.

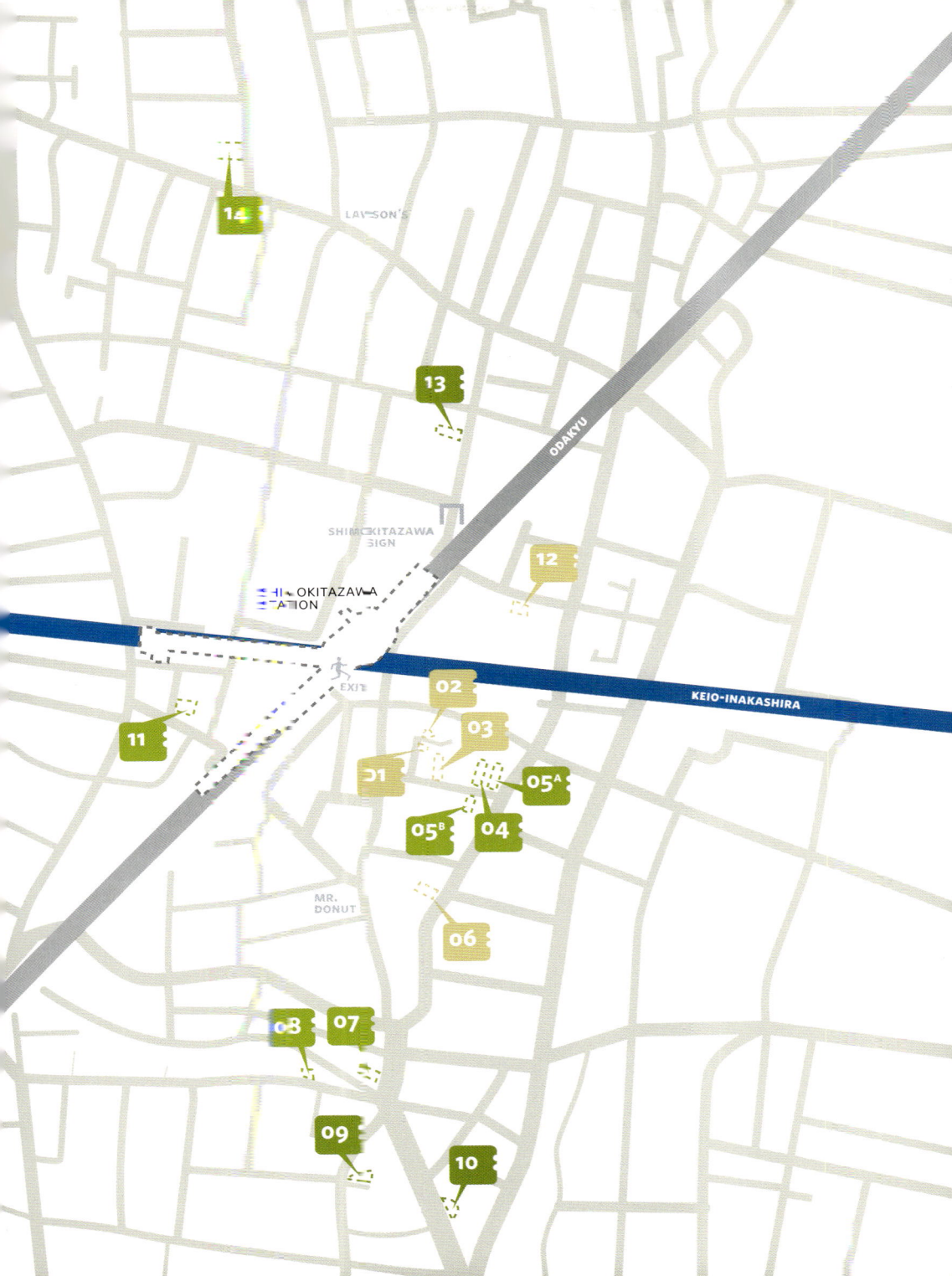

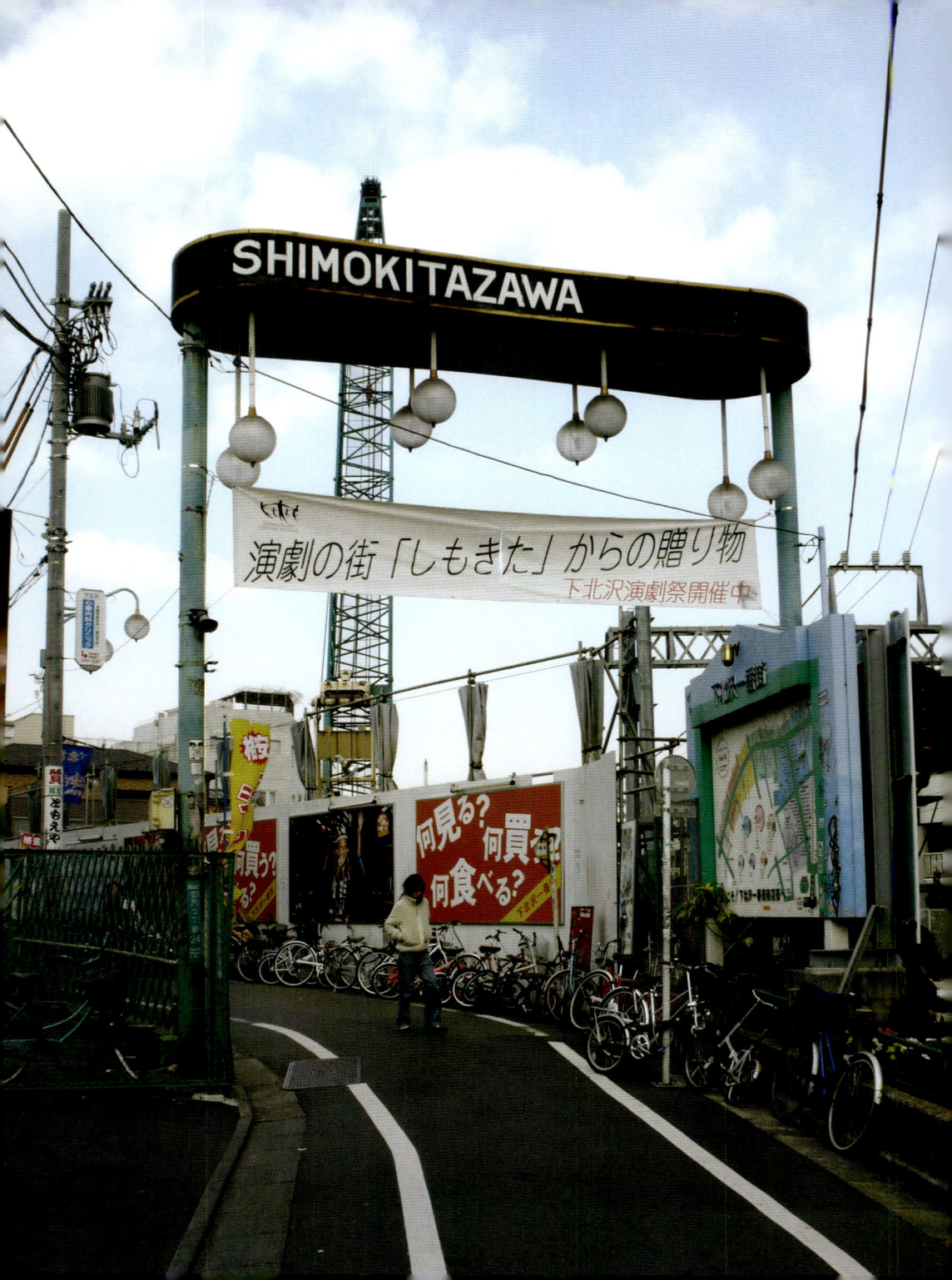

Upon arriving in Shimokitazawa exit the train station at the south exit, where you'll be right in the thick of things. The exit is fairly congested and the streets are laid out at slightly awkward angles, so walk more or less "straight" and take a right onto one of Shimokitazawa's main streets. One block down, turn left and walk half a block farther, where you will see a small alley to the left with several shops. In the back right corner is B Maniacs (01), which sells mostly old paper goods, and upstairs is Hardcore Chocolate (02), an oddball fashion t-shirt company, mixing random horror-movie and punk rock images, that Quentin Tarantino apparently loves.

Back on the street, fashion t-shirt shop Graniph is on the left (03), and just a few stores down is Sunny Co. (04), a shop with all the latest in toy and model kit releases. Next door to Sunny Co., on the corner and across the street, is Dorama (05A, 05B), which offers a great selection of used books. If you are hungry, take a right and head down two blocks to 2x2=8 (06). Located on the second floor, this is an all-you-can-eat Indian restaurant for 900 yen per person, but watch out—the drinks are 300 yen apiece and can drive your price up quickly.

Strolling back down the main road, pass Mr. Donut, and after two blocks, you will see Zemba Shonter (07) on the left, an old-school candy and toy store where you never know what to expect. Just down a narrow side street to the right is Funny Fanny (08), which focuses mostly on small toys, Smurfs, and Peanuts characters. Taking a right at the next fork will get you to Home-Rice (09) on the left-hand side. An amazing vintage toy shop with phenomenal prices, Home-Rice is another of Tokyo's great secrets.

Back on the main drag once again, one more block down on the left is Toys Paradise (10). Looking more like a generic toy store on the outside, Toys Paradise has vintage figures hidden throughout the shop, and cheap gifts of all sizes.

As you return to the train station, turn right and walk along the tracks to the crossover point. To the right, half a block down, is Village Vanguard (12), a purveyor of cheap novelty gifts and books and a favorite shop for artists looking for odd titles from obscure Japanese illustrators.

After you cross the tracks and under the Shimokitazawa sign (shown at left), Natuka Shia (13) is just one and a half blocks up. Located above Zappas, Natuka Shia is a hit-or-miss vintage shop. As you continue one more block, turn left, then walk several blocks down the road to Fewture Shop/Planet-X (14), located just off the main street. The house shop for the Fewture Company, it is full of new and vintage toys, but has very limited hours. Even further up the road is Warugaki Salon (15), a Doraemon collectors' heaven.

For those not wanting to miss anything in Shimokitazawa, Sounds Good (11) is located on the other side of the station. Featuring advertising characters and Hawaiiana, this fun little shop is right off the main street and is indicative of Shimokitazawa's eclectic nature. If you have time, we recommend wandering up and down all the side streets in this neighborhood; something new and unexpected always seems to pop up.

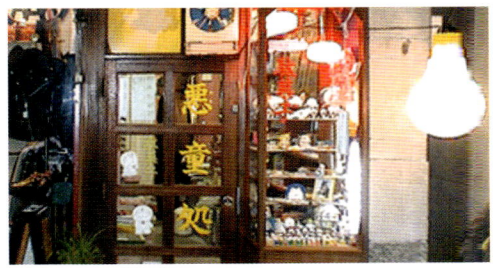

WARUGAKI SALON 15
3-34-4 KITAZAWA KU SETAGAYA
03-3460-1739, BLOG.LIVEDOOR.JP/DAGASIYA63/
HOURS: 18:00 — 3:00

This is a small shop that specializes in Doraemon toys, candy, and other toys of yesteryear. The man who runs it, known as Doraemon Uncle, has a blog all about his daily life, and an obsession with horse racing. Warugaki Salon roughly translates to "naughty boys'" place, so take that as you see fit.

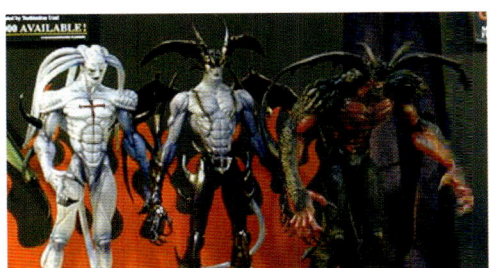

FEWTURE SHOP/PLANET-X 14
3-31-14 KITAZAWA, SETAGAYA-KU
03-3460-9742, ARTSTORM.CO.JP/SHOP.HTM
HOURS: FRIDAY & SATURDAY 13:00 — 20:00

Planet-X is the retail shop attached to toy manufacturer Fewture. There are vintage and new toys, along with Fewture products, and rumor has it that all the vintage comes from a secret warehouse that Fewture owns. Planet-X is only open on Fridays and Saturdays, so plan accordingly.

09

HOME-RICE

5-29-9 DAIZAWA, SETAGAYA-KU

03-3411-5262

HOURS: 12:00 — 19:30

Often referred to as "Oma Rise," Home-Rice is one of Tokyo's best one-stop shops. Carrying a little bit of everything, including tin, die-cast, advertising, twelve-inch figures, jumbos, and vinyl, it is just as enjoyable for looking at toys as it is for buying them. With a helpful and knowledgeable staff, and some of the best prices in the city, Home-Rice is one of Tokyo's toy hunters' secret spots.

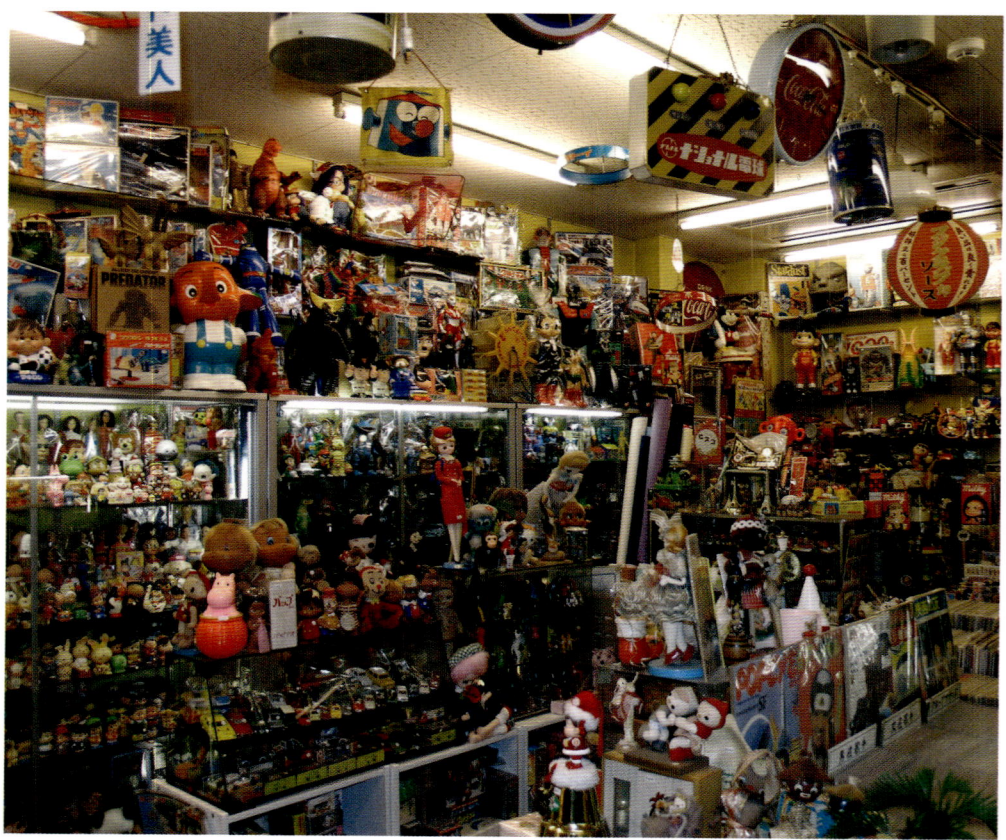

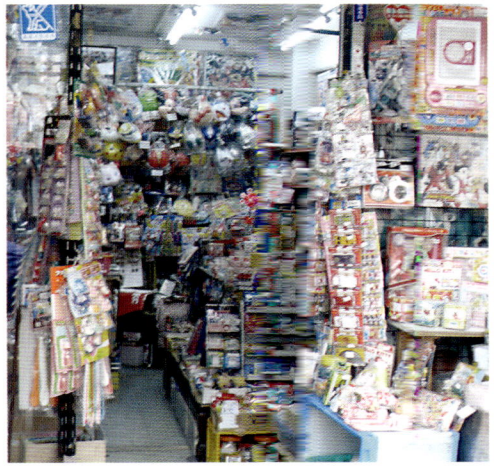

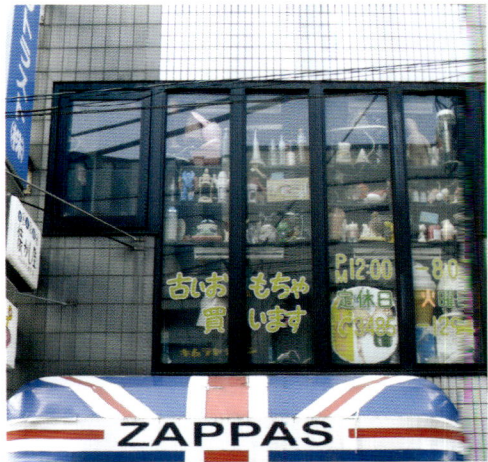

ZEMBA SHOHTEN   07

5-36-7 DAIZAWA, SETAGAYA-KU
03-3414-2079
HOURS: 13:00 — 20:00, CLOSED THURSDAY

In this classic candy store, there are toys tucked here, there, and everywhere. Everything appears random, and if there is a method to their madness, we haven't figured it out. If you were a kid today, this might be your favorite store, but if you are prone to cavities, stay away.

NATUKA SHIA   13

2-31-14 KITAZAWA, SETAGAYA-KU
03-3485-1294, WWW.SHIMOKITAZAWA.NET/I/421.HTML
HOURS: 12:30 — 20:00, CLOSED TUESDAY

Situated above the shop Zappas is another one of Tokyo's older shops, Natuka Shia. Smaller and more cramped than most of Shimokitazawa's shops, it still has plenty to see. Natuka Shia is exclusively for collectors; vintage is all that is available. Most of the stock seems to have been there for quite some time, and new stock does not seem to arrive as quickly as it does in other stores. We recommend visiting if you can, as this shop may not last much longer.

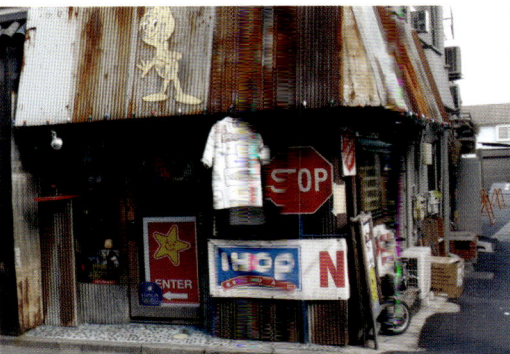

SOUNDS GOOD   11

2-23-6 SETAGAYA, KITAZAWA
03-5433-3758, WWW.HOME.ATT.NE.JP/GREEN/SOUNDSGOOD
HOURS: 13:00 — 20:00

A small shop covered in corrugated metal and display signs, Sounds Good is home to a decent sampling of advertising character toys and Hawaii-oriented merchandise. Although we have never known anyone to actually buy anything in this fun little shop, it sure looks nice.

10

TOYS PARADISE
5-30-3 DAIZAWA, SETAGAYA-KU
03-3419-7256
HOURS: 12:00 — 20:00, CLOSED MONDAY

A mixture of old and new, character and kaiju, Toys Paradise looks like a cheap toy store at first glace, but has many hidden gems lying in wait. This is a shop where digging around pays off, as sometimes even the store owner can't remember where everything is. Claiming to be the third oldest toy store in all of Japan, Toys Paradise has been around forever, but we don't actually know how long forever is. The store owner is one of the nicest you will ever meet, and while the selection may be suspect, your visit is sure to be pleasant.

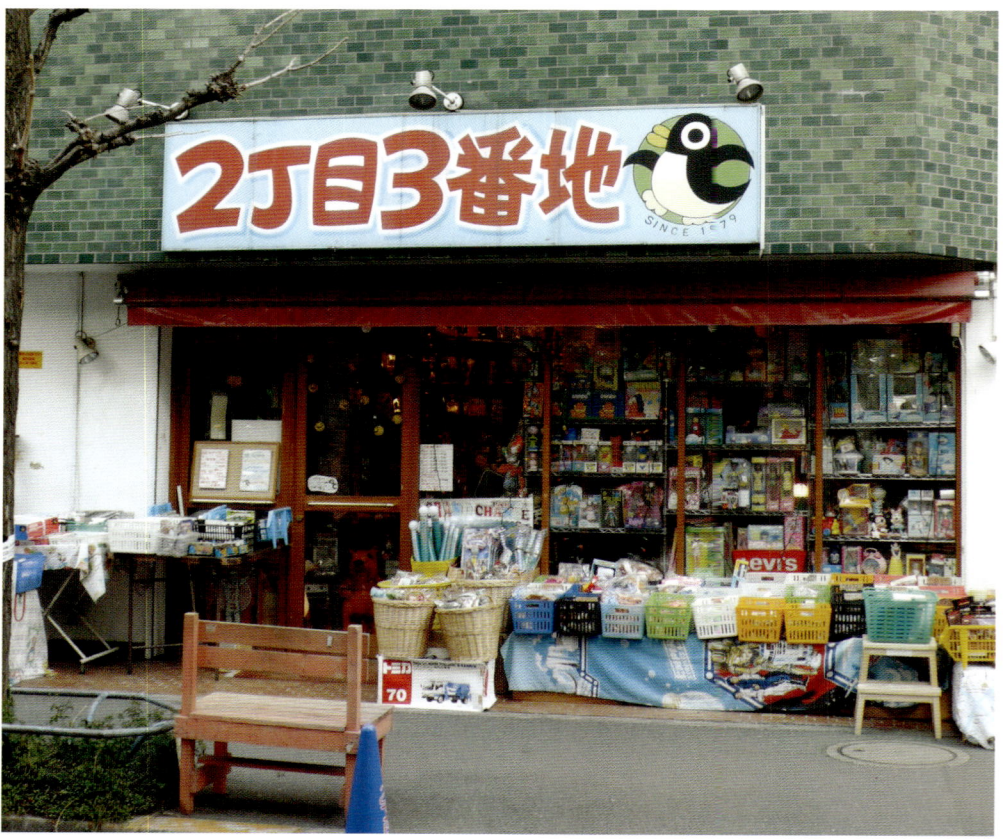

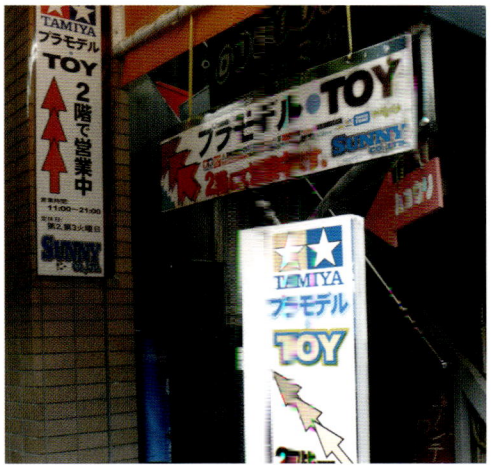

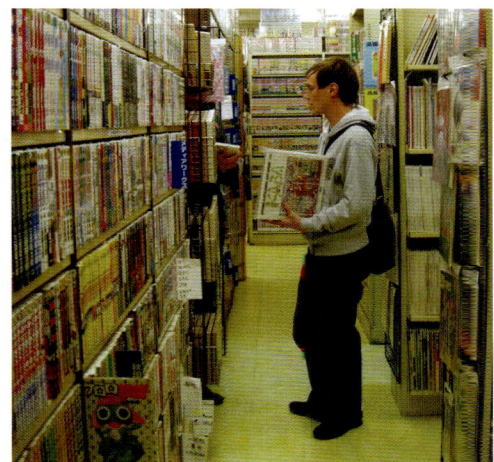

SUNNY CO.   04

2-12-1 KITAZAWA, SETAGAYA-KU
03-3413-0857, WWW.HOBBYSHOP-SUNNY.COM
HOURS: 10:00 — 21:00, CLOSED 2ND AND 3RD TUESDAY

The only two-story toy shop in Shimokitazawa, Sunny Co.'s bottom floor is dominated by model kits, and the second floor houses new Bandai releases and the latest in vinyl and chogokin. While there is nothing here that you won't find at other new toy stores, you may find something here that was sold out in more highly trafficked neighborhoods.

DORAMA   05A 05B

2-12-16 KITAZAWA, SETAGAYA-KU
03-3487-4233, WWW.DORAMA.CO.JP
HOURS: 13:00 — 20:00

While there are several Dorama shops in the Shimokitazawa area. the bookstore immediately to the left of Sunny Co. seems to be the best (05A). Filled with tons of used books and magazines, as well as the occassional toy, it is worth a stop if you are in the area. Dorama (05B) across the street usually sells movies, but changes every so often to a different kind of stock.

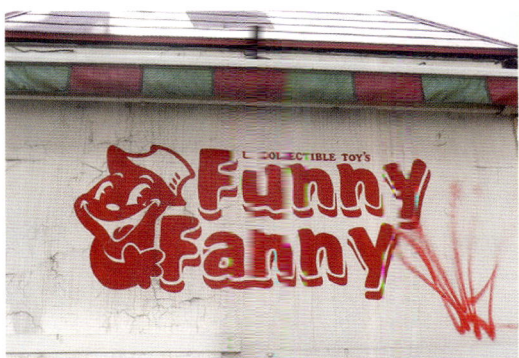

FUNNY FANNY   08

5-33-3 DAIZAWA, SETAGAYA-KU
03-5481-3857, WWW.FUNNYFANNY.BIZ
HOURS: 13:00 — 20:00

Focusing on cute character goods like Snoopy, the Smurfs, and Disneyana, Funny Fanny has tons of PVC desktop collectibles for collectors from five to fifty. Far from our area of expertise, there is always someone shopping, so they must be doing something right.

SINGLE-STOP
TOY SHOPS

MACHIYA
SUGAMO
EKODA
TOYS-R-US

TOY FESTIVALS

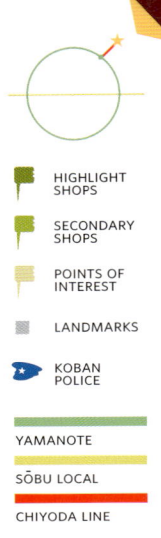

HIGHLIGHT
SHOPS

SECONDARY
SHOPS

POINTS OF
INTEREST

LANDMARKS

KOBAN
POLICE

YAMANOTE

SŌBU LOCAL

CHIYODA LINE

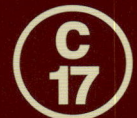

SUBWAY STATIONS:
WHEN TAKING THE TOKYO METRO
SUBWAY, EACH STOP IS NUMBERED
AND EACH LINE IS LETTER CODED
FOR YOUR CONVENIENCE. THE
CHIYODA LINE IS INDICATED BY A
LETTER "C," THE HANZOMAN LINE
BY A "Z," AND THE TOZAI LINE
BY A "T," AMONG OTHERS. THIS
WAY YOU ALWAYS KNOW EXACTLY
WHICH LINE AND STOP YOU ARE AT,
NO MATTER WHERE YOU ARE.

MACHIYA

Machiya is another small neighborhood that most toy collectors have not visited. As it is well off the beaten path, going to Machiya requires taking the JR Yamanote line to Nishi-Nippori, then transferring to the Tokyo Metro Subway system and the Chiyoda line. One stop up the Chiyoda line (Nishi-Nippori is denoted by stop C16) is Machiya (stop C17).

Take Exit 1, and you should be at a street corner by the SMBC building and the Koban. If you don't see them, walk around the station until you do, or ask where the Koban is. From there, walk one very short block to the first right, then one and a half quick blocks down. On the right hand side is Jyarinco (01), indicated by two small signs in Japanese that say "antique toy" in English. Located on the second floor, Jyarinco is packed with just about every kind of toy imaginable, including more Jumbo Machinders than anywhere else in the city. The prices here are incredible, and even better for toys in imperfect condition. Additionally, much like Koenji's Ichiban-Boshi, Jyarinco collaborated with RealxHead to create the Devil Dog and Cyclops Dog figures that were released exclusively through this shop.

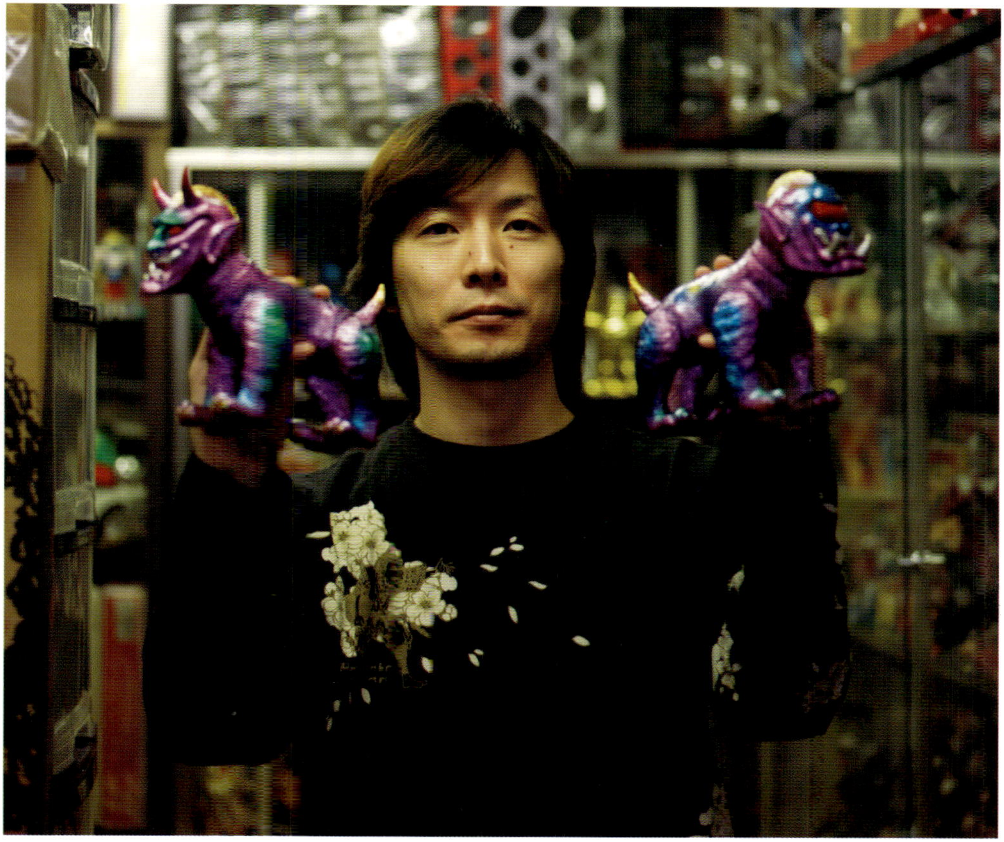

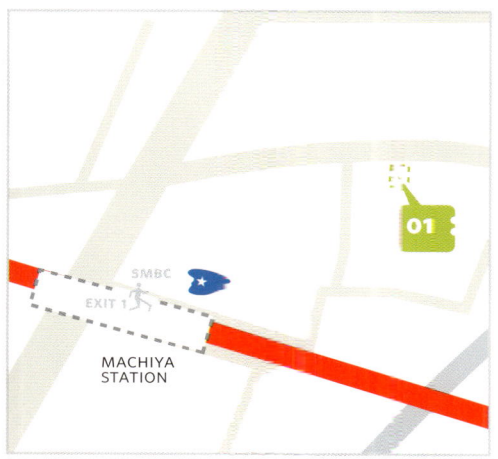

JYARINCO

1-20-9 MACHIYA, ARAKAWA-KU
03-3893-4045, WWW.JYARINCO.COM
HOURS: 12:30 — 20:30

An amazing store with every conceivable kind of toy in stock, Jyarinco is the last of Tokyo's hidden gems. Because it is tucked away in Machiya, few make the trek to Jyarinco, but those who do are rewarded with great deals. Focusing more on vinyl than on die-casts, and featuring a good Jumbo Machinder selection, Jyarinco has a little something for everyone. Not much else is in the area, so it is usually the first or last stop of the day for toy hunters.

MACHIYA
STATION

SMBC

EXIT 1

01

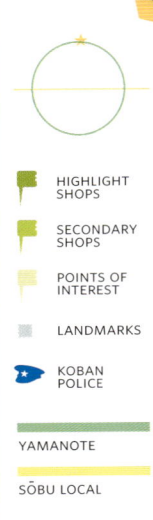

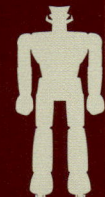

JUMBO MACHINDERS:
EXPORTED INTO THE STATES AS
SHOGUN WARRIORS, THESE FIGURES
ACTUALLY REPRESENT A STYLE OF
TOY CALLED THE JUMBO MACHINDER.
MADE OF POLYETHELENE, STANDING
NEARLY TWO FEET TALL, WITH
WHEELED FEET AND MISSILE-FIRING
MECHANISMS, THE JUMBO
MACHINDER LINE IS ONE OF THE
MOST DIFFICULT OF ALL JAPANESE
TOY TYPES TO COLLECT.

SUGAMO

Hiding on the north side of the Yamanote line, Sugamo is just far enough away to keep a lot of people from stopping in. Originally Tokyo's largest and most diverse toy shop, Forest Gangu (01) used to rule Tokyo's toy community with its brother shops, Third Uncle and Characters (the shop's owners are actual brothers). Since then, Third Uncle and Characters have combined to form one shop, and Forest Gangu held on to a massive shop until just recently. In decline after seemingly forever, Forest Gangu is a pale shade of its former self, as many of the cases and shelves are surprisingly, sadly bare. While it merits a visit as much as any other shop in Tokyo, Forest Gangu almost inconceivably no longer boasts the distinction of being one of the best shops to ever exist. To get there, take the main exit, cross the main road, walk down two blocks, and then turn right for one block. On the left-hand corner will be Forest Gangu.

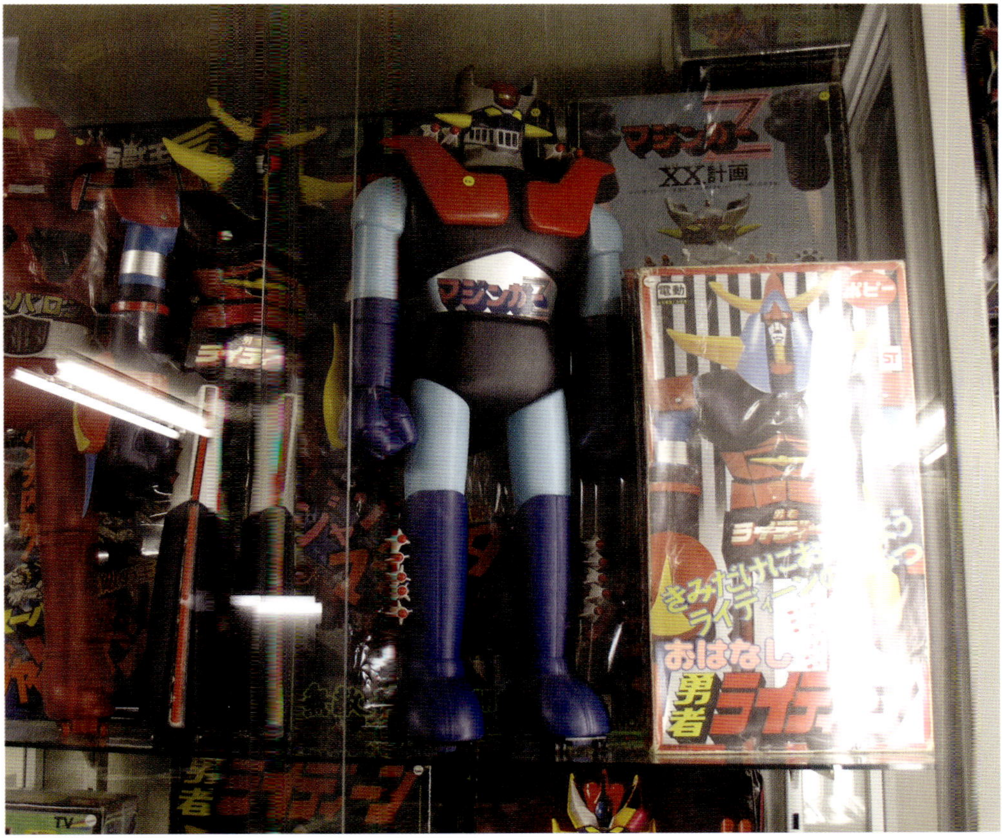

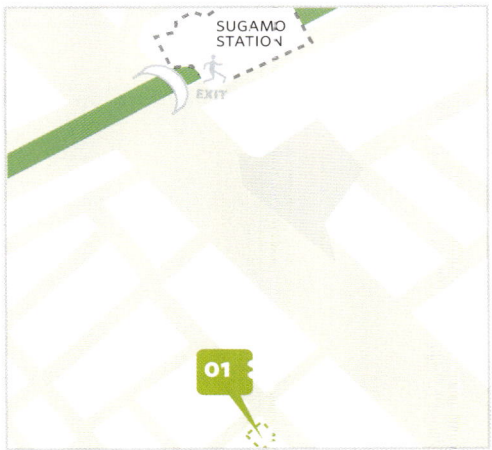

FOREST GANGU

01

1-24-8 SUGAMO, TOSHIMA-KU
03-5978-3278, WWW.FOREST_GANG@SALES.FFN.NE.JP
HOURS: 13:00 — 21:00

One of the original titans of the Tokyo toy scene, Forest Gangu was legendary for its astounding selection and usually correlating prices. This was the shop to which pilgrimages were made just to see the breadth and variety of toys for sale. A massive shop by Tokyo, and even non-Tokyo, standards, Forest Gangu was as much a museum as a store. Regrettably, after selling off many of their rare toys online in recent years, Forest Gangu is not what it once was. Although it is still a great shop to visit, it has lost the luster it had when it was battling Third Uncle and Characters for Tokyo toy supremacy.

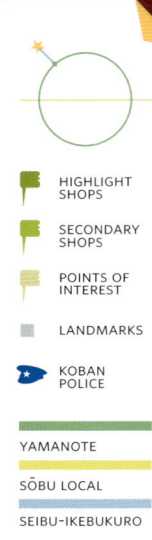

EKODA

Lovely little Ekoda, almost no one knows your name. Hiding on the private Seibu Ikebukuro line, it is such a small stop, many maps don't even list it. Now home to the shop Cosmo Knight Alpha (formerly of Shinjuku), Ekoda is a requisite stop for vinyl collectors.

To get there, take the JR Yamanote line to Ikebukuro and leave the JR system, transferring to the private Seibu Ikebukuro line. Just three stops down the line, the small (and usually unlabeled) Ekoda is quite unassuming. (Make sure you take a local train and not an express, or it will pass Ekoda.) Take the north exit from the station, then take a left, following the tracks.

When you reach the crossover for the tracks, turn right, walking up two and a half blocks until you see a glass sliding door stacked full of vinyl. This is Cosmo Knight Alpha (01), home to more than a few of the rarest vinyls we have seen in years, as well as plenty of much more affordable figures. The shop is packed, and although the staff speak no English, they are very nice and well versed in vinyl minutia.

On the way back to the train station is an action figure and t-shirt shop called Bandit (02), just on the other side of the tracks and two blocks over. This is only worth your time if you are a toy-shop-tour completist or are really into action figures. Most people simply get back on the train and return to Ikebukuro.

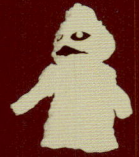

TODAY AND YESTERDAY: THE CORNERSTONES OF COSMO NIGHT ALPHA'S SUCCESS — A NEW BEMON RELEASE ON THE LEFT, ALONGSIDE A STAGGERINGLY RARE BAGGED IKB MOSUGON ON THE RIGHT. IF YOU UNDERSTAND WHY HE IS HOLDING THESE TWO TOYS, THEN THIS IS THE SHOP FOR YOU.

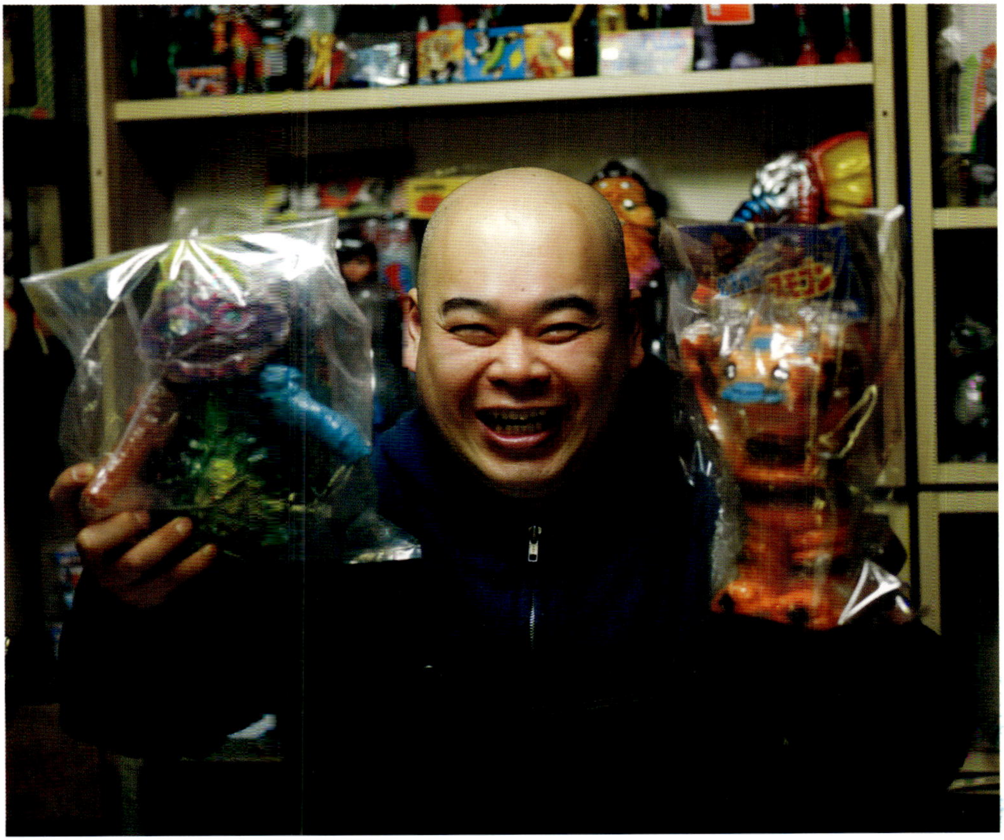

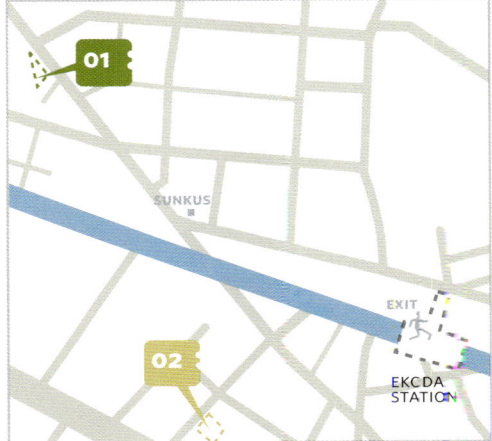

COSMO KNIGHT ALPHA 01

25-17 1F NERIMA SAKAE
03-3557-4616, WWW.SOFV.COM
HOURS: 12:00 — 20:00

One of the best vintage vinyl shops in all of Tokyo, Cosmo Knight Alpha is a wonderful little store tucked away in Ekoda. Off the beaten path for most collectors, it is a vinyl toy lover's paradise. Lined with cases full of rare hero and kaiju vinyls, as well as a decent selection of die-cast toys, Cosmo Knight Alpha always has a few toys you will probably never see again on display. In addition to their staggering vintage selection, Cosmo Knight Alpha is also the most common release spot for new Japanese company Bemon. Although the shop owner may be stoic and speaks little English, he is quite friendly. Cash is preferred, but credit cards are accepted for larger toy purchases.

SUNKUS

EXIT

02

EKCDA STATION

Toys-R-Us

For many toy collectors, the thought of being able to walk into a store like Toys-R-Us and see rows of Godzilla, Ultraman, and Gundam hanging next to Star Wars and Hot Wheels is mind-blowing. It almost seems too easy, like some sort of cheat code for collecting Japanese toys. There are several Toys-R-Us stores in the greater Tokyo area, but these three are en route to the other shops in this book.

IKEBUKURO
After a short walk within the Ikebukuro train station, look for the Sunshine City Mall exit and follow it outside. When you finally make this exit, you will need to cross the street and go up the main road, on your right. Look for Tokyu Hands a couple of blocks down. At the entrance to Tokyu Hands is an escalator to the basement, and a underground walkway to Sunshine City Mall. This is another longish walk. When you finally get to Sunshine City Mall. the Toys-R-Us is all the way at the back left of the mall.

ODAIBA
Along the Kuramamome monorail path headed to Tokyo Big Sight, Odaiba is home to the Aqua City Shopping Mall and a scaled-down reproduction of the Statue of Liberty. (Don't ask us why—it's just what happens in Japan sometimes.) Just across the street from the Statue of Liberty is the Kua 'Aina burger joint on the second floor, and an escalator to Toys-R-Us in the basement.

KAMEIDO
On the Sobu line, four stops past Akihabara (and three stops before Koiwa), there is a Toys-R-Us in the open-air shopping mall just south of the train station. The Toys-R-Us is located in the very back of the mall, a bit hidden away when you first enter.

For information about other Toys-R-Us stores, check www.toysrus.co.jp/truj/store/english/stores/kanto/index.html.

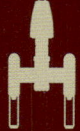

OF SPACE AND TIME:
FOR SOME REASON, TOYS-R-US IN TOKYO ALWAYS SEEMS TO HAVE THE LATEST STAR WARS ACTION FIGURES AND TOYS WELL BEFORE THE SAME CHAIN IN THE UNITED STATES. EVEN MORE CONFUSING IS THE FACT THAT THEY SEEMINGLY HAVE AN ENDLESS SUPPLY AS WELL. APPARENTLY THE FORCE IS STRONG IN TOKYO, AND TOYS-R-US IS A JEDI MASTER.

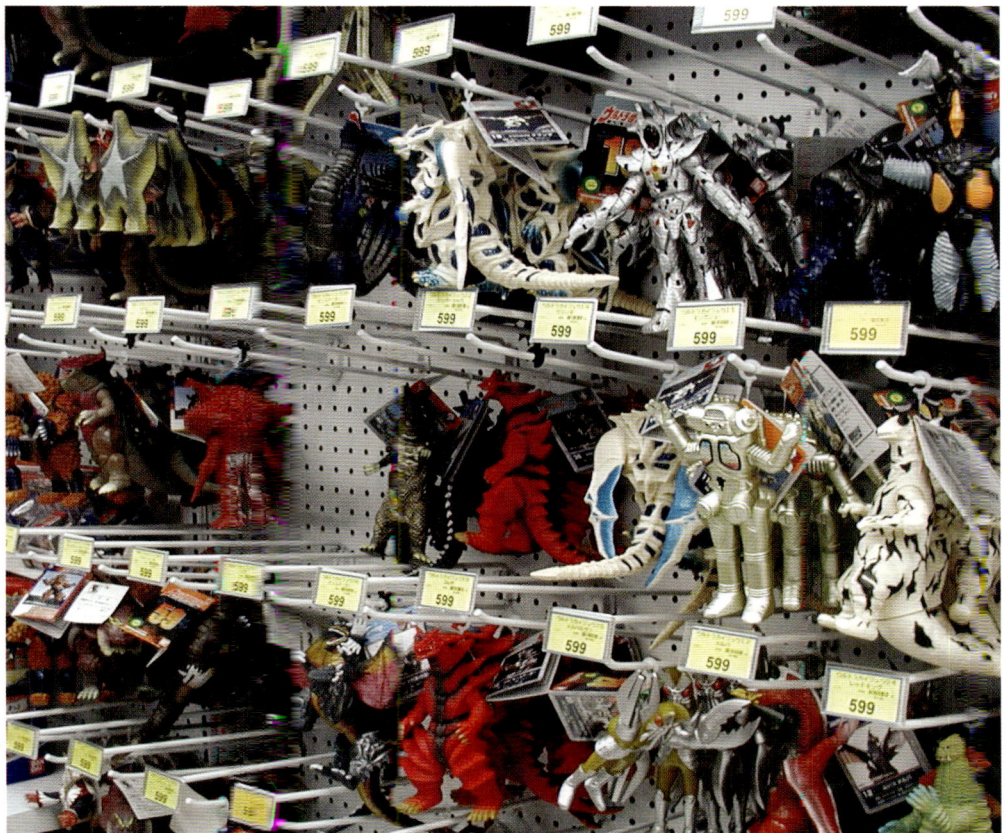

IKEBUKURO, TOYS-R-US
3-1 HIGASHIIKEBUKURO, TOSHIMA-KU (LOCATED IN SUNSHINE CITY MALL)
03-3983-5400, WWW.TOYSRUS.CO.JP/TRUJ/STORE/ENGLISH/STORES/KANTO/ST_IBSUNSHINE.HTML
HOURS: 10:00 — 20:00

ODAIBA, TOYS-R-US
1-7-1 ODAIBA, MINATO-KU (LOCATED IN ODAIBA DECKS AREA)
03-5564-5011, WWW.TOYSRUS.CO.JP/TRUJ/STORE/ENGLISH/STORES/KANTO/ST_ODAIBA.HTML
HOURS: 10:00 — 20:00

KAMEIDO, TOYS-R-US
6-31-1 KAMEIDO, KOTO-KU (LOCATED IN SUN STREET SHOPPING CENTER)
04-7347-2335, WWW.TOYSRUS.CO.JP/TRUJ/STORE/ENGLISH/STORES/KANTO/ST_KAMEIDO.HTML
HOURS: 10:00 — 20:00

Toy Festivals

Many travelers to Tokyo like to synchronize their trip with an event, such as a toy show. In Tokyo, four kinds of toy shows happen at different times of the year. All vary slightly in their coverage, and they all happen at one of two locations: Tokyo Big Sight or the Science Museum Hall. The events always occur on Sundays, and you can usually be finished with a show by 1:00 or 2:00 PM, which gives you ample time to get to other areas of the city.

THE FOUR KINDS OF SHOWS ARE:

WONDER FESTIVAL: The biggest show of the year, Wonder Festival is an all-encompassing event that highlights new toys and model kits above all others. There is very little vintage at this show. What is unique about Wonder Festival is that many companies grant one-day licenses to myriad small companies to make unique one-off toys and models that will never be seen again. The show is held at Tokyo Big Sight, and collectors line up more than twenty-four hours in advance to get their hands on the show's exclusives. Show dates are listed at www.kaiyodo.co.jp/wf.

WORLD CHARACTER CONVENTION: Commonly referred to as WCC, this show features a decent mix of both vintage and newer toys, but only a smattering of exclusives. Unofficially known as the blowout and inexpensive show, this is an event that many dealers use to get rid of excess stock at rock-bottom prices, but it is usually the less popular toys left over from the last few years of releases. Held at Tokyo Big Sight. Show dates are listed at www.wcc-jp.com.

TOKYO TOY FESTIVAL: Traditionally a vintage-only show, Tokyo Toy Festival originally occurred in conjunction with Wonder Festival, but recently has been held on the following weekend. The smallest of all the shows, it is held at Tokyo Big Sight. Show dates are listed at www.toyfes.jp.

SUPER FESTIVAL: A vintage toy show, and the only show held at the Science Museum. Run by Artstorm/Fewture, it happens on a regular basis, always has a fair amount of exclusives, and usually a special guest of some noteriety. Toy dealers new and old come out, as well as most boutique manufacturers. Lines begin forming around four in the morning, with two sets of lines—one for entrance into the show, and another for show-exclusive toys, which are sold in a slightly different area. Selection can vary dramatically from show to show, but there is usually something good for everyone. Show dates are listed at www.artstorm.co.jp/sufes.html.

RISE AND SHINE:
IF YOU PLAN ON BUYING ANY OF THE MORE SOUGHT-AFTER TOY EXCLUSIVES AT ANY TOY SHOW, WE RECOMMEND SHOWING UP EARLY. LINES CAN START FORMING AS EARLY AS SIX TO TWENTY-FOUR HOURS IN ADVANCE — BUT YOU'LL PROBABLY BE UP BY 6:00 ANYWAY.

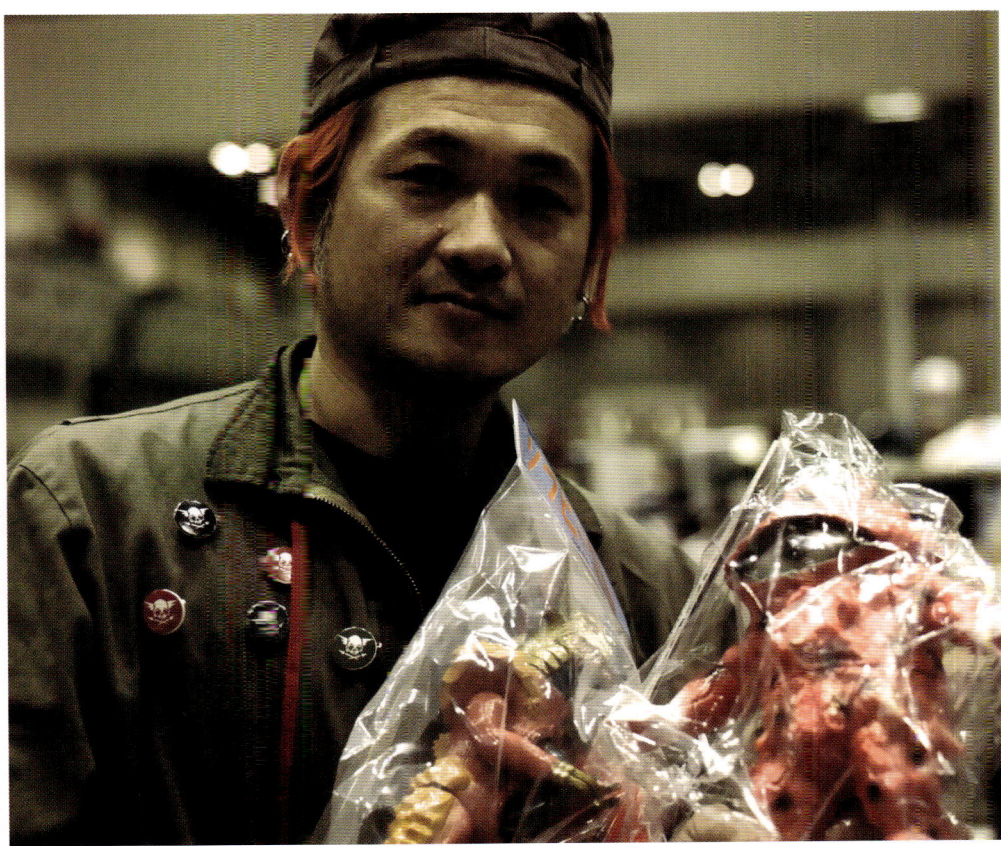

DIRECTIONS TO TOKYO BIG SIGHT:

Take the JR Yamanote line to Shimbashi Station. Look for the Yurikamome Monorail exit. As you exit the JR station, turn right out of the turnstiles. The Yurikamome entrance will be directly in front of you; purchase a ticket to Kokusai-Tenjijo. Shimbashi is the end of the line, so you don't have to worry about getting on a train going the wrong direction. Along the route, you will pass Odaiba Station, which is home to Toys-R-Us. (Most showgoers stop here on their way back from the show, to grab a bite from Kua 'Aina burger and shop at Toys-R-Us.) Upon arriving at Kokusai-Tenjijo, walk across the pathway to the giant inverted triangle known as Tokyo Big Sight. There will be plenty of signs, people, and lines directing you to exactly where you should go. For more information, go to www.bigsight.jp/english/general/access/index.html.

DIRECTIONS TO THE SCIENCE MUSEUM:

From Shibuya, take the Tokyo Metro Subway Hanzoman line (purple) six stops to Kudanshita. Shibuya is the last stop on the Hanzoman line, so you don't have worry about going the wrong direction. (Kudanshita is also indicated by stop Z6.) At Kudanshita, transfer to the Tokyo Metro Subway Tozai line. You will be at stop T7, and you will need to go one stop to Takabashi, stop T8. At Takabashi, take exit 1B and go west, past the Museum of Modern Art and the National Archives. Turn right on the main road and follow the signs to the Science Museum, which is located right next to the legendary music hall Budokan. For more information, go to www.jsf.or.jp/eng/map.

CONCLUSION

That just about wraps it up for us.
If you want to know more, we encourage
you to seek it out, as we have run dry.
(Okay, we may have kept one or two
secrets to ourselves, but we aren't telling.)
Along the way, if you notice shops that
have closed or moved, or new shops
we should know about, don't hesitate to
let us know (contact information is on the
copyright page). Tell the shop owners how
you got there. Show them this book; ask
them to sign their pictures. Strike up a
conversation, buy some toys, and have a
fun trip. You don't get to Tokyo very often,
so make it a memorable experience.

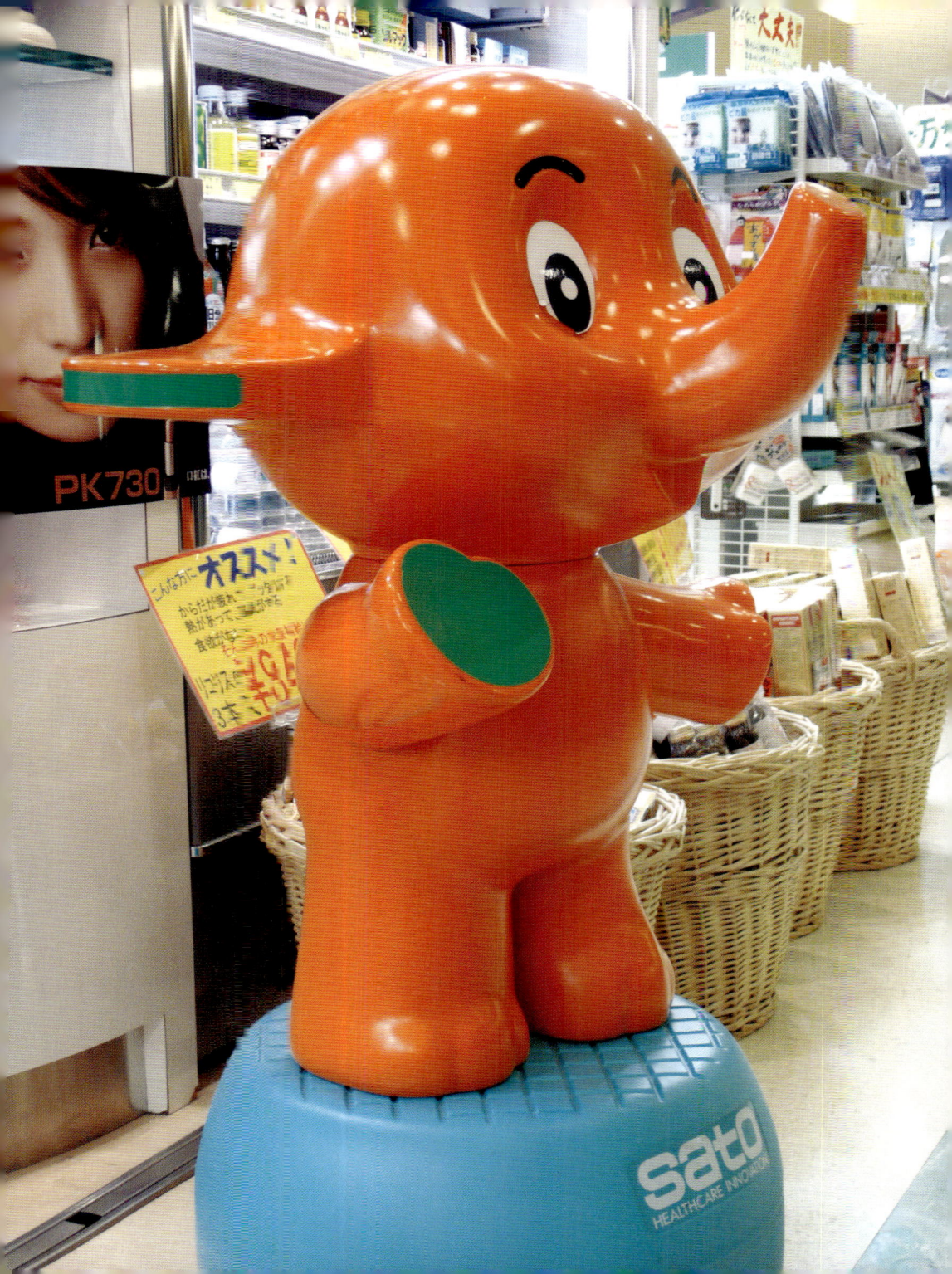

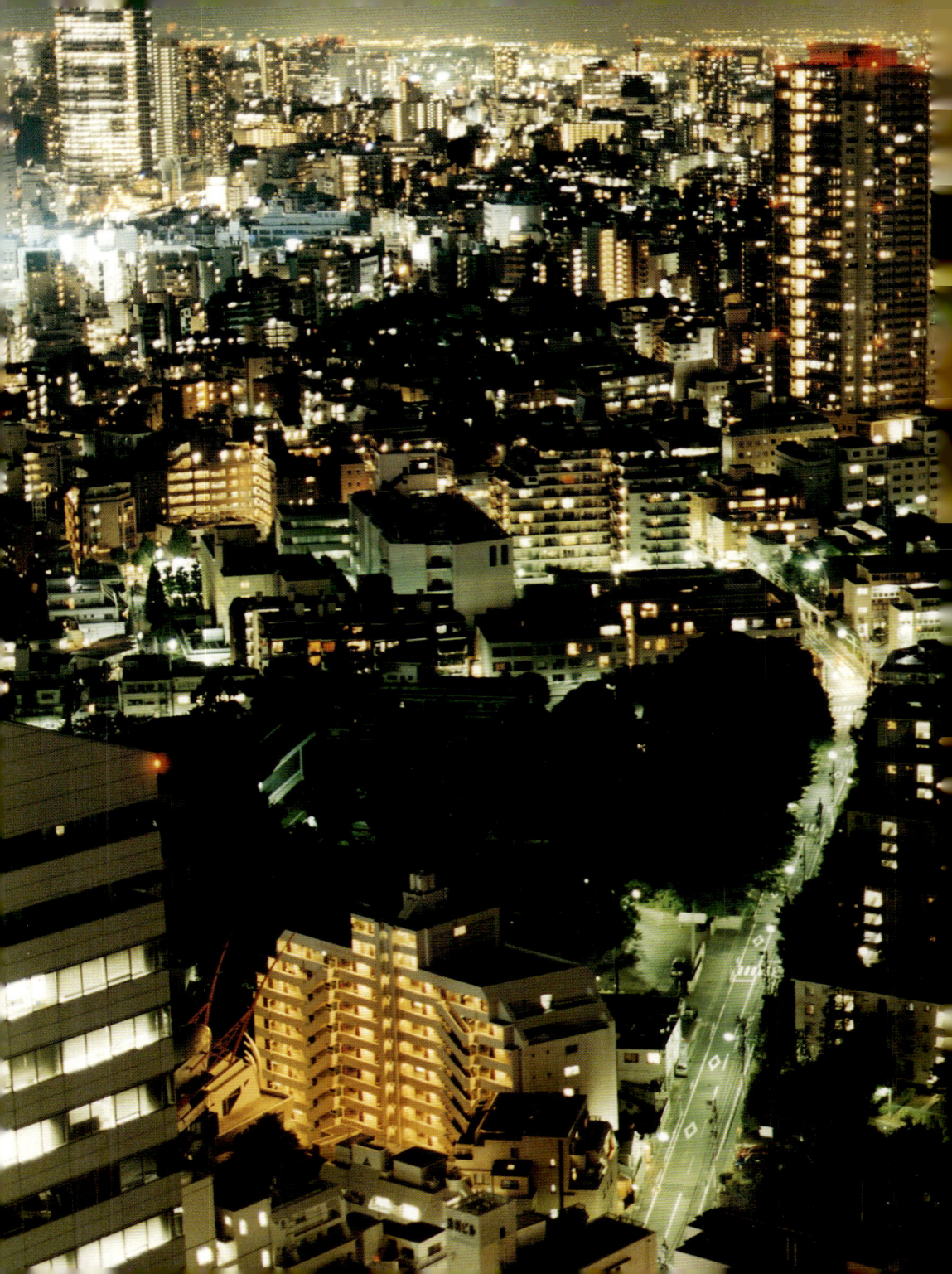

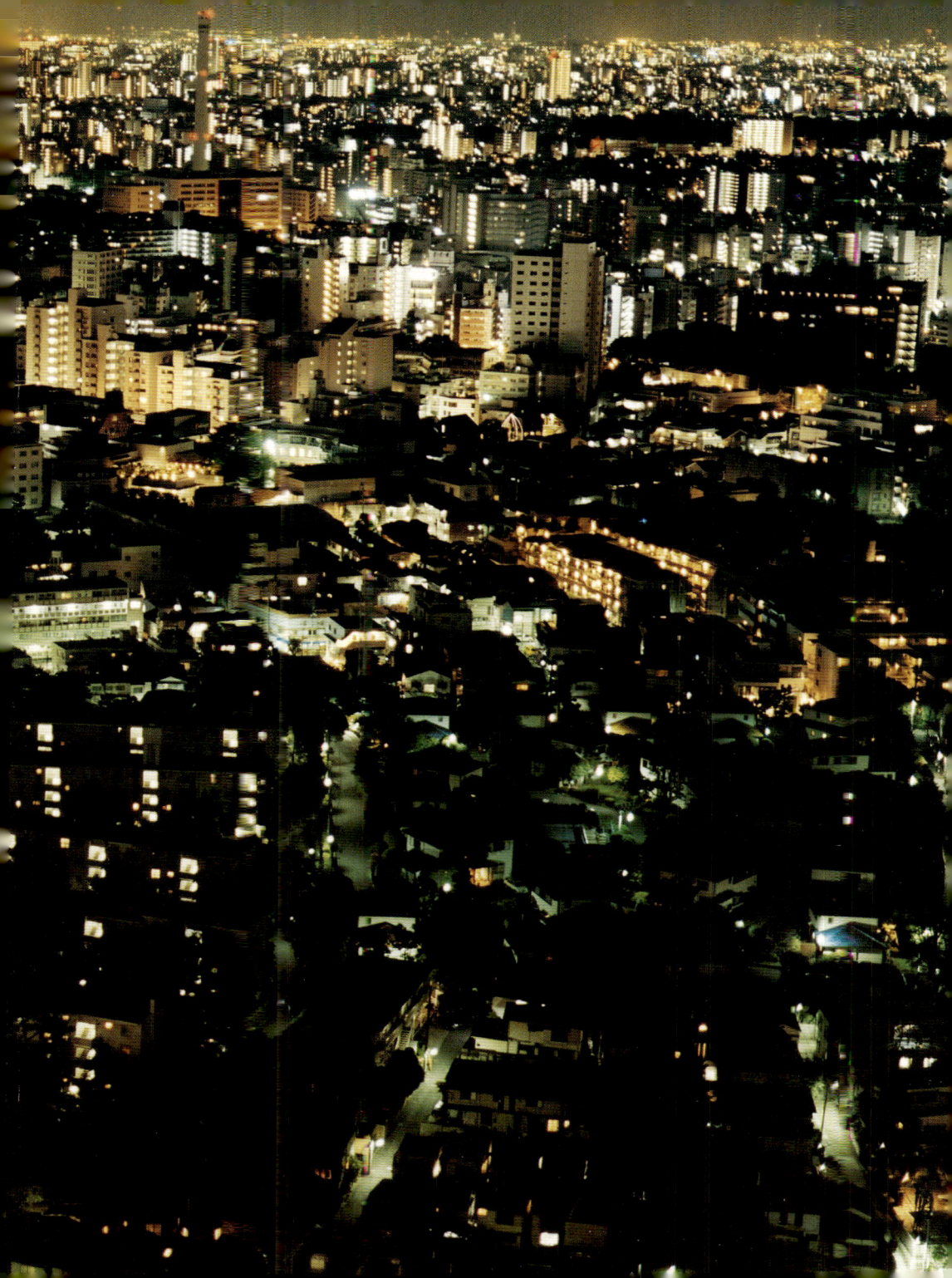

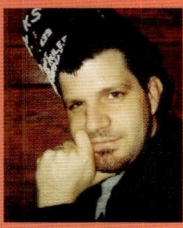

BRIAN FLYNN

Brian Flynn was born in the midst of a hurricane in 1875. After spending his formative years underachieving at various tasks, he decided the world was not ready for his forward-thinking vision of the future and was cryogenically frozen until 1994. After reawakening, Brian hit the streets, and decided that ruling the universe through the hidden mysticism of arcane Star Wars references, binary pulsar radio emission patterns, vintage Japanese vinyls, and Coca-Cola was the only way to go. Brian is the publisher and owner of *Super7* magazine, a partner and founder of Hybrid Design, an award-winning designer, and a highly obsessed toy collector.

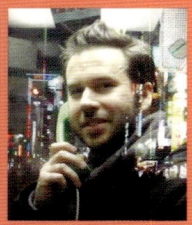

JEFF DEY

Born outside of Detroit, but growing up a stone's throw from NASA in Clear Lake, Texas, Jeff Dey spent his early years obsessing over rockets, spaceships, Batman, a certain dark-haired drama class girl, and losing to Lance Armstrong in bicycle races. After graduating with a design degree and becoming a design director for Nike, Jeff turned to the allure of elaborate photo shoots, realized a childhood dream of going to NASA's neutral buoyancy lab, and exceeded his mother's expectations. Jeff is currently in an exotic locale, shooting beautiful photographs and making bad jokes.

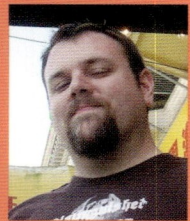

JOSHUA BERNARD

Joshua Bernard was born in Lowell, Massachusetts, in May of 1973. Like many children born at that time, he was raised by *Speed Racer, Force Five,* and George Lucas. In 2001, his obsession for Japanese toys and culture caused him to create CollectionDX.com, a popular website for toy collecting. Since then he has written for *Super7* magazine and made the pilgrimage to Tokyo on several occasions. Joshua currently lives in Massachusetts with his wife, four children, two cats, two guinea pigs, and several dozen fish.

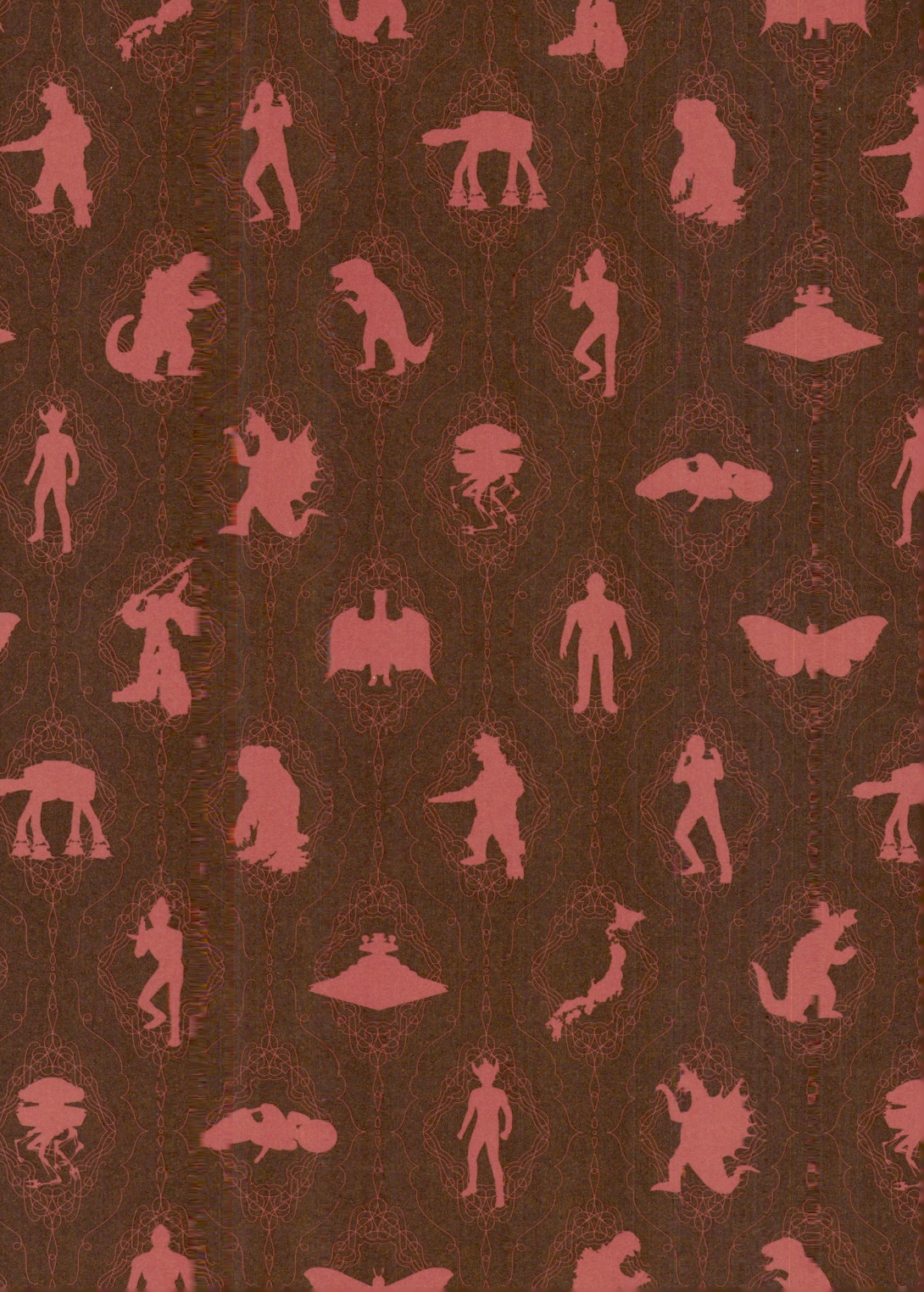